THE CHINESE ROAD TO SOCIALISM

Economics of the Cultural Revolution

by E. L. Wheelwright and Bruce McFarlane

Foreword by Joan Robinson

New York and London

Contents

Foreword
by Joan Robinson

All political struggle is a struggle for power. There have been three milestones on the road to socialist revolution. The first was the Paris Commune. It failed, but through it the proletariat gained valuable experience. The October Revolution was the first successful proletarian revolution. The Cultural Revolution is the first case of a revolution taking place under an already established dictatorship of the proletariat. Why was it necessary to carry through another revolution after power had been seized, and why should the Chinese Communist Party and the Chinese proletariat initiate such a revolution? The reason lies in the objective law of class struggle. Every revolution should be consolidated some time after its initial success. The class enemy will not be reconciled to his fate. After being dispossessed the bourgeoisie struggles for restoration.

The bourgeois revolution leaves property intact. The proletarian revolution seizes property. The propertied class attempts a restoration. Many times in history a revolution has been succeeded by a restoration. In the Soviet Union, counter-revolution was defeated, private property had been transferred to the State, but they failed to make a Cultural Revolution. Bourgeois ideology was not remoulded and proletarian power was corrupted by it. A kind of restoration of capitalism was made by Khrushchev in 1956.

The sad lesson of revisionism in the Soviet Union gives us warning that removing property is not enough; the revolution must be carried into the superstructure of the economic system. In China, also, after the success of the revolution in 1949, class struggle persisted and reactionary forces were attempting restoration.[1]

The sense of history has always been stronger in China, from ancient times, than in other civilizations. Now Chairman Mao and his supporters see themselves in terms of history. They have passed an epoch to open a new phase of historical development. The

7

Soviet Union has proved that a revolution can transform the economic base of society and that planned investment can transform a backward country into a great industrial and military power. It has also proved, as Mao sees it, that transforming the base is not enough to create socialism; it is necessary to carry the revolution into the superstructure. The Cultural Revolution got its name from a debate about culture in the narrow sense—what kind of writing, art, and theater is appropriate to a still-continuing class struggle? It widened into a transformation of culture in all aspects of life, education, and the relations of people to each other. The superstructure reacts upon the base. How do democratic relationships between the experts and the simple workers in a factory affect production? How does the campaign against private profit affect the marketed surplus from agriculture?

The authors of this book know the right questions to ask. They see the Cultural Revolution in the perspective of economic history. "The book is an exercise in political economy." Political economy cannot be understood without considering ideology and morality. They emphasize the moral element in Chinese socialism, at the same time remarking that Chinese policy is designed to avoid putting more weight on the morality than it will hold—the Liberation has offered solid benefits to all except the former privileged few, in improvements in the standard of consumption, social services, and economic security, which have transformed China from one of the most miserable countries in the so-called developing world into one (perhaps the only one) where development is really going on.

The Chinese Communist Party has a very different style from that of the Soviet Union and its disciples. Instead of justifying even the grossest errors as correct or at least necessary political schemes, the Chinese are taught to analyze mistakes in order to avoid them in the future; they do not mind even foreigners knowing that mistakes have been made. Our authors, though sympathetic, have no need to gloss over errors of policy, fake starts, and retreats. On the other hand, they have no need to lard their pages with adulation. A cool account of what they have seen is quite sufficiently impressive.

Since 1960, there have been no overall official statistics from China, though a good deal of piecemeal information can be picked up. The authors cannot give a systematic account of GNP, growth rates, and all that. They give very valuable first-hand reports to illustrate their analysis of Chinese policy and achievements.

Hostile observers (including many professional China watchers) like to discredit the reports of visitors who, they maintain, must have been shown around. There is a great deal of reluctance, both in the Soviet Union and in the West, to believe what sympathetic visitors to China report. Is it possible to carry out industrialization without squeezing and dragooning the peasantry? How can there be discipline in a factory where the workers are free to criticize the boss? How can there be incentives to work without inequality? How can there be socialism with grass-roots democracy? How can a backward country develop by its own efforts, without benefit of "foreign aid" and foreign advisers?

Yet there are certain large facts which no one can deny. Frequent predictions of breakdown, famine, and chaos have proved false. China has paid off all her debts and is now giving aid to developing countries while receiving none. It passed through the bad years, 1959–1961, without inflation and its currency is one of the few that is stable today. Trade is balanced, and it is gradually reversing the "underdeveloped" pattern of importing manufacturers and exporting raw materials.

If Chinese policy has been so foolish, how could these things have come about? Certainly the eye-witness reports of details of economic performance seem a great deal more plausible than the sneers which the Western and Soviet press delight to quote from each other.

Our authors understand orthodox economics. They understand it well enough to see through it. For two centuries we have been following Adam Smith's doctrine that the individual's pursuit of self-interest is the foundation of national prosperity. China, following the "Thoughts" of Mao Tse-tung, has set out to prove the opposite. But it does not expect such a profound reversal to be easily achieved: "The present great cultural revolution is only the first; there will inevitably be many more in the future. In the last few years Comrade Mao Tse-tung has said repeatedly that the issue of who will win in the revolution can only be settled over a long historical period." [2]

Cambridge
May 1970

Notes

1. From a statement made in November 1967 by a member of the committee then forming the "temporary organ of power" in Shanghai. See Joan Robinson, *The Cultural Revolution in China* (London and Baltimore: Penguin, 1969).
2. See p. 231 below.

PART I

Chinese Economic Development
1949-1965

APPROACHING THE CHINESE ECONOMY

How does an economist obtain impressions of an economy? He reads as much as he can of what has been written by other economists on the subject. He studies the official statistics and publications put out by the government and other institutions. He talks to the country's economists. He moves around as much as he can, visiting various units of production over as wide a field as possible. In his travels, he "sniffs the economic atmosphere," which means that he utilizes his previous experiences and observes the condition of the people—whether they appear well fed and healthy, whether there appears to be substantial unemployment (real or disguised), the absence or presence of beggars, standards of cleanliness and hygiene, the quality and range of consumer goods in the shops, other products exhibited in trade fairs and elsewhere, the standard of public housing, the clothing of the people, the leisure habits of the people, and so on. All this is patently subjective, but an experienced observer can use his eyes, his ears, and his nose to supplement his conversation and his study to good effect, in order to get the "feel" of the economy.

The coauthors of this book had the opportunity to do this, each for a period of two months, in two separate visits to the People's Republic of China; Wheelwright in November and December 1966 and McFarlane in April and May 1968. The second trip was designed partly as a follow-up or "in-depth" study of enterprises and communes visited on the first one, and partly to study examples of new economic institutions working under the influence of the Great Proletarian Cultural Revolution.

The aim in both cases was to see big and small communes in cities and in remote areas, large and small enterprises in cities and in country towns, in order to assess the impact of the Cultural

Revolution on economic policy, planning, technology, and production. Both authors also had numerous and illuminating discussions with theoretical economists, political scientists, and ideologists.

What were the main issues we were trying to understand?

First, the broad political, social, and cultural factors which are so important in the Chinese economy. Second, how these operate in detail. In particular, how the spread of Maoism has affected attitudes, incentives, organization, production, efficiency, quantity, and quality; in other words, how the myriads of decision-making bodies are being motivated in such an enormous and populous country, which operates a considerably decentralized planned economy. Our approach was conditioned by the conviction that it is not sensible to look at China through the prism of Western textbook economics, or some "command economy" model constructed by "Kremlinologists," and alleged to be suitable for analyzing the Chinese economy. The textbooks, for example, throw no light on how a socialist economy combines investment planning with the devolution of detailed implementation of plans. Our approach was to examine the institutions which the Chinese State has set up to solve its economic problems and to distribute the power of decision-making. Moreover, we became aware, as the analysis and inspections proceeded, that the performance of the Chinese economy cannot be judged by purely economic standards, such as real productivity per man-hour or rate of return to the State on invested capital, *because noneconomic aims are being "fed" into the planning system.*

Without anticipating the arguments to be developed in this book, we might mention, among these noneconomic objectives, the fear of war, the desire to resist excessive bureaucratic control, the belief in a certain kind of morality, and a revolt against certain imperatives stemming from industrialization.

We have been particularly interested in two questions—in the problem of the relationship between moral and material incentives in the economy, and in the economic element in the Cultural

Revolution, which we have discerned to be the promotion of the human factor in economic development, that is, the breaking down of the great gulf between a senior élite group of technocrats, managers, and Party administrators, on the one hand, and the mass of peasants and workers, on the other. These issues formed the framework of our inquiry.

Substance was added to this framework by directing attention to certain particular issues:

(1) How does the planning mechanism work—"who" or "what" is the "State," in each particular case where a factory or commune has dealings with a higher authority? What is the relationship between each economic unit and the various planning echelons? How much autonomy has each got? Which matters is each free to decide for itself and which not? How is agreement reached between those in charge of the economic unit and the planners? How much autonomy do communes have in comparison with factories?

(2) What is the relative scope for central decisions, market forces, and decentralized decisions? What marketing arrangements exist and to what extent do moral rather than financial incentives influence marketing?

(3) What is the organizational structure of communes, factories, municipal councils, district councils? Who is in authority and how did they get there?

(4) What is the wage spread in factories? How far do financial incentives operate within factories? What role do ordinary workers play in the organization of production, farming, and commerce?

(5) What particular examples—favorable and unfavorable—of reorganization and technological change exist, to illustrate the influence of Maoism and of the Cultural Revolution?

(6) How do the organization and the motivation of the Chinese economy today compare with earlier periods of Chinese economic development?

Mao and the Chinese Communists "make history," but they do so within certain restraints and constraints. As Engels said in his letter to Bloch: "We make our own history, but in the first place under very definite presuppositions and conditions." A "restraint" on modern Chinese economics is China's economic backwardness and the need to create incentives. Other restraints on policy are China's defense needs, and the problem of regionalism with its great historical importance. Finally, there is the all-pervading influence of Chinese morality, history, and culture.

We have been conscious of the fact that China is, above all, a socialist State which has been profoundly influenced by developments in the Soviet Union. The Chinese people were influenced not only by the October Revolution itself, but by the ideas which came out of it and, in recent times, many Chinese have been influenced by what they call the negative example of the development of the Soviet Union since Stalin's death. For Mao Tse-tung's followers, socialism is not merely an engine of industrialization—a means to an end; it is the end itself—a society with high moral standards and a certain style of collective living. Much of contemporary Chinese development can be seen as an attempt to avoid the élite spirit that has characterized other communist regimes, and an attempt also to avoid the mediocrity of a centralized and bureaucratic power system. In a sense, China is trying to give an answer opposite to that of the Soviet Union, especially in the sphere of technological administration, incentives, and mass participation.

The fact that China is a socialist society makes it necessary to isolate and discuss carefully the processes at work in the three different forms of ownership: state, communal, and cooperative. Many people in the West find difficulty in understanding certain aspects of Chinese planning and organization (income distribution, pricing, marketing) because they fail to differentiate these forms.

A major difficulty in explaining the Chinese system lies in the morality—especially as revealed in the thought of Mao Tse-tung, on the one hand, and in the impact of Chinese civilization on China's communism and its value system, on the other. Thus the notion of "serve the people" and the general Maoist fervor do not lend themselves to rigorous analysis. Western academics tend to find them personally embarrassing. Anna Louise Strong has pointed also to the difficulty that Chinese views and exhortations, when translated into English, just do not sound right. To give a simple example—the Chinese character for "bad elements" consists of four separate pictures: ox, devil, snake, and god. In English, this is apt to read "freaks, ghosts, monsters, and demons," which means that language barriers are not always overcome by translation. Other aspects of current Chinese morality are met with incredulity in the West. How does reading Mao's thoughts help a peasant commune to grow better cabbages? This is a typical Western reaction to the waving and reading of the "little red book" of quotations from Mao Tse-tung. The answer lies in the *content* of that "little red book." For the peasants of China, it is an instruction to apply scientific principles; an instruction to learn from veteran workers; an exhortation to work with persistence, overcoming all difficulties, for the good of the society, for the international revolution. If all of these thoughts are really applied in a particular case, the peasants concerned probably *will* grow better cabbages!

The visitor to China also is confronted with a number of local Communist conventions. Emphasis is given to the "three constantly read articles"—Mao's "Serve the People," "In Memory of Norman Bethune," and "The Foolish Old Man Who Removed the Mountain." The last is a fable used by Mao to eradicate colonial cultural inferiority and to inspire faith and confidence in the people's ability to undertake enormous tasks. The others are parables pointing up the moral of working selflessly and, if necessary, dying for the common good. They are attempts to eradicate a selfish, bourgeois, individualistic, competitive morality, and to substitute for it a collectivist, selfless attitude.

Emphasis is also given to the "three constantly read old quotations" and the "three constantly read new quotations." The former comprise:

(1) "The force at the core leading our cause forward is the Chinese Communist Party. The theoretical basis guiding our thinking is Marxism-Leninism."

(2) "We must have faith in the masses and we must have faith in the Party. These are two cardinal principles. If we doubt these principles we shall accomplish nothing."

(3) "Policy and tactics are the life of the Party; leading com-

rades at all levels must give them full attention and must never on any account be negligent."

The "three constantly read new quotations" are:

(1) "You must concern yourselves with State affairs and carry the Great Proletarian Cultural Revolution through to the end."

(2) "Don't rest on your laurels, make new contributions."

(3) "Fight self, repudiate revisionism!"

These articles and quotations—together with ritual readings from the "little red book," several specially written songs ("Sailing the Seas Depends on the Helmsman," "The East Is Red," "Wish Chairman Mao a Long Life!," "Golden Mountain in Peking," and "Long Live Chairman Mao!"), and Mao's "latest instructions" *—play a key part in the spreading of moral incentives. Every society needs a morality which suits its economic development, as Tawney argued in *Religion and the Rise of Capitalism.* Britain had Adam Smith's "Invisible Hand" of self-interest, as the mainspring of its industrialization, which was regulated by competition, so that "private vice became public virtue," as Mandeville put it. For China, Mao presents himself, and the socialist morality he preaches, as the visible bond linking decisions and motivating producers.

The modern Chinese identification of morals, politics, and government is not new, especially among leading statesmen in Chinese political history. Westerners simply do not have this view of politics and find it almost incomprehensible. However, a number of Western anthropologists and sociologists recently have been upgrading the role of the human factor (and therefore, in part, of nonfinancial incentives) in economic development, and pointing to problems caused by the lack of a bond between people and government—a lack arising from the great gulf between élites and the mass of peasants.[1]

---

* The "latest instructions" are sometimes directives from Mao personally, and sometimes quotations from unsigned newspaper editorials by Mao. During the Cultural Revolution, their constant reiteration in press, radio, and mass readings gave them a hypnotic, even magical, character which had to be seen and heard to be believed. A collection of these "latest instructions" appears in the Appendix.

ETHICS, POLITICS, AND GOVERNMENT

Traditionally, Chinese statesmen have identified ethics, politics, and government, and have advocated a moral factor in public administration. Confucius exhorted the rulers to be benevolent to the people and to avoid excessive exploitation; he paid great attention to ethics and demanded strict rules governing the attitudes of inferiors and superiors. Emperor Wen, first of the Sui dynasty, attempted to introduce political reform, improvements in the penal code, and the right of appeal to higher courts in litigation. He also distributed land according to a land equalization system. The influential author Wu Ching-tzu, in *The Scholars*, written in the Ching dynasty, criticized the pursuit of fame and wealth on the part of officials, landlords, and "scholar despots."

Mao Tse-tung and his followers in the Cultural Revolution are firmly in this tradition as far as ideology is concerned. Mao's basic message, repeated in article after article, is the need to "serve the people wholeheartedly and never for a moment divorce ourselves from the masses, to proceed in all cases from the interests of the people and not from one's self-interest or from the interests of a small group." [2] This injunction of 1945 followed similar advice in the 1920's and 1930's to his followers and to the People's Liberation Army. The corollary was that "The organs of the state must practise democratic centralism, they must rely on the masses and their personnel must serve the people." [3] In 1967–1968, the same emphasis prevailed. Two of his "latest instructions" were "fight self" (January 1967)—issued to the Red Guards as an answer to their question about resolving internal differences; and the corollary: "The most fundamental principle in the reform of the state organs is that they must keep in contact with the masses" (April 1968).

The ex cathedra statements of "the great leader, great helmsman, great supreme commander" were of importance in themselves as an influence on economic development, whatever one may think of their practical application. They led, for example, to the abolition of financial rewards, premiums, bonuses, and piecework in Chinese factories in 1967–1968, and to a new motif for stimulating output, so that a supply and marketing cooperative could announce in 1968 that "Our relations with our customers are not business or monetary relations, they are class relations, political relations; when we serve the people wholeheartedly, we are helping to consolidate our proletarian power." [4]

It is not possible to assess the significance of developments in Chinese planning and organization after 1966, unless due weight is given to the presence of ethics in Chinese public administration. For, as Joan Robinson points out, Chinese communes do not keep a clear distinction between the profit *motive* as a stimulus to individual energy, and the profit *criterion* as a measure of achievement: "The objection to profit as a criterion is largely ethical, even thinking in terms of profit in the abstract may be corrupting." [5]

THE HISTORICAL PRESENT

Contemporary social and economic development in China is not sharply divided from history, as shown by allusions to ancient stories, traditional expressions, and language conventions. One of the authors inquired as to how a particular group of workers had been able to overthrow an especially powerful manager at the Shanghai Diesel Pumps and Motors Plant. He met with the following reply: "The golden monkey wrathfully swings his magic cudgel and the jade-like firmament is cleared of dust!"

To understand this answer one had to know two things. First, there exists a very popular ancient story written in the fourteenth century by Wu Chen-en, called "Pilgrimage to the West." It is set in the Tan dynasty (680–907) and is part fact, part legend. The factual part deals with the journey of Tung Chung, a Buddhist monk who traveled to India to find the Buddhist scriptures and remained there for thirty years. The mythical part deals with this monk's companions—another monk (Sa Ho-siang), a man with a pig's head (Chu Pa-che), and the monkey king. The monkey is very wise and tactically astute; he can change into seventy-two different forms and wields a magic cudgel which he can change at will into different sizes—very large, or as small as a needle so that it fits into his ear. Above all, he is very courageous and rebellious and even dares to go to Heaven where he creates havoc and challenges the authority of the King of all Heaven, the Emperor of Jade.

The second thing one had to know in order to understand the reply of the workers is that in 1961 Mao Tse-tung wrote a poem called "In Company with Comrade Kuo Mo-jo." The veteran, Kuo Mo-jo, had seen a Peking Opera and written a poem about it. Mao's poem, in reply, mentions "monsters and freaks" doing evil to the people, being incorrigible and immune to reason. Two of the lines read:

> The golden monkey wields the cudgel
> and the dust of green jade rises everywhere.[6]

Their implication is that *it is justified to rebel and attack the strongest foes*. The background of Mao's attitude was the year 1961 —the year of severe natural calamities in China, the Soviet's withdrawal of its technicians, blueprints, and contracts, and the growing pressure of the United States on China. Since then, the two lines quoted have been used by many people in connection with the Cultural Revolution. The Red Guards represent the monkey, Mao's thought represents the cudgel.

Another example of the wide use of Mao's poems in Cultural Revolution struggle is "Mayflies." Two of the lines read:

> In a tiny group small flies are buzzing
> and Mayflies lightly plot to topple the giant tree.[7]

Here the message seems to be that the reactionaries and imperialists—the mayflies—are plotting, but cannot undermine the revolutionary cause of the Chinese people.

Books which deal with the peasant revolution, and which are widely quoted in Mao's works and among the Chinese people, are *Story of the Three Kingdoms* and *All Men Are Brothers* or *Stories from the Marshy Lands*. The *Three Kingdoms* was written in the thirteenth century and deals with events taking place in 184–280, notably the Yellow Towel Revolt of the peasants against the East Han dynasty. The revolt was repressed, but the dynasty collapsed and broke up into three kingdoms. There are many peasant heroes in the story, as well as Chu Kuo-liang, one of China's great military strategists, a scientist, technologist, and statesman greatly admired by Mao. The Chinese people tend to refer to the *Three Kingdoms* when warning officials against repression and exploitation, and they have referred to it often, for in China there developed an agrarian bureaucracy, upon which the landed élite depended for the preservation of its control over the peasant population. Chinese history has been punctuated by periodic and widespread rebellions. The ones launched in the 1920's and 1930's finally produced a thorough social revolution in which the peasants furnished the main driving force behind the victory of a party dedicated to achieving a supposedly inevitable phase of history in which the peasantry would cease to exist.[8] The peasant revolts portrayed in the *Three Kingdoms* are referred to by Mao Tse-tung in his article "The Chinese Revolution and the Communist Party of China," and in his *On Practice*.

All Men Are Brothers, written by Xy Nai-An in the twelfth century, deals with the period 1120–1128 of the North Sun dynasty. It shows how this dynasty, under pressure of attacks from people of the Kin nationality, pursued a ruthless taxation policy to fight its wars, and thus sparked a peasant revolt led by Sun Kiang, who set up a revolutionary base area in the marshlands of Shantung Province, and exercised a policy of robbing the rich to help the poor. Mao refers to the novel in his *On Contradictions*. In the Cultural Revolution struggles of 1966–1968, many press articles referred to "the strategy used by the imitation foreign devil"—an allusion to *The True Story of Ah Q*, and aimed at the idea that revolution should be permitted only under official approval.

One also has to take into account the enormous popularity of Mao's slogans with the masses insofar as the slogans are expressed in the aesthetically pleasing classical style of groups of four and eight Chinese characters: "fight self, repudiate revisionism" (four characters) and "a single spark can light a prairie fire" (eight characters). Echoes of this can be found in exhortations to pursue the "three-eight" working style (which in Chinese is written in three phrases and eight additional characters). It indicates firm, correct political orientation; a plain, hard-working manner; flexibility in strategy and tactics; and unity, alertness, and liveliness. (The "eight characters," incidentally, were a method of fortune-telling in China based on the examination of the two cyclic characters for each year, month, day, and hour of a person's birth.) The Cultural Revolution has seen the consistent promotion of the "four firsts": the slogan that first place must be given to man in handling the relationship between man and weapons; to political work in handling the relationship between political and other work; to ideological work in relation to the other aspects of political work; and, in ideological work, to the ideas currently in a person's mind as distinguished from ideas in books. The Socialist Education Movement of 1963 also featured the "four clean-ups," in politics, ideology, organization, economy, while the Cultural Revolution saw many demands to destroy the "four olds" (culture, ideas, custom, and habit) and to replace them with "four news" covering the same phenomenon.

Much of what Westerners complain of in the Cultural Revolution, or find perplexing, has its origins deep in Chinese history and culture. Take the repeated slogan "Mao Tse-tung *wansui!*" The Chinese word *"wansui"* is used for "long live," but literally means "ten thousand years," and was the traditional salute to the emperor; it had become a synonym for "emperor." Or take the "inexplicable" fact that many leading Communists have been publicly attacked, even humiliated, but remain at their posts, or reappear after a period of political disgrace. As Hegel points out in his *Philosophy of History*, "No subject in China was too exalted to receive stripes"; princes and officials were equally punished, so that "equality of them all before the Emperor meant that all were equally degraded." Disgrace of an individual was not followed by his demise; the blows received were for discipline rather than punishment. Analogies with the treatment of high State and Party officials during the Great Proletarian Cultural Revolution are obvious.

Another thread connecting the Cultural Revolution with history and culture is the all-important question of regionalism, or what Chi Chao-ting has called "key economic areas." [9] The existence of key economic areas motivated the geographical differentiation in the land system and methods of taxation, and accentuated the natural tendency toward uneven regional development. Differences in the land system, taxation, and the degree of development of commercial and usurious capital meant differences in the social characteristics and power of the local ruling groups, differences in the degree of exploitation, and differences in the conditions of life of the peasants.[10] The attempts of rulers and their local representatives to change the boundaries between public and private landholdings in various regions had social consequences, and localized revolt often followed. As Chi Chao-ting put it:

> When a socio-economic cycle, which usually coincided with a dynastic period drew to a close, when exploitation of the peasants increased and production declined, when extravagance and corruption weakened the ruling power, and when bankruptcy faced the government and starvation confronted the pauperized population, the peasants usually took the road of rebellion, refusing to pay rent, taxes and debts, harassing and expropriating the rich and sacking centres of political power and administration.[11]

In other words, regional autonomy and its association with peasant revolt has been a big influence on Chinese history.[12] Rebellion has flared when a certain sort of regionalism has been allowed to emerge. The pattern of the Chin, Han, and Tang dynasties was that economic development and public administration tended to cluster in the regional cities, where the government was strong. In the countryside, however, warlords arose to replace the weaker regional units of the central government. They, in turn, suppressed the peasants who were driven to rebellion. The importance of regional development in Chinese history has not been lost on Mao Tse-tung.

In the 1960's Mao tried to avoid a repetition of earlier historical patterns by linking regional Maoist groups with the "center"; through ideology and the army he tried to link them more and more with the Cultural Revolution Group under the Party Central Committee in Peking. That is why he allowed regional autonomy to grow only to a certain point and then, in the Cultural Revolution, cracked down on semi-independent "kingdoms"—notably Szechuan and Kwangtung. Take the case of the Southeast Bureau of the Communist Party of China. The former Secretary of the Center-South Bureau, Tao Chu, was responsible for administering the affairs of 200 million Chinese from Fukien (opposite Formosa) to the Vietnamese border. He had direct control of the half-billion dollars of foreign exchange coming in yearly from Hong Kong. Until September 1967, he was never accused of being a "rightist." [13] In fact, he was known as a "leftist" who promoted the Leap Forward of 1958–1959 and the communes (which he lauded in his book, *People's Communes Forge Ahead,* published in 1964). Tao Chu, in August 1966, was also a member of the Central Party Secretariat; he was called to Peking to join the Cultural Revolution Group under the Party Central Committee, and became Director of the Propaganda Department. After this brief admittance to the proletarian headquarters, he was dropped in mid-1967. Clearly, he had been called away from the Central-South area to enable Mao's supporters to break up his regional power base. His successor, Wang Jen-chung, Secretary of the Hupei Party Committee and then Secretary of the Center-South Bureau, met with the same fate.

Of the six first secretaries of the powerful regional bureaus of the Party, four were opposed in some way to the Cultural Revolution in 1966 or 1967: the First Secretary of the Southwest Bureau, Li Ching-chuan; the First Secretary of the Northwest Bureau, Liu Lan-tao; the First Secretary of the North, Li Hsueh-feng; and the First Secretary of the Center-South Bureau, Tao Chu, whose successor, Wang Jen-chung, followed the same course. In 1967–1968 the strongest opposition to the Cultural Revolution was encountered in Szechuan Province, where Lo Ching-chuan had built up a big local following; in Kwangtung Province, headquarters of Tao Chu; in Yunnan; and in Kwangsi. There are very interesting historical parallels here. Liang Chi-chao pointed out[14] that "Whenever there were disturbances under Heaven (meaning in China) Szechuan was held by an independent ruler and it was always the last to lose its independence." There were eight occasions on which this happened in Chinese history after the fall of the Early Han dynasty (206 B.C.–A.D. 25). Other regions which are more or less integral units, when considered geographically and historically, are Shansi, and the Southeastern coastal provinces of Chekiang and Fukien. "Of the two regions, Shansi is strong in defence though weak in economic self-sufficiency, while Chekiang and Fukien are weaker in defence but strong in economic resources. Historically, both have been seats of independent rulers for considerable lengths of time during periods of division. But these two regions were too close to the central domain to defy the central authority for long." [15]

THE CHINESE REVOLUTION, AGRARIAN SOCIALISM, AND THE PEOPLE'S LIBERATION ARMY

Any assessment of Chinese economic strategy after 1950 must begin by asking why the Chinese Revolution itself was successful. It is possible to advance the following reasons:

(1) It was not opposed by traditional religion; the bureaucratic social order associated with Confucianism could be overthrown, to allow for a radically new activation of the latent energies of ordinary people.

(2) China had experienced political and armed uprisings for decades—the Taiping, Boxer, and 1911 Revolts, and a new revolutionary working-class had been created in Canton, Shanghai, and Hong Kong.

(3) Mao evolved a new revolutionary strategy in tune with these conditions, surrounding the cities with peasants as the backbone of revolution.*

(4) Orthodox nationalism had led the country to economic disaster; there was an absence of ideological barriers; there was a chronic revolutionary situation, and a peasant strategy to deal with it—a unique constellation of forces favorable to agrarian communism.[16]

During the 1930's, the People's Liberation Army (PLA) had already taken part in communal production: "As a result, the conception of a Red Army performing the dual function of a mass army and a mass labour force was successfully implemented. The soldiers were taught not only to fight battles but were made to reclaim waste land for cultivation." [17]

---

* A constant theme at all lectures delivered at revolutionary "shrines" in contemporary China is that the Russian Revolution involved the city surrounding the towns, whereas the Chinese Revolution hit first at the countryside where the rule of capital was weak. The Mao stronghold of the 1920's, Chingshan Mountains, is held up as the first rural revolutionary base area in modern history.

This did two things—it initiated the commune[18] system and gave a leading place to the PLA in promoting new social relations and production. The last was of the greatest importance to Mao Tse-tung. His policy was that "As long as the army on its part does this job well, the local government and the people will also improve their relations with the army." [19] He pointed out that "Production by the army for its own support has improved the army's living conditions and lightened the burden on the people." [20] He gave as an example the fact that "In recent years our army units in the border region have undertaken production on a big scale to provide themselves with ample food and clothing and there is a greater unity than ever within the army and between the army and the people." [21] The Great Leap Forward saw the army—a peasant army—taking a large part in public works, construction in agriculture, and in harvesting. The PLA's Chief of Staff, on November 21, 1957, ordered the dependents of officers to return to their native villages to "participate in socialist construction." [22] In 1958, army units were in the forefront of the antidrought works, and contributed 40 million days of agricultural and other labor during 1959.[23] In this sense, the PLA helped to implement a vast scheme of agrarian socialism.

During the Cultural Revolution the army has been a main proponent of Mao's call, issued at the Eleventh Plenum of the Central Committee of August 1966, to "grasp revolution and to promote production," as well as to be a leading force in the "three-in-one" combination (cadres,* masses, and army) which formed the revolutionary committees, the Paris Commune type of administrative structures which proliferated in China in 1967–1968.

RECENT DEVELOPMENTS

We have tried to emphasize the ideological, cultural, and political aspects of Chinese civilization as it affects the economy, the social system, and the people. That is why this book is an exercise

---

* "Cadre," in this book, is used for both the group and the individual engaged in leading political activity—a use in keeping with the Chinese word for cadre, *kanpu*.

in institutional economics or political economy and not a treatise for specialists or "China-watchers." This is not meant to imply that China is simply an inward-looking "special case." It is true that sometimes the statements of cadres and leaders give the impression that China is a closed continent turned in on itself with colossal economic, political, and cultural problems to resolve— problems which absorb the main interest of the leadership. However, there is also a strong internationalism in the ranks. Beyond the national and historical elements specific to the Chinese situation, the Chinese "road" runs through many areas faced by the communist movement as a whole: power, decision-making, bureaucracy, participation, industrialization, technology, and attitudes toward other social systems.

As to the Cultural Revolution itself, we have adopted the attitude that it cannot be understood as a clash of personalities, or as a power-struggle-at-the-top, muted by ideological noise. We have tried to see the elements in it which are relevant to understanding the present state of China's social and economic system: revolt against the power system which industrialization engenders; elements of Narodnik ideology*—even echoes of peasant anarchism and populism; the problem of regional versus central authority; and the role of communist parties as engines of industrialization.

Notes

1. See, for example, D. E. Novack and R. Leckachman, *Development and Society: The Dynamics of Economic Change* (New York: St. Martin's, 1964).
2. Mao Tse-tung, "On Coalition Government," *Selected Works* (Peking: Foreign Languages Press, 1961), Vol. III, p. 315.

---

* "Narodnik" refers to the Russian populist movement, influential after 1860, which sought to move directly from feudalism to agrarian socialism by developing the village "mir" system, in order to skip over the capitalist phase of Russian economic development.

3. Mao Tse-tung, *On the Correct Handling of Contradictions Among the People* (Peking: Foreign Languages Press, 1967).
4. "Supply and Marketing Co-operative Carries Forward Revolutionary Tradition," *Hsinua News Bulletin*, April 14, 1968.
5. Joan Robinson, "Planning and Development," review of "La Construction du Socialisme en Chine," *Co-Existence*, No. 4, 1964, p. 106.
6. See Jerome Ch'ên, *Mao and the Chinese Revolution* (London and New York: Oxford, 1965), p. 355.
7. *China Pictorial*, No. 1, 1968.
8. Barrington Moore, Jr., *Social Origins of Dictatorship and Democracy: Lord and Peasant in the Making of the Modern World* (Boston: Beacon, 1966), pp. 227, 482.
9. Chi Chao-ting, *Key Economic Areas in Chinese History* (London: 1936), p. xiii.
10. *Ibid.*, p. 148.
11. *Ibid.*, p. xiv.
12. Tung Chi-ming, *A Short History of China to 1840* (Peking: 1965), pp. 47–50, 114–115, 128–129.
13. According to charges by Canton Radio on December 6, 1967, Tao Chu had experimented in the Hsienchien Brigade of Shaho Commune in Kwangtung Province, with a scheme of redistribution of land to families according to their labor potential, and called it a "production responsibility system." He was also accused of promoting material ahead of spiritual progress in stating that "The idea of socialism is to use every means to ensure rapid national industrialisation." See *Far Eastern Economic Review*, February 1, 1968, p. 192.
14. Quoted in Chao-ting, *Key Economic Areas*, p. 31.
15. *Ibid.*, p. 33.
16. P. Worsley, *The Third World* (London: Weidenfeld and Nicholson, 1964), p. 94; and Barrington Moore, Jr., *Social Origins*, Ch. 9.
17. Ping-chia Kuo, *China, New Age and Outlook* (London: Penguin, 1960), p. 66.
18. "During the War of Resistance against Japan, for instance, an agricultural producers' co-operative of a socialist character appeared in Ansai county in northern Shensi." Mao Tse-tung, *On the Question of Agricultural Co-operation* (Peking: 1956), p. 3.
19. Mao Tse-tung, "Policy for Work in the Liberated Areas for 1946," *Selected Works*, Vol. IV, p. 77.

20. Mao Tse-tung, "On Production by the Army," *Selected Works,* Vol. III, pp. 327–328.
21. Mao Tse-tung, "We Must Learn to Do Economic Work," *Selected Works,* Vol. III, pp. 243–244.
22. H. C. Hinton, "Intra-Party Politics and Economic Policy in Communist China," *World Politics,* July 1960, p. 513 n.
23. *Ibid.,* p. 523 n.

Chapter 1

ECONOMIC STRATEGY UP TO 1957[1]

The economy inherited by the new regime was a shambles. Since the fall of the Manchu dynasty in 1911, extensive areas of China had been wracked by revolution, war lordism, civil war, foreign invasion, and flood and famine. Industry and commerce had almost come to a standstill in major urban centers. The industrial base in Manchuria had been looted by the U.S.S.R. of more than $2 billion worth of machinery and equipment. Dams, irrigation systems, and canals were in a state of disrepair. Railroad lines had been cut and recut by the contending armies. Inflation had ruined confidence in the money system. And finally, the population had suffered enormous casualties from both man made and natural disasters and was disorganised, half starved, and exhausted.[2]

In 1949 China was a poor and backward country. The modern industrial sector was small and predominantly foreign-owned. It was concentrated along the Eastern seaboard and in Manchuria, in a few large cities such as Shenyang, Harbin, Tientsin, and Shanghai, where foreigners had been able to obtain special privileges. It was mainly light industry, although the beginnings of heavy industry existed. Steel output never exceeded one million tons, and machine-building industries were almost nonexistent. A few modern power stations supplied electricity to the large cities, but in the countryside electricity was virtually unknown. The transport system was inadequate—only about 12,000 miles of railway existed, mostly in Manchuria and linking the cities on the Eastern seaboard. Vast areas of the country were inaccessible to motor vehicles.

Most manufactured goods in everyday use still were made by traditional methods, either in the home or in very small handicraft

31

industries, especially in the remote interior where the products of the Western commercial enterprises could not penetrate. About four-fifths of the population was employed in agriculture, which provided the bulk of the national income, and most were poor peasants. It was found, at the time of the land reform of 1949–1952, that landlords and rich peasants, constituting less than ten percent of the total population, owned seventy percent of the land. However, Chinese inheritance laws, which divided a father's land equally among his sons, inhibited the emergence of very large estates, such as existed in Russia and Eastern Europe in the nineteenth century; hence a Chinese landlord who owned 120 *mou** would be thought to be a man of considerable substance. He would rent out his land in small lots, and even those lots would be split up by the families farming them into a number of widely scattered strips. Modern agricultural technology had not reached China, and in any case its adoption would have been very difficult in the face of such extreme fragmentation of holdings and the existing social organization of agriculture. Consequently output per man and per acre were very low; landlords commonly took up to fifty percent of the crop in rent; most peasants had no chance to accumulate capital, and many were permanently in debt to money lenders, who were often also the landlords, charging extortionate rates of interest.

The Chinese economy was thus predominantly feudal, with enclaves of foreign capitalist industry in the coastal cities. The industrial base and infrastructure was smaller than that possessed by Russia in 1914, and smaller than that of India when it became independent. In addition, much of what industry existed had been run down, agricultural production drastically reduced, and the primitive transport system severely disrupted by decades of war—culminating in the worst inflation of modern times.[3]

REHABILITATION OF THE NATIONAL ECONOMY: 1949–1952

The immediate strategic objective clearly had to be the rehabilitation of the national economy, in a way which would lay the

---

* Six Chinese *mou* are equivalent to one acre.

groundwork for the future socialist transformation of the economy and society. During this period economic control was secured over the "commanding heights" of the economy, such as banking, trade, railways, steel, and other key industries; and land reform redistributed the estates of landlords and rich peasants. But neither in agriculture nor in industry was there any large-scale nationalization, with the exception of industrial assets belonging to supporters of the Kuomintang, who were allied to foreign interests, and characterized as "bureaucrat capitalists," as opposed to "national capitalists," whom the government tolerated. The latter were smaller businessmen who had tried to build up independent industry. They were looked on as a progressive force, and possessed valuable skills which the regime could not do without; policy was not to expropriate them but gradually to assimilate them into the socialist sector. They continued to receive interest on their investments, and were paid fairly high salaries to continue managing their enterprises. Many produced under contract to the state, and by 1952, twenty-two percent of industry by value was in this position. Simultaneously the government was setting up joint State-private enterprises, and creating completely State-owned industry in the capital goods sector.

Land reform was begun before 1949 in the liberated areas,[4] and was completed by 1952. Over 300 million peasants benefited from the redistribution, but the equalization of land holdings was not complete; rich peasants were treated relatively lightly, and middle peasants also shared in the distribution, so that after the reform, although the number of middle peasants greatly increased, rich and poor peasants still remained. Most landlords were allowed to retain sufficient land to support themselves. A completely egalitarian land reform would have alienated the middle peasants and disrupted production.

Thus, at this stage, China became a country of small owner-cultivators. The ultimate aim of the regime in respect to agriculture was stated from the first to be its full socialization, yet neither the material nor the political conditions for this existed during this period. The material conditions necessitated a high degree of mechanization, scientific manpower, and a skilled and educated labor force. Also, a high level of political and social consciousness would have been necessary to enable the peasants to work collectively instead of individually. Hence a policy of gradualism was begun by the widespread formation of mutual aid teams, which were already established in Northern and Western China before 1949. Originally organized on a temporary basis, these teams consisted of about five households, formed to compensate for shortages of manpower, draft animals, and farm implements during busy seasons. They developed into more advanced teams, on a permanent basis, consisting of up to ten households, which held some property such as tools and animals in common, and combined their efforts in farm production and subsidiary occupations all the year round. Members were compensated according to their contribution, and could withdraw if they wished, taking with them their share of the common property. By 1952 over forty percent of households were members of such teams.

The policies adopted during this three-year rehabilitation period were remarkably successful. By 1952 all sectors of the economy had reached the pre-1949 production levels, and some had surpassed them. Ashbrook, in his contribution to a report of the Joint Economic Committee of the U.S. Congress, writes:

. . . in a remarkably short time the new government had
—suppressed banditry.
—restored the battered railroad system to operation.
—repaired and extended the badly neglected system of dikes.
—replaced the graft-ridden bureaucratic system of local government with apparently incorruptible Communist "cadres."
—introduced a stable currency and enforced a nationwide tax system.
—begun an extensive program of public health and sanitation.
—provided a tolerably even distribution of available food and clothing.
. . . Chinese economic policy in the period of Rehabilitation (1949–52) gets full marks for drawing all China together in one national economic unit and laying the groundwork for the transformation of the economy to a Soviet-type command economy. The objectives of this period—the establishment of economic law and order, the seizure of the commanding heights of the economy, and the restoration of existing productive facilities—were all achieved.[5]

THE FIRST FIVE-YEAR PLAN AND THE SOCIALIST TRANSFORMATION
OF INDUSTRY AND AGRICULTURE, 1953–1957

The aims of the First Five-Year Plan were to lay the foundations of a comprehensive industrial structure as quickly as possible. Priority of investment funds (over fifty percent) was given to the capital goods industries, which were planned to grow faster than the consumer goods industries, although output of the latter was also to be increased. The proportion of the State budget devoted to agriculture was relatively low (6.2 percent), but investment in agriculture by the peasants themselves was not included in the State budget. The economic strategy followed was that pioneered by the Soviet Union: the slogan was "Learn from the Soviet Union," but the Chinese applied the Russian model in a less extreme form. Originally, planning was highly centralized, and all-important targets were fixed by the ministries in Peking responsible for the various industries. But in a country of China's size and complexity, this system led to a certain amount of waste and dislocation. Hence the control of industry was considerably decentralized at the end of 1957; consumer goods industries came under the control of provincial authorities. The central authorities continued to control directly the capital goods industries, and exercised broad supervision over the rest of the economy, fixing the rate of investment, allocating raw materials, and determining wages and employment levels.

The Soviet Union had agreed to provide, in the course of three Five-Year Plans (1953–1967), about 300 modern industrial plants of all kinds, and to train the Chinese to run them, at an estimated total cost of about $3 billion in the form of loans. By the end of 1957, 68 of these projects had been completed, and by 1960, when the Soviet technicians were withdrawn, 154 had been finished. At that time the accumulated Chinese debt to the Soviet Union was about $1.5 billion, but less than one-third of this was connected with economic assistance, the rest being related to the liquidation of the Soviet share in several joint Sino-Soviet stock companies, payment for certain Soviet assets in Port Arthur, and payment for Soviet supplies to the Chinese army in the Korean War.[6] (By the end of 1964 all debts to the Soviet Union had been repaid, by the export of specialty foods, textiles, and processed ores—notably tin, antimony, and tungsten.) The main Russian contribution was thus in the form of technical assistance in modern methods of which the Chinese had not had any experience, rather than in the form of capital, as the loans were repaid in about ten years.

The Chinese financed the great bulk of their capital investment themselves. According to one foreign estimate, during the First Five-Year Plan, gross fixed investment rose from 5.5 percent of Gross National Product in 1950, to 17.9 percent, and during the Great Leap Forward, it reached 25 percent.[7] China also invested in people, in their education and health. Between 1949–1958, 431,000 students graduated, of whom 130,000 were engineers; this was more than double the number produced in the previous twenty years. A public health program, with emphasis on preventive medicine and better hygiene, virtually eliminated lethal diseases such as cholera, typhoid, and plague, and controlled debilitating diseases such as schistosomiasis.

Most industrial targets of the First Five-Year Plan were achieved and some surpassed. Heavy industry constituted 48 percent of industrial output by 1957. Over the period of the plan, crude steel output increased from 1.35 million metric tons to 5.35 million; coal from 66.5 to 130.7 million; petroleum from 0.44 to 1.46 million; cement from 2.9 to 6.9 million; sulphuric acid from 190 thousand metric tons to 632 thousand; and electric power from 7.3 billion kilowatt hours to 19.3 billion.[8]

According to official figures, the gross output value of all industry, including handicrafts, increased by 128.4 percent during the plan, an annual average increase of 18 percent. Scholars in the West, for various reasons, have considered this an overestimate; Field's estimate is a 100 percent increase, giving an annual average increase of 14 percent,[9] but even the lowest estimate concedes an increase of 85.9 percent over the five years.

Agriculture

In agriculture, the strategy was to extend collectivization gradually, by stages, developing from the mutual aid teams. The next stage was the development of cooperatives, in 1955–1956. The movement toward cooperatives advanced slowly, but speeded up in the latter half of 1955 after a major policy intervention by Mao Tse-tung, who feared a reversion to capitalist agriculture: "The spontaneous forces of capitalism have been steadily growing in the countryside in recent years, with new rich peasants springing up everywhere, and many well-to-do middle peasants striving to become rich peasants. On the other hand, many poor peasants are still living in poverty for lack of sufficient means of production . . ." Mao's 1955 program, *On the Question of Agricultural Co-operation,* was largely an ideological document aimed to encourage the mutual aid teams to develop into cooperatives and to reduce the role of the private peasant. He also argued, however, that agricultural cooperatives, by the impetus they gave to public work projects, would be able to achieve larger crops than those produced by individual peasants and mutual aid teams. He concluded: "If we cannot solve the problem of agricultural co-operations in a period of roughly three five-year plans, that is to say, if our agriculture cannot make a leap from small-scale farming with animal drawn farm implements to large-scale mechanised farming, including extensive state-organized land reclamation, by settlers using machinery, then we shall fail to resolve the contradiction between the ever-increasing need for marketable grain and industrial raw materials, and the present generally low yield of staple crops; we shall run into formidable difficulties in our socialist industrialization and shall be unable to complete it." [10]

Lower cooperatives were formed, consisting of from 20–40 households; the income of members came from payment for labor services, and payment for property contributed to the cooperative. Higher cooperatives, containing from 100–300 households, were formed from the merger of a number of lower cooperatives, and payment for property contributed ceased, although peasants whose animals were taken over were compensated. By the end of 1956, 88 percent of peasant households were members of higher cooperatives, which embraced whole villages, and thus became the basic economic unit in the countryside.

Cooperatives had four main economic advantages. *First,* they could mobilize the surplus labor power available in the slack seasons, especially on small-scale irrigation works at the village level

—the building of ditches, ponds, canals, small dams, and reservoirs. During the First Five-Year Plan, close to 200 million *mou* were added to the irrigated area of China—nearly half during 1955–1956 by the cooperatives. In addition, there was much terracing of the fields and large-scale tree planting. Both types of activity were undertaken by large numbers of people using primitive tools and mobilized from within the cooperatives.

Second, the cooperative can marshal the savings of its members. Its possibilities for productive investment are greater than those of an individual and so can benefit all of its members. The risk of failure also is shared; if a project fails, members do not face destitution. *Third,* the cooperative can effect more rational management of agriculture, by the pooling of small fragmented plots into fields of a more economic size. *Fourth,* the cooperative can develop a better social security system; it can set aside a welfare fund available to all its members, on the familiar principle of social insurance.

These are well-known advantages of larger economic and social units over small ones—better utilization of labor, greater saving and investment potential, more rational use of physical resources, and better social welfare provision. The potential disadvantages are equally well known—the increased complexity of management, and the possible loss of incentive to work for and with the larger group, rather than independently and for one's self, resulting in a reduced effort. The central problem of cooperatives everywhere has been to provide efficient management, especially where the population is largely illiterate, as it was in China in 1955–1956. We met a number of commune administrators who had been illiterate, but who had benefited from the adult literacy and education programs. They described their difficulties when the cooperatives were first formed; often they were learning to read and write, and to keep accounts, at the same time as they were learning to administer the cooperatives. Naturally many mistakes were made, but with more widespread education, and the rise of a literate younger generation, the problem of developing competent administration became less difficult.

On the important question of incentives, more will be said later, especially in Chapter 8, which discusses moral incentives. Here it

will be sufficient to stress that although moral incentives have
been a key component of the ideology of the Chinese Revolution
from the beginning, there has nevertheless been a mixture of both
material and nonmaterial incentives in practice, although there
have been changes of emphasis in certain periods. On joining the
cooperatives the peasants were allowed to keep small private plots
on which they could produce for themselves and for the free
market, and their share of the net income of the cooperative was
assessed on the basis of work points accumulated, which were determined by the extent and arduousness of the work put in by
each member.

Official statistics indicated that over the period of the First Five-
Year Plan, the gross output value of agriculture increased by 24.7
percent at 1952 prices; the output of food grains increased by 19.8
percent. As the population increased by about 11 percent, this
would represent about a 9 percent increase in per capita food
grain production, or an annual rate of about 1.5 percent per year.
Some Western economists, while broadly accepting these statistics,
argue that the real increases in crop and livestock production occurred between 1952 and the completion of the 1955–1956 cooperative drive, but that agricultural stagnation had already commenced in 1957.[11] Whether this is true or not, the significant
achievement is that during the First Five-Year Plan, when the
major emphasis was on the expansion of heavy industry, and agriculture received only 6.2 percent of the total investment allocated
by the State budget, a major collectivization of agriculture was
carried through without a decrease in output per head, and probably with a small increase. Ashbrook writes:

> The Chinese Communists did not try to begin the large scale
> mechanisation of agriculture in the First Five-Year Plan period and
> this was sound economic policy. Industrial effort had to go toward
> expanding the industrial base . . . Agriculture was to continue to
> benefit in this period from the restoration of peace, and the estab-
> lishment of a strong central government. Continued improvement
> in flood control and irrigation systems depended on the organisation
> and discipline of large bodies of men; the new government was well
> suited for this kind of task . . . Another major line of improve-
> ment in agriculture was largely beyond the capacity of the economy

in this period; namely the development and application of improved techniques of production, especially the increased use of chemical fertilisers and the introduction of superior strains of rice and other crops . . . In this period the Chinese Communist leadership should be graded high for its economic policy and its economic achievements at this stage of development . . . In addition to a several fold increase in the production of major industrial products, the Chinese Communists, with Soviet help also

—modernised and increased the capacity of major branches of modern industry.

—trained thousands of skilled and semi-skilled workers.

—laid the groundwork for a Soviet-type planning and statistical system.

—obtained sufficient growth in agriculture to keep up with the growth of population.

. . . By the end of the First Five-Year Plan period Communist China had achieved an enviable momentum in economic development. This momentum was translated into high morale and enthusiasm among a large part of the population . . .[12]

Nevertheless there were problems. Agriculture was not developing fast enough; neither was light industry, which received only 11.2 percent of total investment during the period. This created problems for peasant incentives. Just as in the Soviet Union in the 1920's, the encouragement of a marketable surplus in agriculture depended largely on investment in agriculture, and on making available supplies of light industrial goods for peasants to buy in exchange for their produce, so in China it was found that, under conditions of only gradual collectivization, peasant productivity lagged as a result of lack of incentives. Without steadily growing surpluses of agriculture, not only were there problems in supplying food to urban areas, but the financial backing (derived from taxation on agriculture and State profits from resale of agricultural deliveries) for industrialization was not there. Lack of export surpluses did not permit the alternative method of industrialization, of exporting grain to obtain imported machinery.

In 1956–1957 the State procurements of grain and taxation in kind fell to 25.1 percent of the value of all grain produced, compared to 29.1 percent in 1953–1954.[13] This encouraged Mao to attack the looming problems in industrial growth by three methods:

rapid growth of agricultural collectives in 1955–1956; the commune system in agriculture in 1958; and the encouragement of the Great Leap Forward in industry of 1958–1959.

Regionalism and the Decentralization of Industry

Another problem was regionalism and the location of industries. The new Communist government was, from the first, dissatisfied with the concentration of China's industrial plants in coastal areas. Planner Li Fu-chun announced, in the First Five-Year Plan, a policy of "appropriately locating new industries in different parts of the country so that industrial production will be close to the sources of raw materials and fuels as well as consumer markets." [14] By 1956, however, planning authorities seem to have been unwilling to develop new economic areas at the expense of the general rate of economic expansion. True, the picture of actual regional development since 1952 was that of a widening area of decentralized control of industry. But what kind of industry? Small and medium firms had been promoted in the regions and inland cities, but the large-scale modern sector had remained concentrated in the old economic coastal centers, where technocracy and "bourgeois experts" were firmly entrenched. (This, as we shall see, was to become a major issue of the Great Proletarian Cultural Revolution launched in 1966.) Later statistics showed that even after the considerable effort during the Leap Forward years of 1958–1959 to develop industry in remote areas, this pattern of concentrated industrial capacity still existed. Thus in 1960–1961 the value of annual industrial capacity in Shanghai was more than five times that of the next largest industrial center, Tientsin, and over six times that of the third largest urban complex, Wuhan. Over half the total estimated modern sector in industry was still concentrated in Kiangsu, Hopeh, and Liaoning Provinces.[15]

Notes

1. This chapter makes extensive use of Nicholas Brunner's excellent pamphlet, *China's Economy* (London: Anglo-Chinese Educa-

tional Institute, 1969). Unless otherwise indicated, its statistics have been taken from this source.

2. Arthur G. Ashbrook, Jr., in *An Economic Profile of Mainland China* (New York: Praeger, 1968), p. 18.

3. See Han Suyin, *Birdless Summer* (New York: Putnam, 1968) for a graphic account of the situation in the decade before 1949. She records that average prices in February 1944 were 250 times those of the summer of 1942 (p. 294), and that when her husband died fighting for the Kuomintang in October 1947, she received the sum of *ten million Chinese dollars* from the Chiang Kai-shek government; this came to about *three pounds sterling* (p. 313).

4. See William Hinton, *Fanshen: A Documentary of Revolution in a Chinese Village* (New York: Monthly Review Press, 1966), for an extensive account of the process in the village of Long Bow, Lucheng County, Shansi Province, in the spring and summer of 1948.

5. Ashbrook, Jr., in *An Economic Profile of Mainland China*, pp. 18, 20.

6. *Ibid.*, p. 22.

7. W. W. Hollister in *China Quarterly*, January–March 1964, p. 40. Cited by Nicholas Brunner, *China's Economy* (London: Anglo-Chinese Educational Institute, 1969).

8. Ashbrook, Jr., in *An Economic Profile of Mainland China*, p. 25.

9. *Ibid.*, p. 275.

10. Mao Tse-tung, *On the Question of Agricultural Co-operation* (Peking: 1956), p. 19.

11. For example, see Marion R. Larsen in *An Economic Profile of Mainland China*, p. 257.

12. Ashbrook, Jr., in *An Economic Profile of Mainland China*, pp. 24–25.

13. S. Ishikawa, *Long Term Projections of China's Mainland Economy* (Tokyo: 1965), p. 32.

14. Li Fu-chun, *Report on the First Five-Year Plan of Development* (Peking: 1955), p. 50.

15. Yuan-li Wu, *The Spatial Economy of Communist China: A Study on Industrial Location and Transportation* (New York: Praeger, 1967).

Chapter 2

THE GREAT LEAP FORWARD: 1958
AND THE CRISIS YEARS: 1959-1961

THE GREAT LEAP FORWARD

Up to 1957, Western economists, as we have noted, had, by and large, given guarded approval to the Chinese strategy of economic development. With the Great Leap Forward, which saw the creation of the communes, and the industrial policy of "walking on two legs" (which meant the simultaneous development of medium, small, and large industry, and the simultaneous use of indigenous techniques and modern methods), disillusion set in. Most Western economists regarded these policies as a disastrous failure, responsible for the crisis years of 1959–1961, and embarked upon mainly for political reasons.

We cannot agree with these propositions. As we hope to show in this chapter, they are rooted in misconceptions of the Leap Forward as a mixture of the creation of communes and the development of "backyard" iron production. The aim of the commune system was the intensification of agricultural socialism to increase the marketable agricultural surplus and widen local agricultural and other investment opportunities. The industrial policy of "walking on two legs" aimed to tap the sources of industrial growth inherent in widely spread, easily mined coal and iron ore deposits, and small-scale indigenous technology, by the rapid development of small and medium industry in the interior of the country, both *within and without* the communes. In this respect it can be viewed as a kind of "crash industrialization" program, but within the context of developing agrarian socialism, without large-scale labor transfers to the cities.

Industrial Policy and "Walking on Two Legs"

This policy was sketched in the year 1955 when Chief Planner Li Fu-chun said:

> Our task is to arrive at a proper distribution of investments among big, medium and small enterprises in the course of industrial construction, and to effect co-ordination and mutual support in the construction of these various enterprises, so as to guarantee not only construction of the necessary priority projects, but also quick returns from investments. Many medium and small scale enterprises can be built in a short time, bringing quick returns on investment and adding to our productive capacity. They not only play an important role in increasing supplies of industrial products and supporting agricultural production but they also constitute an indispensable factor in increasing accumulation of funds in supporting and assisting construction of big priority projects.[1]

Indeed, it was probably only because there were too few large enterprises to form a backbone for industry that the policy was not widely implemented until 1958.

The policy embraced many branches of the "heavy" field, previously identified in communist literature* as requiring large-scale investments and large-scale, capital-intensive plants in the coal, iron and steel, chemical, and machine-building industries. Usually the policy of "walking on two legs" involved industrial decentralization by communes and provinces, which supervised the effective mobilization of manpower in projects which were labor-intensive.

Clearly this widespread use of labor-intensive, small-scale production units represented an adjustment to the "factor proportions" situation in China, that is, to the abundance of human labor power and the relative scarcity of capital. However a group of additional economic advantages arose from the development of *local* small industry in the "heavy" field. These advantages can be summarized as follows:

---

* It has become increasingly clear that the Soviet division of industry into "heavy" and "light" is outmoded. "Heavy" includes capital goods, some of which are produced by small plants, while "light" includes a product such as paper which requires large-scale and capital-intensive investments.

(1) Where raw materials and markets were close to the communes, a wider distribution of enterprises was possible, reducing transport bottlenecks and keeping down required transport investments. This facilitated local regional self-sufficiency, which has been a continuing objective of Chinese economic planning.

(2) Linked to this is an improved geographical location of industry which develops "backward" areas.

(3) Smaller enterprises are less demanding of quality of construction. The poorer raw materials used in both construction and production often forced new technological solutions which reduced costs.

(4) The construction period and "gestation" period of investment are reduced, because of the smaller scale of enterprises.

(5) Low capital intensity is achieved, provided adequate local labor is available.

Savings in construction and operation costs were noted by a number of Western experts who visited China in 1958–1959. Bettelheim referred to the invention of plants for the extracting of shale-oil, which were built within three days and cost only 300 *yuan*.* [2] Their annual capacity was only 100 tons of crude oil each, but since there were over 10,000 such plants (as well as 100 medium plants and 500 medium refineries), they produced 1.2 million tons of oil annually—about four-fifths of total output in 1957. Bettleheim also noted, in Wuhan, a small blast furnace of 3.5 cubic meters, capable of producing 180 tons of steel per year and employing eighteen people in three shifts. This cost only 200 *yuan* and was constructed by twelve people over nine days. Adler claims[3] that, in 1958–1959, a large number of small blast furnaces of capacity of up to 100 cubic meters each, and a total capacity of 43,000 cubic meters, were established; also some medium furnaces, of total capacity of 24,000 cubic meters, which produced 50 percent of total pig-iron output; and that the quality was good. (The pig-iron output-to-input coefficient, which shows tons of output per cubic meter of furnace volume, in September 1959, was 0.85 for small furnaces, compared to 1.49 for big furnaces. The cor-

---

* Two *yuan*, in Communist China, are equivalent to one U.S. dollar, according to the 1970 basic rate.

responding coefficients for the Soviet Union and the United States were 1.4 and 1.0.) In the steel industry, small and medium converters, taking less than 3 tons, were widely used, and produced 3 million out of the 11 to 12 million tons of steel produced in 1958. Pig iron from medium and small blast furnaces was, in the main, up to international standards in 1958.[4] In coal mining, medium and small mines produced 40 percent of output in 1958 and 1959. The Chinese claimed that during 1958, 81 percent of all coal was mined by modern methods, and of this about 24 percent was won by modern methods in *small* mines.[5]

These observations correspond with contemporary Chinese press reports. Early in 1959 a network of small chemical works was established. The works were run by locally improvised methods and turned out acid, soda, fertilizer, and insecticides; by May 1959, there were 2,000 small acid and soda works in the countryside. (Five million fertilizer plants were also claimed, but many of these were probably village compost depots.) The interesting point here is that the local chemical works reduced costs sharply by substituting pottery and glass for metal equipment.[6] In Kiangsu, in 1959, 40 small sulphuric acid factories, each with a capacity of 400 tons, were established in two months, using simplified equipment (consisting of pottery, oil barrels, and strips of cast iron) designed by technicians of the Yung Li Chemical Works. It seems rather hard to argue, as many Western economists have done, that these low-cost factories, introduced to *supplement* the large chemical works at a time when rapid expansion of steel output was putting a strain on supplies of sulphuric acid and caustic soda, could have inflicted damage on the economy.

Small-scale works of the kind discussed above are also alleged by Western writers[7] to have diverted labor away from more urgent tasks—especially in agriculture. However, in the chemical works mentioned, only 34 technicians and 300 workers were required for operation.[8] It would seem that any reallocation of such labor to agriculture or to the large plant sector would have had only a very marginal effect, if any. Many of these chemical factories widened bottlenecks in the supply of scarce products, and they did so by actually using waste materials—by processing the existing surplus of sweet potato and rice husks, turning out alcohol and glucose.

On a more macroeconomic level, Western writers argued that the allocation of labor resources to small industry was uneconomic, that its opportunity cost was high, because three-quarters of the increase in the industrial labor force was taken away from more productive activities.[9] Little real evidence has been produced to support this theory, and it is not clear whether women workers were included in the notion of an "increased industrial labor force." It seems doubtful whether millions of women could have been released for employment without the reorganization of the division of labor, and a restructuring of the economic activities of the communes.

The case of the small chemical industry also shows that "walking on two legs" did not involve the *sacrifice* of the development of big industries and the large plant sector in the interests of rural industrialization. Large industry continued to make the decisive contributions in iron, steel, heavy machinery, machine tools, and power. In the power industry, although many people's communes constructed small power plants, large hydrostations were completed and put under construction, raising hydropower capacity to 10 million kilowatts in 1959,[10] and some large thermal units were also constructed (for instance, the 225,000-kilowatt station at Tsinan).[11] The contrast is shown by comparing the 125 small power stations of total 6,800 kilowatt capacity built in Kiangsu (East China coast)[12] with the construction in 1958–1959 of big hydropower stations at Tankiangkou (900,000 kilowatts); Hsinan River (652,000 kilowatts); Hsitsin Station; and Kwangsi (210,000 kilowatts).[13] Similarly, in the iron and steel industry, the burst of medium and small plants occurred simultaneously with the conscious development of giant, complicated steel-rolling equipment, with individual sets having a capacity of up to 700,000 tons of steel blooms per year (notably in Shenyang and Dairen).[14] The Chinese continued to recognize that once full employment was attained, extra productivity would have to depend on new techniques, and while these were to some extent developed in small and medium plants, their application could be widened substantially only in the large plant sector, with its ability to obtain economies of scale resulting from specialization.

A point to note is that the whole Leap Forward strategy, with its Emulation Campaigns, resulted in the discovery of many new techniques.[15] Thus, in the Tayeh Steel Mill in Central China, it was discovered that by adding slag from an electric furnace to molten steel from an open-hearth furnace, the melting time of a heat of steel was reduced by one hour, with an average increase of 7.6 percent in the rate of production. It was found that high quality carbon structural steel could be turned out using this method, harnessing pig iron with a substantial sulphur impurity content.[16] The manufacture of pellet iron ore, which raised the output of an ordinary blast furnace by twenty percent, was developed in Anshan during 1959.[17] New hot air blast pipes which increased pig-iron output and reduced coke consumption were successfully developed at the Wuhan Steel Company, Central China. These saved 30,000 *yuan* annually for each blast furnace with a volume of more than 1,000 cubic meters, and coke consumption was reduced by 12 kilograms per ton of pig iron produced.[18]

The picture drawn here is in conflict with the widespread view in Western countries that medium and small enterprises were not set up as economic enterprises but for purely political reasons; that they were costly, that the quality of output was poor, and that these inadequacies forced their eventual collapse and closing. Some of this thinking is rooted in misconceptions about the role of the "Backyard" Iron and Steel Campaign of early 1958. This campaign was a mass movement development, which took place before the main Leap Forward; at most it can be regarded as a prelude to the wider use of small industry. It was halted by the government when it became clear that the quality of output was low and too big a strain was being placed on the transport system. Such was *not* the case with commune small industry. Most of the output of this form of small industry—even in iron production—was satisfactory and transport was relieved rather than burdened. It is probable that skepticism about small and medium industries in China, and the belief that they involved low quality output, has its roots in the confused and incorrect identification of "backyard" steel with commune industry. Rather, the conscious development of small and medium furnaces and converters within commune industry, the growth of small chemical and machine-building works, and similar activities, should be clearly differentiated from the short-lived "Backyard" Campaign. Western writers would understand Chinese strategy more clearly if they ceased to describe the Leap Forward as a mixture of communes, "backyard" iron production, and "walking on two legs."

The Development of the Communes

The communes were not only a new administrative unit or a method of decentralizing the location of industry. They were primarily exercises in agrarian socialism—in collective labor, a collective way of life, a method of bringing new activities to the village. They were also a means of improving the division of labor in the agricultural sector, and they developed out of the earlier experiments in agricultural organization, the cooperatives.

The advantages of larger-scale cooperation for irrigation and canal building and for water conservation works were recognized; and 1957 saw the merger of cooperatives into embryonic communes in some areas. By September 1958, after official approval for this kind of development, the 750,000 agricultural cooperatives had become organized into 23,384 communes embracing 90 percent of peasant households. Their size varied from 5,000 to 100,000 people. (Later their number was increased to some 70,000, and the size reduced considerably, as many of the initial formations were too large and unwieldy.)

Everything that has been said about the cooperatives can be applied with equal or greater force to the communes. However, they were not simply production units but governmental units as well; they were also responsible for education, health, and defense. Some communes adopted very advanced policies—for example, in some cases private plots were abolished, in others a system of free supply was instituted; people received a food ration, and sometimes other basic necessities, irrespective of work performed. These advanced policies, before long, had to be reversed.

With the development of communes came problems of ownership and the question of whether the village, the team, or the commune should be the basic unit for accounts, planning, and distributing incomes. By the end of 1958 the peasants had already pooled their major items of property—mainly farm tools and draft animals, but at first, in most cases, the communes did not involve the pooling of small private agricultural plots. Later this was done, but in 1959 about twenty percent of the general income of the villages (production brigades) was still taken up by the share of small individual plots.*

In the first stage of the communes, exclusive ownership of major assets—land, capital goods, and production—was in the hands of the communes rather than of brigades, teams, or administrative districts. Problems arose, however, from the amalgamation of cooperatives of unequal wealth and ability, particularly in those cases where egalitarian wage-payments in kind were introduced. After the Wuchang Resolution of December 1958 had revoked payment according to need and reestablished payment according to work, the production brigades (villages) became more prominent "units of account" and this was formalized in the Lushan Resolution of August 1959. These changes have led some observers to think that the communes ceased to exist, except in name. But this is not so; the reforms described were directed primarily against those communes which had advanced furthest toward centralization and free supply. The commune still retained ownership of industrial plants and control over relations with State organs. (The production brigade as the "unit of account" was the structure still prevailing in much of China in 1968. However, in some areas the commune was the "unit of account," and in others it was the production team, depending partly on the economic geography of the area and the political consciousness of commune members.)

The commune, like the cooperative, can apply a system of deferred wages, or a system of unpaid collective labor—but on a larger scale—provided moral incentives are maintained. Where a number of different crops can be produced on the same land, and the earnings of the commune are affected by different tax levels on the various crops, there will be a tendency to apply something like marginal principles and switch labor effort between crops to maximize commune incomes. In practice, however, the plan will

---

* Even in 1966–1968, the authors found that some twelve percent of village income came from these plots.

largely set the pattern of output and restrict the freedom to choose relative crop outputs.

The advantage of the commune in this regard—the use of non-wage labor—applies not only to cultivation but also to water conservation and irrigation, again on a larger scale than the co-operative. Provided there are adequate inspections, checks, and incentives, labor can be organized to create such physical capital without putting money-wage pressures on the supply of food and "wage-goods."

Rather strangely, the Resolution of the Central Committee of the Communist Party of China on the "Establishment of People's Communes in Rural Areas" of August 29, 1958, did not go into the question of irrigation, nor did the Wuchang Party Session Resolution of December 10, 1958. However, the idea of the commune as a more optimal unit of organization of labor for such projects was clearly implied in the first of these resolutions, and the work achieved in irrigation and water conservation was summarized in a document[19] issued in January 1960.

This is not to say that all of this collective labor was utilized in an optimal manner. Mistakes occurred. Water conveyance systems from reservoir to field were often neglected in the great rush to build dams.[20] Not enough care was taken to complete detailed studies of topography, silt content, river flow, and weather patterns. An excessive number of irrigation canals were dug as part of a network which aimed to crisscross the area between the Yellow, Yangtze, and Huai Rivers, but not enough drainage canals. Since many irrigation canals were too small, they created problems for future farm mechanization, without providing adequate protection in times of flood. Many canals leaked,[21] and this seepage, causing waterlogging, accentuated the alkalinization of the soil where seepage came from drainage canals which had a higher proportion of salts than irrigation canals. Nevertheless, there were solid achievements in irrigation work by the communes in the three years 1958–1960, and more than an additional 16.5 million *mou* of land were brought under irrigation.[22] On the whole, the achievements probably outweighed the errors, even though, for short periods in 1960–1961, in some areas, these disadvantages would have reinforced the effects of the natural calamities that China had to cope with.

The commune was not, however, only a method of improving cultivation or of constructing more public projects to improve agriculture. It also embraced, as we have seen, indigenous and small industry: iron and steel, use of waste materials for making acid, fertilizer, food processing factories, and so forth. In addition, the commune was a unit of State power to better exploit the productivity of existing manpower and resources. Thus, the average number of workdays per farm in 1930 came to 190, whereas the number of workdays per year envisaged in the people's communes was more than 250 for able-bodied men, and 120 for able-bodied women.[23] The application of this labor by reorganization of the division of labor converted human labor directly into physical assets on a spectacular scale, despite mistakes and excesses. The year October 1957 to September 1958 saw the removal of 58,000 million cubic meters of stone and earth, which is equivalent to the digging of 300 Panama Canals. Agricultural results in 1958 were solid, although much below the original claim that grain output would be doubled in that year. A thirty percent increase was probably achieved. Other results, such as a more balanced economic life and greater public welfare expenditure, are also important.

The Chinese experiences in 1958–1959 appear to show that the direct transformation of labor reserves into physical capital may work best in decentralized units, such as communes, where agriculture and industry and services are coordinated.

Where natural resources existed and were readily winnable, the communes allowed:

(1) The use of the agriculturally unemployed on construction works in local areas, thereby yielding "Nurkse-type savings." [24]

(2) The supply of wage goods to workers in the area, rather than the offer of higher money wages to workers to encourage them to move to large plants in cities. This kept down pressure on foodstuffs, brought about the rapid extension of consumption on the communes following 1958, and reduced the inflationary potential inherent in rising money wages confronting a short-run inelasticity in the supply of food and consumer goods.

(3) Careful attention to the danger of those remaining in agriculture stepping up their consumption of foodstuffs.

(4) Development of a complementary relationship between agricultural and medium industrial development, in which small and medium industrial plants supplied tools and machinery, fertilizers and insecticides for agriculture, while agriculture supplied food and also agricultural raw materials for processing in the chemical and other light industries.

This seemed to be the principal rationale of the system of industrial growth within communes.

THE CRISIS YEARS

Natural disasters, the withdrawal of Soviet economic aid in 1960, and organizational problems in the communes, compelled a slowdown in the rate of expansion. In heavy industry, mainly, the sudden withdrawal of Soviet technicians in the mid-summer of 1960 caused very serious problems. Some 150 enterprises were being constructed, in which over a thousand Soviet technicians were engaged. In one month all of these enterprises stopped. The Soviet technicians withdrew, taking their blueprints with them, and no further equipment was supplied. We were told in factory after factory of the tremendous problem this created for Chinese industry—"It was like taking the dishes out in the middle of a meal." The readjustment was painful, for Chinese technicians had to work out, slowly and laboriously, the operational design of unfamiliar processes, and to learn how to make the essential equipment which was no longer forthcoming. This withdrawal obviously set back China's industrial progress by several years; it obviously had an impact on Mao Tse-tung, causing him to stress even more the policy of self-reliance and technological independence. The sudden withdrawal probably motivated Chinese technicians, scientists, and workers more strongly than exhortations from within could have done; gradually the new processes were understood and the essential equipment constructed, and the fact that most capital equipment can now be designed and built in China is probably due, in no small part, to the sudden withdrawal of Soviet assistance.

In agriculture, 1958 was certainly a good year, though not as good as had been thought. The three succeeding years were extremely bad. In 1959, almost a half of the cultivated area was affected by heavy floods or serious drought. In 1960, drought, typhoons, floods, and pests struck 800 million *mou*, more than half of the cultivated area, and seriously affected another 300 to 360 million *mou*, some of which bore no crop at all. The Yellow River practically dried up for a month in Shantung, an almost unheard of event.[25] A serious food shortage developed, but famine was avoided by rationing and collective effort. The commune system, by its ability to mobilize large numbers of people, undoubtedly helped in avoiding famine in these difficult years.

It is a familiar experience that underdeveloped countries tend to founder under an inadequate marketable agricultural surplus. When agriculture stagnates, food imports edge out important industrial imports; it becomes more difficult to divert labor to capital works, since food does not follow the flow of labor. To the extent that industrial policy was modified in China after 1959 it was largely in response to agricultural short-falls. This gave rise to some zigzags in priorities, and the relative priorities to be accorded agriculture, heavy industry, and light industry changed in a confusing manner. Eventually the policy of giving first priority to heavy industry was reversed, resources were switched back into food production, and the slogan "Agriculture as the foundation of the economy and industry as the leading sector" was adopted.

For industry, the policy of "walking on two legs" was restated categorically in 1960. In February an official exhortation read:

> It is absolutely possible to operate a large number of small enterprises with greater, faster economic results. Guided by this policy China has doubled the speed of its agricultural, industrial, transport and other economic development achieved in the First Five Year Plan. During 1960 our targets are the building of large numbers of small modern enterprises in the non-ferrous metal, chemical, petroleum and electric power industries.[26]

In August 1960, a further call to implement this policy was made:

> The large-scale development of productivity at the moment calls for further organization of production, co-ordination, close combina-

tion of State industry with commune industry, of big enterprises
with medium and small enterprises, and of indigenous methods with
modern methods of production. It demands multi-purpose utilization and diversified undertakings . . . As close co-ordination is
achieved between big, medium and small enterprises, and as State
industry gives more help and support to commune industry after
the formation of combined enterprises, it is possible to concentrate
the technical forces for break throughs in the technical revolutions
and to popularise advanced experiences . . .[27]

Physical evidence from power, chemical, and coal-mining industries during 1960-1962 shows definitely that the concept of
small-scale and medium-scale development continued to be applied. Small hydropower stations increased in number in several
provinces. In Chekiang Province, for example, 900 small power
stations were constructed between 1958 and the end of 1961, with
a total capacity of 22,000 kilowatts.[28] Ten thousand people were
trained in communes to operate them, and some communes could
manufacture the turbines required.[29] The use of small coal mines
was favored throughout the period. A new drive to open up small
mines was launched in May 1960, and there were reports of many
new mines coming into operation. In Hopei Province new mines
amounted to 66 percent of total new capacity added.[30] In Kiangsi,
1,000 new mines were put into operation in May and June 1960—
all small-scale.[31] Kwangtung Province, previously deficient in coal,
opened 800 small pits, and by September 1960 its output was six
times that of 1958.[32] In the chemical industry, the policy of rapid
expansion of small works was continued in 1960 and 1961. In
Harbin, 2,800 small plants were set up in the first six months of
1960. (Only 7 plants existed there in 1957.) When the output
value of 500 of these is added together, it comes to double that
of the biggest modern plant. But while the modern chemical plant
took three years to construct, the 500 small ones took only six
months.[33] In nine months of 1960, some 1,500 small chemical
plants were set up in 40 of China's cities to meet rapidly increased
demand.[34] In 1961, rapid expansion and new operation of small
chemical works continued, especially in Shanghai, Kiangsi Province,
and Nanking.[35] What particularly pleased Chinese leaders was
that many of these plants were using gas, waste liquids, and other

discarded materials to turn out ammonium sulphide, calcium superphosphate, and DDT.

However, the policy of "walking on two legs" was increasingly associated with increased emphasis on mechanization and modernization of small and medium enterprises, and with the spread of technological improvements. Press reports continually mentioned technical improvements of small coal pits and iron mines.[36] In the machine-building industry, three innovations were frequently mentioned: (1) the substitution of precision casting for the previous system of cutting with machine tools,[37] (2) the development of a simplified *set* of multiple machine tools, designed at the Chiluan Machine Works and suitable for small industry and commune-run plants (these innovations were popularized at the end of 1961),[38] (3) the development of a low-cost pump which could lift 45 tons of water per hour to a height of 12 meters, and which cost one-eightieth as much as an ordinary engine-driven plant. This was also popularized at the end of 1961.[39]

This emphasis on modernization, better techniques, mechanization, and so forth, seems to indicate that the momentum of innovation was slowing up toward the end of 1960, and that this process continued in 1961. In that year official statements began drawing attention to the failings of some small enterprises in obtaining satisfactory coefficients of utilization of inputs, as compared to large plants.[40] But whether this represented a retreat from medium firms is doubtful, in view of the evident growth of these enterprises in 1960–1962.

Decentralization

Some new developments took place in remoter areas in these years—mainly in light manufacturing production. In 1960 textile production was no longer limited to Shanghai, Sian, Chengchow, Harbin, and Shihchiachuang. Glassware, plastics, and rubber goods had shifted from coastal cities. Sugar refineries which, before 1958, were sixty percent concentrated in South China, had been constructed inland. In 1961, in Tsinghai Province (West China), 10,000 types of light articles were being turned out in factories set up only in 1958 or later.[41] Inner Mongolia was producing consumer goods in 3,000 factories in 1961.[42]

Attempts were made to decentralize heavy industry—in the sense of small and medium plants turning out iron and engaging in machine building. By 1960 iron was produced in eighteen administrative regions. Machine-building industries using a modest level of technique were established by 1960 in all provinces except Tibet, Ninghsia, and Tsinghai.

Large Plant Development

The main feature of large plant development after 1958 was the greater emphasis on *quality* of output and expansion of a variety of types in the product-mix. The Chinese planners regarded this as *equivalent to a quantitative increase in output*. In a major speech of December 1961, the Vice-Minister of the Metallurgical Industry[43] explained that "The improvement of quality and increase in variety of steel products also means, in a certain sense an increase in quantity . . . a higher quality product will last longer. A steel rail which lasts forty years is as good as two steel rails which last only twenty years . . ." He explained further that the greater stress on quality rather than on sheer output was a reflection of a more mature industry:

> In the Leap Forward Years of 1958 and 1959, it was still impossible to concentrate forces on tackling this problem, because an increase in variety must rest on a certain quantitative basis . . . It was only after the great quantitative development as a result of the three years of Great Leap Forward, that we were in a position to concentrate on the problem of variety.[44]

During 1961 the press commented continually on the increase in quality and variety of steel and machinery. Among the claims made were that 400 new varieties of rolled steel were produced in 1961; that 93 percent of converter steel produced in 1961 reached first-class quality (compared to 87 percent in 1960); that most of the *new* kinds of steel products were high-grade alloy steels never made in China before.[45] It was always said that these results were equivalent to increases in output of lower-grade steel.

It is likely that this improvement in the large plant sector was greatly aided by the assistance to *total* output given by those small plants which were producing usable output. Further, the ability of the large-scale sector to specialize was made possible by a division of labor between the two sectors. In the chemical industry, the large plants were able to concentrate on high-grade products and the smaller on simpler products—clearly an economic proposition.[46]

Thus in February 1960, there was a reaffirmation of the policies of 1958–1959. It was expressed in these terms:

> Some people said that the establishment of industry in the people's communes occupies too much labour power and therefore affects agricultural production. But actually the extensive building of industry in the people's communes has vigorously urged agricultural production to take a continued forward leap. Commune industry has turned out large amounts of farm implements, working tools, chemical fertilisers, and insecticides, creating favourable conditions for increasing agricultural production.[47]

Policy Changes

However, in March 1960, came the first indication of a change in priorities:

> . . . we should see that in industry, production is stepped up without increasing the number of hands in industry. The commune economy may not take up more than five per cent of agricultural labourers, and during the busy farm season, commune-owned undertakings are to transfer as much labour as possible to agriculture.[48]

Yet in the same month we also read:

> The guideline of adopting agriculture as the foundation with industry taking the lead, and of simultaneously promoting industry and agriculture, with priority given to industrial development is China's steadfast guideline for carrying out socialist reconstruction . . . The priority development of heavy industry is still necessary today and will remain so in the communist society of the future. This is because heavy industry supplies the branches of the economy with technical equipment and new techniques.[49]

By December 1961 there was a definite switch to a policy of agricultural priority, but with a "contradictory" emphasis on heavy industry:

Agricultural output occupies a specially important position. In the process of expanded reproduction, the growth of agriculture and light industry match that of heavy industry. The aim of socialist production is, in the last analysis to develop the production of articles of consumption.[50]

This "transitional" statement may be compared with the later and more definite instruction of 1962, for heavy industry to mark time. Consider, for example, the Ten-Point Program announced on April 16, 1962, by Chou En-lai at the National People's Congress:

(1) To strive to increase agricultural production, primarily of grain, cotton and oil-bearing crops.

(2) Rational arrangement of production of light and heavy industry, and increased output of daily necessities as much as possible.

(3) Continued retrenchment of capital construction and use of material, equipment and manpower where they are most urgently needed.

(4) Reduce the urban population and the number of workers and officials to an appropriate extent by persuading those coming from rural areas to return to rural production.

(5) Make inventories of stock and examine and fix the funds for each enterprise, so that unused materials and funds can be used where these are most needed during the present adjustment.

(6) Ensure that the purchase and supply of commodities are effective and that market supply conditions are improved.

(7) To work energetically to fulfil foreign trade targets.

(8) Adjust cultural, educational and scientific research.

(9) Carry out firmly the policy of building the country, and with diligence and thrift and hard work to reduce expenditure and increase revenue.

(10) To continue to improve the work of planning to ensure the all-round balance between the branches of the national economy in the order: *agriculture, light industry and heavy industry*. (Italics added.)[51]

The implementation of this policy can be seen in the investment of 300 million *yuan* in a new form of long-term interest-free loans to rural communes between July and September 1962. The aim of these was to aid agricultural development. The figure compared with 827 million *yuan* given to *all* branches of the economy in the 1957 budget.[52]

Investment priority after 1962 was given to agriculture and light industry. Heavy industry was expected to finance more of its expansion from its internal accumulation of capital. In the first quarter of 1962 it was revealed that internal resources mobilized by large capital construction units amounted to ten percent of total capital construction investment. This was welcomed as allowing less financial appropriation to the "heavy" sector, thus saving funds for use elsewhere.[53]

However, in all of these changes, there was no evidence of a complete abandonment of the policy of "walking on two legs," or the policy of developing both small and large plants *within* the heavy and light industry sectors.

CONCLUSIONS

A major effect of the Leap Forward, the setting up of the communes, and the decentralization of industry was to bring a very large proportion of industry under local administrative control. This proved to be irreversible—and is a continuing factor in Chinese economics and politics. The changes brought by the events of 1958–1959 in industrial administration are shown here:[54]

	1957	1958	1959
Central control (percent)	46.0	27.0	26.0
Local control (percent)	54.0	73.0	74.0

Central control and direction of planning in the provinces is weakened by the sheer size of China, and by the limited railway network, which is only two-thirds that of Britain and one-third that of India.* Hence the importance of regionalism cannot be

* Railways carry eighty percent of all freight. The railroads were the recipients of ten percent of all capital investment by the State in the First Five-Year Plan. During the Great Leap Forward the freight carried by the railroads rose by 170 percent due to the demands placed on the railways; even so, lack of railways held up industrial and construction programs in regions. Plans to switch from steam to diesel and electric traction announced in 1959

overemphasized. The two most important physical bases for regionalism are the river systems and the mountain ranges. The difference between the North and South of China proper, represented by the Yellow River Valley and the Yangtze Valley, remains crucial. Taking the Central-South and Central-West regions, one notices immediately the groupings of Kwangtung-Kwangsi, Hupei-Hunan, Szechuan-Yunnan, and the seaboard territories Fukien-Chekiang. The Hupei-Hunan area is the hub of the Yangtze Valley; Fukien and Chekiang have been unable to develop an agricultural surplus but have been politically and militarily semi-autonomous—as they are today.

In the case of Kwangtung and Kwangsi, their regional integrity can be seen clearly from the topography. Encircled by the mountains and by the ocean, the economic and cultural life of the region is self-sustained, with comparatively few horizontal planning or policy connections with adjoining provinces. Farther west, equally distinct regional autonomy is evident in Szechuan-Yunnan. The Red Basin of Szechuan is encircled by high barrier ranges; anything which can be grown anywhere in the country may be produced there. Thus Szechuan, with its easily defended boundaries and rich and varied resources, is remarkably fitted for a relatively independent and self-sufficient economic existence. There is also a basic contrast between agricultural or "Inner" China and non-agricultural or "Outer" China.[55] "Agricultural China" embraces China south and east of the Great Wall. While much of the area is mountainous, there are alluvial plains and wide lowlands. North China, with its poorer, tawny soil is climatically marginal for rice; its porous soils can grow only soybeans, millet, high-cost wheat, and cotton. The hill areas are thinly peopled and are scarce of soil and timber, the grass roots having been dug up over the centuries for fuel. Central and South China is the center of rice, bamboo, and tea production, while the far-South is tropical, yielding two

---

have been only partly begun, but by 1960 the Chinese railroads were carrying three times as much freight as in 1957. With a renewed effort after 1959, more than 22,000 miles of rail had been completed by 1965, comprising Peking-Canton (part double-tracked), Tientsin-Shanghai (part double-tracked), Szechuan-Shensi (1961); Szechuan-Yunnan (1966), Chengtu-Chungking (1955); Paoki-Lanchow, Wuhan-N.W. Hupei (1968).

crops of rice a year, as well as many fruits. Afforestation on a large scale has transformed the hill country of agricultural China, and terraced plantings of trees are to be seen everywhere, notably in Hopei Province. Flood control and irrigation have partly countered the erratic behavior of China's rivers.

A new pattern of industry is emerging, following a reassessment of the mineral potential of the mountains and basins of the thinly populated interior. Abundant hydroelectric power resources, and the vast market represented by the growing standard of living among the peasant masses, form cornerstones of a future pattern of regional development, in which particular provinces will eventually reach the industrial and agricultural levels of individual European countries.

Under these conditions, a regional enterprise is encouraged to make its own machinery, rather than to rely on deliveries from established industrial centers.

This pattern has made for self-reliance in locally controlled factories, and for strengthening of centrifugal tendencies in politics. These tendencies became acute in the New Economic Policy period, 1961–1964, forming a major reason for the promotion of the Cultural Revolution, the overthrow of regional Party committees, and the establishment of provincial revolutionary committees as new organs of Maoist authority in 1967–1968.

Further, the general strategy of economic growth and the high targets set in nonagricultural sectors were overtaken by the natural catastrophes of 1959–1961, which deprived the industrialization program of the solid support of a rising net marketable agricultural surplus. The strains of this deprivation, as well as disruptions arising from man-made errors of implementation of planning goals, gave rise to sharp political and ideological struggles over economic policy in industry and agriculture in the years which followed.

Notes

1. Li Fu-chun, *Report on the First Five Year Plan* (Peking: 1955), pp. 48–50.

2. C. Bettelheim, "China's Economic Growth," *Monthly Review*, March 1959; see also *Survey of Chinese Mainland Press* (Hong Kong), hereafter cited as *SCMP*, May 9, 1959, p. 14, which describes these plants and foreshadows their contribution at coal pitheads to produce (with coke) tars, tar-oil, and petroleum.

3. S. Adler, lecture at Indian Statistical Institute, New Delhi, December 26, 1959.

4. *Ibid.*; see also *SCMP*, May 15, 1959, p. 30, for the development of small and medium converters in Sinkiang Province, which increased steel output by four times in 1958.

5. Adler, lecture at Indian Statistical Institute.

6. *SCMP*, May 6, 1959, p. 19.

7. E. Jones in *Problems of Communism*, No. 1, 1963, pp. 17–25.

8. *SCMP*, May 6, 1959, p. 19.

9. Jones in *Problems of Communism*, No. 1, 1963, p. 20.

10. *SCMP*, May 16, 1959, p. 15.

11. *Ibid.*, p. 12.

12. *SCMP*, May 7, 1959, p. 19.

13. *SCMP*, May 19, 1959, p. 25.

14. *SCMP*, May 9, 1959, p. 13.

15. For an account of these campaigns and their results, see *SCMP*, April 20, 1959, p. 32 (for Dairen and Peking); May 4, 1959, p. 20 (for Anhwei and Changchun); May 7, 1959 (for Anshan); May 22, 1959, p. 30 (for other areas).

16. *SCMP*, May 19, 1959, p. 21.

17. *Ibid.*, p. 21.

18. *Ibid.*, p. 20.

19. *Fast Progress in Water Conservancy in China* (Government of China: January 1960). See Chao Ku-chun, *Agrarian Policy of the Chinese Communist Party* (Peking: 1960), Appendix 4.

20. Valentin Chu, "The Famine-Makers," *The New Leader*, June 11, 1962.

21. *Ibid.*

22. Han Suyin, *China in the Year 2001* (New York: Basic Books, 1967), p. 53.

23. Y. Gluckstein, "The Chinese People's Communes," *International Socialism*, Spring 1960, p. 22.

24. Ragnar Nurkse in his *Problems of Capital Formation in Underdeveloped Countries* (New York: Oxford University Press, 1966) regarded underemployed agricultural labor as potential but disguised "savings," since the direct application of this labor to capi-

tal works, with the use of simple tools, could accelerate capital construction without great financial outlays.

25. Nicholas Brunner, *China's Economy* (London: Anglo-Chinese Educational Institute, 1969), p. 20.
26. Editorial statement, *Jen-Min Jih-Pao*, February 8, 1960; see *SCMP*, February 1960, p. 1.
27. Kuan Ta-tung, "The Question of Organising Production Co-ordination and Combined Enterprise in Urban Communes," *Jen-Min Jih-Pao*, August 19, 1960, from *SCMP*, August 1960, p. 15.
28. *SCMP*, April 23, 1962, p. 21.
29. *Ibid.*
30. *SCMP*, August 14, 1960, p. 3.
31. *SCMP*, July 27, 1960, p. 5.
32. *SCMP*, September 24, 1960, p. 16.
33. *SCMP*, August 18, 1960, p. 4.
34. *Ibid.* See also *SCMP*, September 24, 1960, pp. 17–18.
35. *SCMP*, November 17, 1961, p. 25.
36. *SCMP*, August 21, 1960, p. 16; December 11, 1961, p. 21; No. 2621, November 1961, p. 24.
37. *SCMP*, August 21, 1960, p. 16.
38. *SCMP*, December 25, 1961, p. 20.
39. *SCMP*, November 9, 1961, pp. 21–22.
40. Editorial statement, *Jen-Min Jih-Pao*, November 14, 1961; see *SCMP*, No. 2629, November 1961, p. 9.
41. *SCMP*, November 16, 1961, p. 22.
42. *Ibid.*
43. Kao Yang-wen, "Exert the Utmost Efforts," *Peking Kung-Yen Jih-Pao*, December 30, 1961; see *SCMP*, No. 2655, p. 11.
44. *Ibid.*
45. *Ibid.*
46. *SCMP*, August 18, 1960, p. 4.
47. Editorial statement, *Shansi Jih-Pao*, January 12, 1960; *SCMP*, February 16, 1960, pp. 20–22.
48. Huang Yen, "The Development of the National Economy Must Be Based on Agriculture," *Jen-Min Jih-Pao*, August 2, 1960; see *SCMP*, No. 2325, August 1960.
49. Ch'en Ying Chun, "Not Detours But Spiral Progress," *Canton Nan Fang Jih-Pao*; *SCMP*, No. 2338, August 1960.
50. Yang Ch'i-hsien, "On the Need to Arrange National Economic Plans in the Order—Agriculture, Light Industry and Heavy In-

dustry," *Peking Ta-Kung Pao*, December 11, 1961; *SCMP*, No. 2649, December 1961.

51. *London Times*, April 17, 1962.
52. *London Times*, October 23, 1962.
53. *Ibid.*
54. Cho-ming Li, "China's Industrial Development, 1958–63," *China Quarterly*, No. 17, p. 16.
55. Keith Buchanan, "The Many Faces of China," *Monthly Review*, May 1959, pp. 8–18.

Chapter 3

NEW ECONOMIC POLICY: 1961-1964

The economic crisis brought on by poor agricultural results in 1959–1961 led to a new strategy of economic development and a new series of economic policies. The greater scope given for market forces and free price movements, the shift to profitability as a motive force in agricultural and industrial production, and the increased authority of managers, planners, and technical personnel (by comparison with local cadres), justify describing the new course as a New Economic Policy (NEP).

NEW STRATEGIES: 1961–1962

At the Ninth Plenary Session of the Eighth Congress of the Chinese Communist Party, in January 1961, it was decided to reinforce the agricultural front by making agriculture the foundation of the national economy and giving industry second priority. It was pointed out then, and later, that the Chinese countryside constituted eighty percent of the market for light industrial goods, as well as a large market for heavy industrial goods.[1] It was proposed to adjust the rate of development of industry to the amount of raw materials and foodstuffs that agriculture could supply, and that industry should supply the flow of goods made necessary by agricultural development to help mechanize the rural sector.

A new theory of economic development appeared—in part to rationalize what had happened in Chinese practice, in part as a recognition of necessity, and in part as good economic sense. This was the notion of "spiral growth," according to which the rate of growth of the Chinese economy would oscillate around a trend line, giving rise to "undulatory advances." [2] According to this theory, the annual rate of growth in China would fluctuate according to (1) changes in the number of laborers entering into production each year, (2) variations in labor productivity from year to year, (3) the allocations of fixed capital investments from year to year, and (4) the efficiency of utilization of capital funds from year to year. This new approach set the ground for a forthcoming period of "readjustment, consolidation, strengthening, and perfection" of branches of the economy—to follow the accelerated growth rate of 1958–1959. This "readjustment" policy was adopted in 1962.

The decentralization of authority had also proceeded apace in 1958, not only with the commune and the responsibility invested in the brigade and the team, but with the decentralization of industrialization administration itself. By the middle of 1958, for example, the central government controlled virtually none of the output of manufactured consumer goods.[3]

As the economic crisis of China deepened with the crop failures of 1959–1961, the New Economic Policy emerged. It aimed to strengthen the authority of management and of ministries, while giving more scope for the operation of free market forces in agriculture and industry, at the expense of the authority of decentralized political cadres.

Market Forces in Agriculture: The "San Zi Yi Bao" Policy

One of the first moves was the gradual introduction of a free market in rural areas.[4] Later there appeared the policy of "*san zi yi bao*" which involved (a) the restoration of private plots, (b) the use of the household as the main accounting unit in communes, (c) the assumption by enterprises in communes of sole responsibility for profit and output quotas.

In addition, a black market price was tolerated. In Shanghai in 1961 the official price of cooking oil was 0.61 *yuan* per catty* while the free market price was 30 *yuan*. "Free" rice prices in Nanking were three times the official price.[5] Trade and speculation in farm produce grew apace. A kulak peasant class began to appear, causing concern to some officials: "Some well-to-do peasants have said that the government needs only to control the collection and purchasing of grain; it should not bother about how agricultural

---

* A catty is equivalent to 1.1 pounds or half a kilogram.

production is done . . . the new and old upper middle peasants have a comparatively strong spontaneous tendency towards capitalism." [6]

The contribution of private plots to production was greatly extended. By 1962, the private grain harvest in Yunan was larger than the collective harvest, and private cultivated land rose to fifty percent of the total.[7] In Kweichow and Szechuan Provinces there was, even as late as 1964, more private than collective tilling.[8] Open markets for agricultural products developed, as official policy relaxed the administrative regulation of market prices, and indicated that the level of profits should be made the criterion for operating even the State farms. On the communes, new opportunities were given for the peasants to engage in "sideline" production such as the growing of pigs and vegetables. *"San zi yi bao"* was in full swing. All of this added up to a recovery program of the kind advocated by Bukharin in the 1920's in the Soviet Union —"riding into socialism on the peasant's nag."

In the communes that the authors visited, the 1960–1964 period was remembered vividly. Basically, the impression given to us was that peasants in the production team began to hoard seedlings and grain, to market goods privately, and to use their leisure hours for private plots or "sideline" production. The Party had to concern itself directly and constantly with the problem of balance between individual and communal needs. The Party branches were not always able to do this effectively, as ideological levels plummeted downward. Within the production brigades, people received "work points," and their income was adjusted to the amount and quality of the work. Peasants enriched themselves, rather than "serving the people."

Market Forces, Profitability, and Expertness in Industry

Another directive of the Ninth Plenum of the Eighth Congress was that small and medium firms were permitted to buy raw materials directly from the market, rather than through the wholesale corporations whose allocations were determined by the central plan. There was a redirection of China's industrial sector to consumer output after 1961, designed as part of a program of relying on material incentives, bonuses, and prizes to encourage productivity in manufacturing.

If the Great Leap Forward was primarily a phase in the political history of Chinese Communism, a "leftist" revolt, with "politics in command," against the bureaucratization of the Revolution, the policies set in train by the Ninth Plenum saw a dramatic halt to the revolt. Not only were profits put "in command," but many traditional patterns of industrial organization and ownership which had been effaced during the years of "radicalism" reappeared.

Most significant was the shift from output targets to profit targets *within* the enterprises, and the changeover in the locus of power, from control by trade-union and Party committees to control by managers, professional staff, and technocrats. Above all, the modus operandi of work shifted from nonmaterial (ideological, political) incentives to financial incentives. With this came the reemergence of intellectuals, technocrats, and managers—all with close connections with regional Party authorities. "Expertness," rather than "redness," was what counted in making economic decisions. As Schurmann said at the time, "While the ideology remains orthodox, the country as a working system of organization seems at times suspiciously similar to Yugoslavia." [9]

The authors saw many examples of what all of this had meant in practice during visits to some thirty enterprises:

(1) At the Shanghai docks, according to a member of the Revolutionary Committee:

Only three periods a week were given over to study of any kind. In fact these three periods were used to study technique and safety and for the assessment of prizes. Such prizes and bonuses were the main means of management, and involved monthly, quarterly and yearly prizes for "economy in work," "quality," "safety," "rational suggestions," etc. This set worker against worker. The managers made the dock an independent kingdom, which sought only to build up profit. For example we loaded rice for a grain corporation. If a rice bale broke, we made this corporation's staff patch it. If they borrowed needles from us they had to pay twice as much per hour as the cost of a needle. Did this "serve the people"? Or, again, warehouses here were used to store goods, and if enterprises did not collect them in time, we rented the warehouses to other enterprises, after putting the original goods in the open air where their quality was affected. Before the Cultural Revolution the bosses here got one to two times the wage of ordinary workers. Since the Cultural Revolution these irrational salaries have been cut.

(2) At the Hsinhua Printing House, Changsha, a member of the Revolutionary Committee said:

Between 1961 and 1963 the enterprise tried to use capitalist management methods. The industrial charter—what we now call Liu Shao-chi's "seventy sinister points"—was the controlling force. This document emphasized that production was in command, and full responsibility was given to the Director. Regulations controlled man rather than vice versa. The essence of the system was that those who produced more got rewards, and those who produced less were penalized. Political consciousness was not trusted, nor the initiative of the masses. We concluded in 1966 that the "seventy sinister points" should be seen as a control, a check, a stimulating and punishing device. There was a complicated bonus system, with prizes for equality, productivity, safety, savings on raw materials, and the number of meetings attended. Penalties were levied if machines broke down, for poor quality production, for failure to meet quotas or to attend meetings. This emphasis on material incentives divided the workers. But even if the workers paid attention to money alone, the productivity gains were not spectacular. Piecework was finally introduced for a few workers in the transport branch, but we refused to agree to piecework as such and operated mainly on prizes. When we swept aside material incentives in 1966–1967, the management counterattacked by offering to divide up the circulation fund. About 100 workers accepted and a squad of scabs calling themselves the "385 Brigade" was formed. We seized control of the plant and did not allow lump sum payments to be paid. At the end of 1966, about 300 workers went on strike to oppose us. We stayed at our posts and with the support of the revolutionary rebels outside we eventually forced a return to work.

(3) At the Peking No. 2 Textile Mill, the Secretary of the Revolutionary Committee concluded:

In 1961–1964, some workers were not careful enough in political study and they gave the bourgeois line too much room to maneuver. The results of this were that decisions were taken only by technical staff in a bureaucratic way, and material incentives for work and especially for innovation were operative. Selfishness was encouraged: overalls were distributed to those who did not actually need them.

(4) At the Double-Rhomb Clock Factory, Peking, a member of the Revolutionary Committee claimed:

> For a period, Po I-po, the Planning Chief, imposed a bourgeois line which was reflected in our factory. While we did make steady progress, they tried speed-up techniques and finally tried to close down the plant because it did not meet their profitability norms. The management was obsessed with getting more profit, and adjusted its outlook and management techniques to this aim. So they ignored the people's outlook, and the potential of the human factor in innovation and production. Under their control, the output quotas per machine were inflexible so that the machines controlled the masses instead of the masses controlling the machines. The managers heavily emphasized material incentives and promoted self-interest by the use of the innovation bonus, the safety bonus, the overfulfillment bonus and the long-service bonus. The essence of the Cultural Revolution here, at this plant, is the struggle between public interest and group (or personal) interest. Among the workers there is still considerable influence of bourgeois ideology and we have to get to the root of it.

(5) At the Camel Hump Railway Switching Yards, Peking, members of the Revolutionary Committee stated:

> Between 1961 and 1964 we had great difficulty in obtaining copies of Comrade Mao Tse-tung's works. During this period there were three main features. First there was technocracy. The Railways Ministry thought that technical problems should be solved by outside experts rather than by the masses. Second, there were the material incentives—which we hated, but which were imposed. Third, there were the capitalist management ideas in the Railways Ministry— a hangover of the old days. The old system of management, far from being overthrown, was held up by the Railways Ministry as a model. Its basic structure was complete responsibility to the Director; the wide use of financial incentives; bureaucratic control from the top; the division of the workers by the bonus system—the number of wagons shunted per day, etc.

(6) At the 555 Clock Factory, a member of the Revolutionary Committee summed up the period 1961–1964:

> Here the Director and his deputy were using the "seventy sinister points"—the industrial charter—for regulating industry. Prizes and bonuses abounded. We used to say: "The more prizes we allocate, the more bitter become relations among the workers." There was a technocracy in the factory. The administrative staff became larger and larger. There were 850 workers, yet there were 120 staff divided into 10 sections—and all this for a small factory. Management regulations were bureaucratic and complicated. If a worker developed an innovation, to get it accepted and a reward paid he had to go through seven different levels and fill in many forms. This imposed restrictions on the initiative of the workers, and anyway we got fed up with being bribed to work well.

(7) At the Shanghai Diesel Pumps and Motors Plant, a cadre member of the Revolutionary Committee noted:

> The Director was strongly for the piecework system, and through this there arose tensions between young workers and veteran workers and maintenance workers. Finally, under pressure, the élite were compelled to cancel the piecework system. We put up character posters which said "politics in command, not money in command."

(8) At the Pearl River Paper Mill, Kwangtung Province, a member of the Party Branch noted:

> We opposed the principles of profit in command and production in command. We had quarterly and monthly prizes for safety, quality and above-quota output. Piecework was operating in our transport section. Now we understand that work is not for the sake of work, but for revolution. It is not for the sake of getting large money rewards. All of that is now buried.

Summarizing the NEP trend inside factories, we can say that it resulted in:

(1) Adoption of the conception of a factory as a highly rationalized production unit, putting productivity before such noneconomic criteria as self-reliance, mass participation in decision-making, and "public service" as an element in factory planning.

(2) A growing differentiation in take-home pay (though not in stipulated minimum wages), due to bonuses, prizes, and piecework.

(3) A reasonably successful element of market forces in the distribution of consumer goods, with some revival of "bourgeois" economic theory and management technique.

ECONOMISTS' DEBATE

Managers and technical personnel and the controllers of the Right economic policy received strong support from academics and intellectuals. A great debate began about the role of profits in the Chinese economy[10] and the importance of "rational" relative prices for goods.[11] Yan Jien-pei and his followers, Ho Chien-chang and Chang Li, argued that productive funds should be channeled to those enterprises which had proved capable of achieving a profit rate higher than the uniform "average" for industry, and not to those whose performance fell short of this. In addition to measuring performance, the profit rate would become part of the ethos of the firm—part of a "stick and carrot" approach which would force enterprises to select advanced techniques and eliminate waste. Here these arguments resembled the well-known "Liberman" proposals suggested for Soviet industry between 1962 and 1965.[12] They also had their critics, notably Dai-yuan Shen,[13] who adopted a very familiar position—that the concept of an average rate of profit is basically part of the capitalist system, and that any attempts to introduce it would only run the risk of making profits become an automatic mechanism at the expense of economic planning itself; moreover, the "real" aim of the socialist system is not profit, nor investment, nor even industrialization as such, but the fulfillment of "social needs."

In the price discussions, a number of economists favored the inclusion of a differential rent in agriculture prices (reflecting different productivities and fertilities of land).[14] Undoubtedly their view was related to the practical difficulties arising from the "*san zi yi bao*" policy in agriculture, for without such a differential rent, with private plots growing, and with brigade incomes depending on work points, there arose a number of disparities in income, with adverse affects on peasant incentives in poorer areas. In the industrial sphere a number of suggestions for measuring costs more accurately, and deriving relative prices from them, were put forward.[15]

POLITICAL CHANGES AND NEP

Of course all of this could not have taken place without a shift in political power at the top. Managers, technocrats, and university professors were appointed by regional and municipal Party committees. They had to be followers of the NEP line, the "profits in command" line.

In higher Party circles, the early 1960's saw the reemergence of the leading critic of the Leap Forward, the main spokesman for "careful planning, good management, and technical competence," Chen Yun. It is also clear that by 1962, Liu Shao-chi and other previous exponents of the Leap Forward were now leading "rightists" in economic policy.

On November 9, 1962, the *People's Daily* announced the appointment of seven new Deputy Chairmen of the State Planning Commission. Four of these had been strong critics of the Leap Forward, particularly Li Fu-chun (head of the Planning Commission), Yang Ying-chieh (previously dismissed from the Planning Commission in 1959), and Po I-po (Politburo economist and Director of the Office of Industry and Communications).

SOME RESULTS OF THE NEP

The economy certainly improved after 1960. How much of this was due specifically to the NEP is difficult to say, but certainly the incentive system encouraged productivity. The point is that this is not a conclusive test in Maoist terms.

Moreover, some of the economic achievements in the period were due to factors that had little to do with the NEP. Among these must be included the investment projects, commenced in the Leap Forward period, which came to fruition in 1961–1964; improvements in the tax system made in 1958, which introduced proportional rather than progressive taxation in agriculture; and the replacement of a multiplicity of industrial and commercial taxes by turnover taxes, which probably helped incentives. Then there were the benefits of the significant investment in education and health undertaken in the 1950's. By 1962, 820,000 students were enrolled in full-time higher education—a sevenfold increase over the 1949 figure.[16] There had been a huge investment in public health, with the number of people taking degrees in medicine increasing from 1,313 in 1949, to 25,000 in 1963.[17] As Gurley put it:

> . . . some of the sources of economic growth in Communist China can be found in her industrial enterprises . . . But I do not think that China's economic growth can be properly understood only in those terms—without reference to the gains she has made in education, medicine and public health and scientific research. And . . . ideas may have been more important than machines in China's economic development.[18]

Whatever the cause, output, which had declined in 1960 and 1961, had certainly recovered by 1963, and the economy was moving ahead, if at a growth rate below that of the 1950's. Investment, renewed after 1961, also played its part and probably reached 20 percent of national output by 1962. The result was that industrial production was able to record an average annual rate of growth of output of 11 percent from 1949 to 1965, despite a slowdown in the early 1960's.[19] One official estimate is that industrial production rose by 15 percent in 1964, and more than this in 1965.[20]

But the all-important question of the scope to be given to ideology as against management techniques was not definitively solved in this period. The struggle between these two criteria continued throughout the period 1960–1965. Many planners and political figures in China rejected the overemphasis on material incentive. They were determined that China, once its temporary economic setbacks were overcome, should seek an economic system in which man, while seeking a better life, would not pursue this aim only through personal consumption and by handing over the creation of an industrial society to technocrats, academics, and planners. As it turned out the NEP was a transition period, not the beginning of a new market-socialist economy; the latter possibility was nipped in the bud by the Cultural Revolution launched by Mao Tse-tung early in 1966.

Notes

1. Chung Huang, "Basing Industry on Agriculture," *Peking Review*, May 10, 1963, pp. 11–15.
2. Lui Ku-kang, "Spiralling to Socialism," *Peking Ta-Kung Pao*, June 2, 1961, reprinted in *Far Eastern Economic Review*, October 12, 1961.
3. Audrey Donnithorne, "Central Economic Control," *Bulletin of the Atomic Scientists*, June 1966, p. 11.
4. Audrey Donnithorne, "The Organisation of Rural Trade in China Since 1958," *China Quarterly*, October–December 1961, pp. 77–91.
5. Yuan-li Wu, *The Economy of Communist China* (New York: Praeger, 1965), p. 96.
6. Editorial statement, *Southern Daily* (Canton), quoted in Yuan-li Wu, *The Economy of Communist China*, p. 153.
7. R. Wilson, "The China After Next," *Far Eastern Economic Review*, February 1, 1968, p. 193.
8. *Ibid*.
9. Franz Schurmann, "China's New Economic Policy: Transition or Beginning?," in *Industrial Development of Communist China*, Chomin Li, ed. (New York: Praeger, 1964).
10. G. W. Lee, "Current Debate on Profits and Value in Mainland China," *Australian Economic Papers*, June–December 1965, pp. 72–77.
11. Nai-ruenn Chen, "The Theory of Price Formation in Communist China," *China Quarterly*, July–September 1966.
12. B. J. McFarlane and I. Gordijew, "Profitability and the Soviet Firm," *Economic Record*, December 1964 and December 1965.
13. Dai-yuan Shen, "Criticism of the Theory of Production Prices and the Average Rate of Profit," *Jingyi Yangjiu*, September 1964.
14. Chen, "The Theory of Price Formation in Communist China," *China Quarterly*, pp. 44–46.
15. *Ibid*., pp. 40–41.
16. Chu-yuan Cheng, *Scientific and Engineering Manpower in Com-*

munist China 1949–1963 (Washington: National Science Foundation, 1965), pp. 72–73.

17. *Ibid.*, p. 78.
18. John G. Gurley, "The Economic Development of Communist China" (Stanford University, mimeographed), p. 1.
19. *An Economic Profile of Mainland China* (New York: Praeger, 1968), p. 273.
20. *Far Eastern Economic Review*, September 29, 1966.

Chapter 4

IDEOLOGICAL STRUGGLE AND
ECONOMIC POLICY: 1959-1965

IDEOLOGY OF MARKET SOCIALISM

The attitude toward planning and toward material incentives in China has varied with shifts in the political line of the Communist Party of China. A period of orderly central planning, with a large degree of freedom for enterprises in contracting, and quasi-market systems in agriculture and wholesaling, occurred in 1952–1957 and again in 1961–1964. During 1958–1960 and 1965–1967, the Chinese authorities tended to emphasize two basic points about planning. First, that the economy could skip over historical stages, that there was no "domino" theory in Marxism that required socialism and communism to wait upon a prior development in the level of productive forces. Second, that social organization, moral outlook, and relations between people are more important than a one-sided emphasis on raising the level of production.

A number of important ideological questions are involved here: the attitude toward the transition period between capitalism and socialism, the role of market forces (the law of value) under socialism, the relative scope to be given to material incentives as against moral incentives. These ideological views, in the circumstances of China, were most important in influencing the actual course of market socialism in China.

Nature of the Transition Period

In the late summer of 1958, the claims put forward in China for the communes (with their complementary relationship between agriculture and industry and their careful organization of the social division of labor) suggested that communism was no longer a long-run objective; the Chinese implied that they were shortening the transition period. Soviet leaders at the time accused them of attempting to jump historical stages, and openly criticized these claims to foreigners.[1]

As an issue of strategy of socialist construction in the Communist international movement, these views were openly discussed in April 1960, at a Peking celebration of Lenin's birthday.[2] The compromise Moscow Statement issued after the Summit Conference of Communist Parties (November 6–30, 1960) even appeared to repudiate the supposed Chinese view, when it concluded that "To provide a material basis for communism, it is indispensable to achieve a high level of production through the use of the latest techniques and electrification of the national economy, without which it is impossible to provide the abundance of consumer goods required by a communist society." [3]

Closer examination of Chinese statements, however, shows that the Chinese gradually were coming to view the Soviet Union as a social system which was freezing into a mold, rather than pressing on with the uninterrupted revolutionary process which the Chinese saw as a sine qua non for the transition to a fully communist society. This analysis of Soviet developments became fully developed in the Chinese critique of the doctrine of the "state of the whole people" and of the reappearance of bourgeois economic groups in the Soviet Union.

An early statement of the Chinese position was the resolution, "Concerning Some Questions of People's Communes," drawn up at the Sixth Plenary Session of the Eighth Central Committee of the Chinese Communist Party on December 10, 1958. The resolution had this to say on the steps of the transition:

> In connection with the question of transition from socialism to communism, we must not halt our advance at the stage of socialism, nor must we indulge in the dream of skipping the socialist stage and jumping right into communism . . . The transition from socialism to communism must depend on a certain level of development of the productive forces. Three years of hard battle plus several years of energetic work may bring about a great change in the economic face of the country. But even then there will be a considerable distance to go to reach the goals of a higher degree of mechanisation; and there will be an even longer distance to go to reach the goals

of an enormous abundance of social products, of a sharp reduction in working hours. Without all of these, it is, of course, impossible to talk about entering a higher stage of development in human society—communism.

We should not groundlessly make declarations that the people's communes will "realise ownership by the whole people immediately" or even "enter communism immediately," and so on.[4]

The Chinese view seems completely orthodox. However, it implied criticism, namely that the Soviet Union was not pressing on to communism, despite a relatively high level of industrialization.

Between this resolution and the Moscow Statement, other official statements on this issue were published: none upheld the skipping of historical stages thesis. Thus T'ao Chu in an official statement on August 5, 1960, argued:

> We must treat the transition from capitalism to socialism as an integral process of development; we must treat socialism which represents the early stages of communism as a society of a transitional nature, and *must not take it for an independent social form and perpetuate it.* Unless we do that we shall commit mistakes . . . Of course, when we say that we must treat the transition as an integral process, we do not preclude the possibility of dividing it into several stages and *much less suggest the skipping of any historical stage.* (Italics added.)[5]

In their hard-hitting letter to the Central Committee of the Communist Party of the Soviet Union on June 14, 1963, the Chinese again touch on these points:

> In their present level of economic development all socialist countries are still far, far, removed from the higher stage of communism. Therefore it will take a long, long time to eliminate class differences, and . . . it is impossible to say that there is no longer any need for the dictatorship of the proletariat.[6]

Here again we have one of the first criticisms of Soviet doctrine, namely that the Soviet Union is becoming a "state of the whole people," one in which political coercion and centralist economic administration is becoming less necessary. As the Chinese put it, "To deny . . . the necessity of thoroughly completing the socialist revolution on the economic, political and ideological fronts is wrong, does not correspond to reality, and violates Marxism." [7]

The Law of Value and the Economics of Socialism

In Marxist economic thought, great attention is paid to the "law of value"—a shorthand expression for the factors which determine long-run prices in a market economy. Marxist economic doctrine holds that when two commodities exchange, their values, as determined by social labor and other outlays, will be equal. Whether or not prices set by a communist government need to take such factors into account in the transition period between capitalism and communism, has long been debated in communist literature.

The general Chinese position on this issue in 1963 was expressed by Tao Chu:

In the period of transition from capitalism to communism, vestiges of the old relations of production and the old superstructure continue to exist, and some of the old economic categories such as commodity, commodity production and law of prices are still active . . . There is no alcohol which is 100% pure, there must be some foreign matter in it . . . Our job is to preserve, utilize and restrict those old things which must be temporarily preserved. We must restrict them to pave the way for their eventual elimination . . . The more radically these vestiges . . . are removed, the smoother will be the transition to communism.

In as much as the new society carries with it the vestiges of the old until the arrival of the new, we must strive to eliminate these vestiges, and *the more radically the vestiges are removed, the smoother will be the transition to communism.* (Italics added.) [8]

Continuing on the subject of the life to be granted to "capitalist" economic categories, Tao Chu concluded that:

We gradually create the conditions for the elimination of some of the old economic laws.

This applies, for instance, to the price laws. In our country the production and exchange of commodities still exists, and within this sphere, the price law has a role to play, and we must gear it to the needs of socialist construction. We must for example consider the role of the value law in fixing our economic accounting and price policies, and if we do not do that, our economic work will suffer. But in our economic work, we must not have our eyes on the price law alone, and must not concentrate on things economic without regard for political matters.[9]

Within China itself, there seems to have been, up to 1959, a struggle between different views on the speed with which the law of price could be eliminated. The view that the categories of the market will persist may be found in the document published by the Chinese Communist Party Central Committee and State Council in 1959: *Decisions on How to Improve Financial and Trading Management in the Countryside in Adapting to the Post-Commune Situation:*

> Although part of production is disposed of within the people's communes after communization in the countryside, commodity production and commodity exchange, viewed against the situation as a whole, are not curtailed, but expanded. Despite the fact that production is primarily regulated by means of the policy of letting politics assume supreme command, and of the state plan as guide, and that the role of the law of value is restricted, commodities, value, price money and credit will not cease to play a role very soon, but will continue to play an active role.

The emergence of the communes prompted discussion on the future operation of the law of value both after the successful establishment of communes and also under "full" communism.[10] In the first situation, one group of economists and political theorists held that the law of value still plays a minor role, although commune production is basically regulated by the State. The other view was that the regulative role remains, because communes are basically nonstate enterprises, and funds required for expansion still depend on the level of production and income. Where the State's leadership could cover the whole field of commune activity under "full" communism, the *minority* view was that commodity production would come to an end, but the law of value still would continue, since "Value implies a socially necessary average amount of labour, and that law of value governs the determination of this value. In communist society, the role of accounting is bound to exist, and the idea of socially necessary labour for production will also exist in our minds." However, strong opposition came from the majority, which denied that value is the same as "socially necessary labor" under communism: the former exists in all societies, but value is a "social historic norm." [11]

After 1961, when economic policy approximated to a New Economic Policy, but even earlier during the Leap Forward, discussions continued about "destroying old economic categories" and the role of prices and value categories in postcommune society. There was a considerable debate about the role of these categories in the "socialist" system, that is, the period between capitalism and communism. [12] The debate arose partly because "A correct study of commodity production, commodity exchange, monetary system and a law of value has a practical significance of utmost importance to our present economic construction." [13] Summarizing this 1959 controversy, we find roughly three schools of thought on the *role* of the law of value under socialism, and five views on the *influence* of the law. The schools of thought on the law's role were:

(1) That with the basic transformation of agriculture and capitalist industry, the scope for the free market will be curtailed; as resources are transferred to public ownership, the law of value remains only for small commodity producers and capitalist societies.

(2) That with the achievement of recent major reforms, the law is restricted, but still has broad scope, and the real issue to be decided is *at which points* of the economy its role will be manifested.

(3) That the law of value will play an even greater part under socialism, because previously it was hampered from carrying out its proper role of making prices equal to values. With public ownership, socialism dictates that while the national economic plan must suit the law governing the planned and proportional development of the economy, it must also make full utilization of the law of value. By doing so, the price and value of each commodity may tend to be equal.

The views on the influence of the law of value were:

(1) That the "law of value allows spontaneity of the economy whereas the law of planning allows *regulation*." Thus the law of value is to be distrusted.

(2) That the law of value is contradictory to the law of proportionate development.

(3) That the regulating role of the law of value is an *internal* one, that is, in the circulation of consumer goods, and in the payment of new workers to attract an adequate supply of labor (it determines the supply price and demand price in the labor market).

(4) That the regulatory role depends simply on the "depth of the role" played: if the law of value does have a wide application, its role is a regulatory one. If its application is restricted to a narrow sphere of the economy, it is not to be regarded as a regulator of economic development.

(5) That the law plays a regulatory role through two kinds of dialectical contradictions: the contradiction between "prices" and "values" of commodities, and between simple or "concrete" labor and "socially necessary" labor time. "If the law of value (through the contradictions between price and value) regulates the output of various products and readjusts the supply of manpower and the means of production among different production departments, it plays a regulative role," and "If the law of value plays a role over prices, cost and profit by utilizing the difference between the labour time expended by individual labourers and the socially necessary labour time (but has nothing to do with distribution of manpower), then it plays an influence-exercising role." [14]

After continuing debate during 1959, an official summing-up remained noncommittal. It simply referred to the importance of the debate for price policy, without mentioning its implications for decentralized planning or the degree of freedom for market forces. The conclusion reads rather lamely:

> Some held that the law of value does not play a regulatory role over prices, for under socialism price does not oscillate around value but is determined primarily by the major socialist economic laws, being only supplemented by the minor law of value. For this reason, the law of value cannot be said to be the regulator of commodity price.
>
> Some argued that not the law of value, but the law governing the planned and proportional development of the economy can be said to be the regulator of socialist production. The law of value

plays a role in the *circulation* (distribution) only of products turned out by the state-operated light industry.

Comrades in opposition to this said the law has a role for some categories of products—for example when a commune decides to specialize on the most profitable type of product depending on comparative costs between regions and communes.[15]

These disputes partly reflected the uncertainty in earlier Chinese practice during 1950–1959, zigzags in price policy, and continuing experience in the organization of the communes. In 1953, a dual pricing system had been introduced, one for State-operated factories and the other for the free market (mainly private industry and handicraft). The former was an ex-factory price, while the market price was ex-factory cost plus transport charges plus profit margin. The attitude toward this system during the First Five-Year Plan was one of reluctant recognition of necessity:

> Raising or lowering of the prices of industrial or agricultural products must be carried out with discretion and only after due regard is given to the overall situation of supply and demand, remuneration of labour and the operation of the law of value.[16]

By 1960–1962, however, growing hostility to wide application of market forces and profits can be discerned; this came, presumably, from supporters of Mao Tse-tung:

> Some people . . . often look at economic accounting in the socialist enterprise from the bourgeois point of view, go after value of output and profit blindly, and neglect the improvement of quality of products contrary to certain economic policies of the Party and the State.[17]

Or again:

> The existence of such a category as the cost of the product is decided by the objective certainty that an enterprise has to compensate for its expenditure with its income. The profit of the enterprise is the difference between price and cost.
>
> Since socialist economy is planned economy; and since socialist profits are a condition for the maximum satisfaction of society as a whole, the question of profit must be considered from the viewpoint of the development of the entire economy . . . For the sake of the planned, proportional and high speed development of pro-

duction . . . it is permissible for some production departments and newly operated enterprises to make little or no profits or even to sustain losses for a time.[18]

It will be recalled that the commune experiment came between these two statements. The Wuchang Resolution of December 1958 called for payment according to work and not to *needs*, and foreshadowed graduated cash payments. Then in August 1959, the retreat from a system without value categories was made complete with the Lushan Resolution, which revoked the notion of full commune ownership of property, when the production teams were given ownership of small plots of land and minor agricultural implements. These experiences accounted for the reluctant acceptance of the law of value at that time.

"Bukharinism"

We have already mentioned the growth in practice of "expertness" as against "redness" and the shift in favor of putting "profits in command" between 1960 and 1964. Other views expressed resembled "Bukharinism"—the doctrine pursued by N. I. Bukharin in the Soviet Union in the 1920's. Like Bukharin, many Chinese policy-makers argued that agricultural output should be encouraged by improving financial incentives: improving the prices paid for farm produce and lowering the prices of industrial goods supplied to the peasants. Bukharin proposed looking after agriculture first; the peasants should "enrich themselves." [19] With agriculture as a sound foundation, industry could be developed, but light industry and not heavy industry. This line was resurrected in China in almost every detail. Two leading economists said:

> As the foundation of the national economy, agriculture demands that all production departments including those of industry, all construction units and all cultural and educational undertakings develop themselves with the actual conditions of agricultural production as the starting point, and give due consideration to the quantity of commodity grain and industrial raw materials, and to the sizes of the market and the labour force which agriculture can supply . . . It is only after agricultural production has been rehabilitated and expanded and after agriculture, the foundation of the national economy, has been consolidated, that industry, com-

munications and transport, and cultural and educational undertakings can be better developed.[20]

One rather strange phenomenon was the uncanny similarity between Bukharin's view that "our economy exists for the consumer and not the consumer for the economy," [21] and a Chinese pronouncement:

> Under ordinary conditions, should arrangements be made first for the necessary consumption of the people throughout the country, and then, if circumstances permit for accumulation? Or, should arrangements be made after accumulation has been guaranteed? According to the basic aim of socialist production it should be the former, not the latter.[22]

Many of these views were not readily apparent to the outside observer and researcher. Most Chinese economic journals kept up a barrage against "bourgeois" economic theories of socialism because they: (1) neglected inquiry into production relations between men, made a fetish of economic relations, and made scarcity and optimal allocation of given resources the chief concern of economics; (2) ignored the historical relativity of economic laws; (3) detached distribution from production; (4) emphasized formal quantitative analysis rather than qualitative analysis.

Moreover, between 1962 and 1965 attacks were stepped up in the Chinese press on the whole idea of market socialism as it operated in Yugoslavia. The Chinese articles criticized the growth of market forces in petty-commodity production such as crafts, services, and catering in Yugoslavia. They denounced workers' self-management as a device for allowing a system of bourgeois cooperatives to develop.[23] The Chinese accused the Yugoslavs of introducing payment to work and material incentives into income distributions, thereby encouraging a profit-motive fetish.[24] This had brought about attempts to "replace the socialist economic principle of planning, by the capitalist economic principle of profit, leading to the degeneration of Socialist economy." [25] As part of this process, Yugoslav theorists were becoming "more and more receptive to the fashions and vogue of bourgeois economic theory." [26]

Despite the verbal attacks on Yugoslav theory and practice, the

Chinese themselves, as we saw earlier, had permitted the growth of actual markets and financial rewards on a wide scale after 1960.

By 1964, the practice of the New Economic Policy had increased the earnings of factory managers, technicians, and better-off peasants. This, and Bukharinist ideology, threatened Mao's plans for agrarian socialism and increased the variety of sectional interests opposed to egalitarianism and "politics in command."

The main point to be understood in the development of Bukharinism, then, is that the practice and ideology of economic policy during 1960–1964 fell into the hands of the Right (which included a leading Party figure such as Liu Shao-chi who had appeared to support the "leftist" drive to agrarian socialism during 1958 and 1959). The Cultural Revolution had, as part of its objective, to wrest power from this group of economic policy-makers and to resume a Maoist strategy of economic management.

PHILOSOPHY

It is often said that developments in philosophical thinking reflect contradictions and changes in society. One of the most significant struggles in philosophy took place in China during 1964. A principal figure in the controversy was Yang Hsien-chen, Director of the Advanced School for Party Cadres. The topic was one of Marxist dialectical philosophy: whether the revolutionary essence of the dialectic resides in "one divides into two" or in "two fuse into one." The principles of the "unity of opposites" and of the "fusion of the two into one" were defended by Yang Hsien-chen and his followers. The supporters of Mao and other leaders of Chinese Communism held, by contrast, that only through the full assimilation of the concept "one divides into two," by the masses and militant cadres, can philosophy "become a powerful ideological instrument permitting the solution of the present situation in the class struggle, internal as well as international." [27] Continuing the criticism, the Maoists counterattacked:

> At this very moment the frantic spreading by Comrade Yang Hsien Chen of the concept "two fuse into one" is deliberately designed to satisfy the needs of modern revisionists and to help them

in their propaganda in favour of peace between classes, class collaboration and the reconciliation of contradictions. At the same time it is deliberately designed to satisfy the needs of the bourgeoisie and the vestiges of feudal forces in the country, by supplying them with theoretical weapons to thwart the socialist education movement.

Towards the end of the nineteen-twenties society in the Soviet Union experienced a period of vast changes.

The development of the movements for agricultural collectivisation and the socialist industrialisation together with the desperate resistance of the kulaks and bourgeois forces made the class struggle in Soviet society very bitter. At that moment the anti-Party group of Trotsky and Bukharin appeared in the ranks of the CPSU.

It was at this critical moment that the anti-dialectical philosophic conception of Deborin became the ideological weapon of the anti-Party group and the Central Committee of the CPSU led by Stalin severely criticised and categorically rejected the philosophic concept of Deborin's school.[28]

It is quite apparent that there is a certain scholasticism in this whole dispute, and that both sides have reduced the essence of the dialectic to a simplistic formula in a way which indicates that a low level of philosophical education in cadre schools prevailed at that time. The dispute, though, is by no means insignificant. It indicates the extent to which intellectuals took advantage of the "liberalization" of economic and political administration in 1960–1962, and shows that they had resisted efforts to reform their views. In the early 1960's, Mao's own philosophical works and their application were discussed in Party circles. A common point pursued by cultural workers of the Right was that the "four philosophical essays" by Mao (*On Practice, On Contradiction, On the Correct Handling of Contradictions Among the People,* and *Where Do Correct Ideas Come From?*) were classics which were adequate for obtaining a background in Marxist theory or for "remolding one's world outlook." For this purpose, the "three constantly read articles" ("In Memory of Norman Bethune," "The Foolish Old Man," and "Serve the People") were regarded as unnecessary.

The dispute in philosophy also foreshadowed the wholesale attack to be launched on the cultural front by the Maoists in 1965.

LIBERALISM IN CULTURAL AFFAIRS: 1960–1965

In 1962 a Conference on Literature and Arts was held in Northeast China. It proved to be something of a peak in the strength of cultural workers opposed to Mao and seeking liberalization of the arts. At the conference, many writers said that very hard times had come to the peasants due to mistakes in Mao Tse-tung's general line of the people's communes and Great Leap Forward. Others complained that they were under pressure to depict characters in their works in a primitive manner, that heroes were permitted to perform only exemplary acts. Chou Yang, Vice-Director of the Propaganda Department of the Party Central Committee, appears to have tolerated and possibly encouraged the dissenters. Chou Yang opposed turning the Museum of the Chinese Revolution into the Museum of Mao Tse-tung's Thought. While inspecting the exhibition before the opening, Chou Yang had asked: "Why all those quotations from Chairman Mao hanging everywhere like labels?" And when he saw a huge statue of Mao in the first hall he commented: "You should not have the Chairman as a sentry at the entrance."

Intellectual dissent and criticism of the Maoist line was not, of course, a new event in 1962. In 1954, Hu Feng presented a 300,000 word document to the Central Committee, strongly criticizing the Party's policies and Mao's teachings on art and literature. In 1957, a Peking woman university student, Liu Hsi-ling, acted as spokesman for critical youth. But the New Economic Policy of 1961–1964 seems to have stimulated a larger number of cultural workers to express their ideas, ranging from straight criticism of socialist realism in art, and of proletarian culture, to support for a modified capitalism with pluralist elements in political life. Among the most vociferous were a group of intellectuals associated with the journals *Frontline* and *Peking Daily*. In 1961 in these journals Professors Wu Han, Liao Mo-sha and Teng To—all prominent leaders of the Peking Municipal Committee of the Communist Party—used Aesopian language in their articles ("Evening Chats at Yenshan" by Teng To and "Notes from Three-Family Village" by the three authors) to criticize Party-line interference in culture and to demand more pluralism in political and ideological life. The articles advocated "letting a hundred flowers bloom," but actually attacked the dismissal of "rightists" from cultural posts, and openly discussed the man-made contributions to economic difficulties in the country. They also criticized those who failed to "treasure labor power" [29]—the Communist Party group who supported the Great Leap Forward. Teng To had earlier, on May 11, 1957, published an article under the pseudonym of Pu Wu-chi in the *People's Daily*. This was entitled "Abolish Philistine Politics." As a result, Teng To was removed from his post on the *People's Daily* by the Central Committee of the Party. In 1966 ferocious criticisms against Wu Han and Teng To were launched.[30]

COUNTERATTACKS BY MAO TSE-TUNG: 1960–1964

Mao had criticized "rightist" trends in culture in the 1950's, notably in his "Give Serious Attention to the Discussion of the Film 'Life of Wu Hsun'" (May 1951) and "Letter Concerning Studies of the Dream of the Red Chamber" (October 1954).[31] Faced with a "rightist" upsurge in culture and economic policy between 1960 and 1964, he again launched counterattacks.

In a speech at the Tenth Plenary Session of the Eighth Central Committee Mao criticized the upsurge of opposition to "leftist" policy, the wide application of market forces in the economy, and the *"san zi yi bao"* policy in agriculture. He rallied his forces with the slogan of "Never forget class struggle!" At the Central Committee on May 20, 1963, he pushed through a document, "Some Problems in Current Rural Work," which called for less encouragement to private peasants and more attention to disciplined work teams acting on nonmaterial incentives. On June 14, 1963, the Central Committee agreed also to the issue of the Mao-drafted "Proposal Concerning the General Line of the International Communist Movement," which was served on Moscow and Eastern Europe.

On December 12, 1963, Mao issued, through editorials in Party newspapers, an "instruction on literature," which clearly warned the liberals in the cultural field. According to this instruction:

Problems abound in all forms of art such as the drama, ballads, music, the fine arts, the dance, the cinema, poetry and literature, and the people involved are numerous; in many departments very little has been achieved so far in socialist transformation. The "dead" still dominate in many departments. What has been achieved in the cinema, new poetry, folk songs, the fine arts and the novel should not be underestimated, but there, too, there are quite a few problems. As for such departments as the drama, the problems are even more serious. The social and economic base has changed, but the arts as part of the superstructure which serve this base still remain a serious problem. Hence, we should proceed with investigation and study and attend to this matter in earnest.

Isn't it absurd that many Communists are enthusiastic about promoting feudal and capitalist art, but not socialist art? [32]

Then, in the first part of 1964, Mao raised two new slogans, "Learn from Tachai" and "Learn from Taching," eulogizing the efforts of peasants in Tachai Brigade to pull themselves up by their bootstraps, and praising workers of Taching Oil Field for herculean efforts expended without financial reward. Tachai Brigade in Northern Shansi operated in the worst possible conditions—stony hills and eroded gullies. The brigade painfully and successfully terraced the hillsides and filled them with desperately scarce soil. In 1963 a deluge destroyed the terraces. However, the brigade refused State aid (to which it was entitled) and rebuilt its cultivation plots, achieving very high yields. In 1964, opponents of Mao challenged the figures of crop yields put out by Tachai, but after an expert team was sent in by Chou En-lai to measure every plot and count every grain, the brigade was vindicated. The slogan of "Learn from Tachai" spread to many brigades, with the message to raise the ideological content of work and ease out the system of financial reward. It implied an attack on *"san zi yi bao,"* strategies pursued in certain areas of China controlled by the "rightist" leaders of economic policy. A further Maoist critique of the cultural front followed, with the issue of another "instruction" on June 27, 1964:

In the last 15 years of these associations, most of their publications (it is said that a few are good) and by and large the people in them (that is not everybody) have not carried out the policies of the Party. They have acted as high and mighty bureaucrats, have not gone to the workers, peasants and soldiers and have not reflected the socialist revolution and socialist construction. In recent years they have slid right down to the brink of revisionism. Unless they remould themselves in real earnest, at some future date they are bound to become groups like the Hungarian Petofi Club.[33]

Broadly speaking, Mao's technique in 1960–1964 was to prepare and issue warnings about the implications of the "rightist" trend in economic policy and culture, and to counterpose "the revolutionary tradition of the masses," the need to train reliable successors to the revolution who would not follow the Soviet road, the need for everyone to be a soldier, and the need to implement, wherever possible, the line of "from the masses to the masses," which had fallen into disarray with the "seventy points" in industry and the *"san zi yi bao"* policy in agriculture. Mao also took certain organizational steps, notably in obtaining the adherence of the People's Liberation Army and General Lin Piao. The army was used, not only in production and defense, but in implementing cultural policies more in line with Mao's approach. Thus a novel by a member of a People's Liberation Army troupe, *The Song of Ouyang Hai*, was an important literary event promoted by Maoists in the early 1960's, while Lin Piao issued his *Long Live People's War* in 1963—an out-and-out Maoist document dealing with revolution in Asia and Latin America.

By 1965 the tensions in Chinese society were building up. The official ideology of the Chinese Revolution remained Maoist. But the State organizations and enterprises, and large sectors of cultural and ideological life, were governed by different rules. The years 1964 and 1965, in particular, saw the beginning of the struggle to resolve the question—"Which will transform which?," between State and Party practice, and Maoism? In this sense, 1965 marked the prelude to the Great Proletarian Cultural Revolution.

Notes

1. Hudson, Lowenthal and MacFarquhar, *The Sino-Soviet Dispute* (A *China Quarterly* publication: 1961), p. 5.

2. *Ibid.*, p. 12.
3. *World Marxist Review*, December 1960.
4. *Sixth Plenary Session of 8th Central Committee of the Communist Party of China* (Peking: Foreign Languages Press, 1958), pp. 23–27.
5. "An Inquiry into the Question of the Law of the Transitional Period," *Jen-Min Jih-Pao*, August 5, 1960. See *SCMP*, August 23, 1960.
6. *Peking Review*, June 21, 1963, p. 17.
7. *Ibid.*, p. 16.
8. *Ibid.*, pp. 2, 4.
9. *Ibid.*, p. 11.
10. "A Discussion on the Problem of Value and the Law of Value Under the Socialist System," *Peking Kuang-Ming Jih-Pao*, March 30, 1959; see *SCMP*, No. 2014, pp. 15–22.
11. *Ibid.*
12. *Ibid.*, pp. 15–22.
13. *Ibid.*, p. 15.
14. *Ibid.*, p. 18.
15. *Ibid.*, p. 19.
16. *The First Five Year Plan for the Economic Development of the People's Republic of China 1953–57* (Peking: Foreign Languages Press, 1956).
17. Jen Pei-ch'ing, "On the Economic Accounting System," *Jen-Min Jih-Pao*, November 14, 1962; see *SCMP*, No. 2631, p. 8.
18. *Ibid.*, p. 19.
19. Quoted in Alexander Erlich, *Soviet Industrialization Debate* (Cambridge, Mass.: Harvard University Press, 1960).
20. Lu Hsun and Li Yun, "On the Practice of Economy," *Jen-Min Jih-Pao*, August 21, 1962; see *SCMP*, No. 2817, 1962.
21. Quoted in Erlich, *Soviet Industrialization Debate*, p. 79.
22. Yang Ch'i-hsien, "On the Need to Arrange National Economic Plans in the Order—Agriculture, Light Industry and Heavy Industry," *Peking Ta-Kung Pao*, December 11, 1961; see *SCMP*, No. 2649, December 1961.
23. "Behind the Yugoslav Strike," *Peking Review*, May 8, 1964.
24. Chou Yang, "The Fighting Task Confronting Workers in Philosophy and Social Sciences," *Peking Review*, January 3, 1964, p. 20.
25. *Ibid.*, p. 21.
26. *Ibid.*

27. *Peking Information*, September 21, 1964.

28. *Ibid.*

29. "Notes from Three-Family Village," *The Great Socialist Cultural Revolution in China: 1*, Yao Wen-yuan, ed. (Peking: 1966).

30. *The Great Socialist Cultural Revolution in China: 1* and *The Great Socialist Cultural Revolution in China: 2* (Peking: 1966). Each of these contains journal articles criticizing the "gangster inn" of "Evening Chats at Yenshan" and the three men—Wu Han, Teng To and Liao Mo-sha.

31. Mao Tse-tung, *Five Documents on Literature and Art* (Peking: 1967).

32. *Ibid.*

33. *Ibid.*

PART II

Impact of the Cultural Revolution
1966-1968

Chapter 5

PRELUDE TO THE
CULTURAL REVOLUTION

The precise origins of the Great Proletarian Cultural Revolution are not clearly known; what is certain is that the Cultural Revolution was in the direct tradition of Mao's conception of revolution as a continuing process. "Central to this conception is the idea that the existing situation must be constantly reviewed and called into question to prevent the re-emergence of the former exploiting classes in positions of influence, in the form of repeated 'class struggle' movements, and a whole series of policies of 'thought reform' and 'rectification' movements." [1] This idea has been put into practice on many occasions in the last thirty-odd years since Mao has been in charge of the Communist Party, both before and after it came to power in 1949. There are numerous examples: the Land Verification Movement of the early 1930's, in which land reform was regarded by Mao as a political, quite as much as an economic, measure, and at the same time a process of education of the peasantry; the Rectification Campaign conducted among the cadres of the Party in the early 1940's; the Thought Reform Campaign among the intellectuals in 1950; the Three Antis Campaign conducted among the Party cadres in 1951—against corruption, waste, and bureaucracy; the Five Antis Campaign in 1952, directed against bribery, tax evasion, fraud, theft of government property, and theft of State economic secrets, by merchants and industrialists who were still operating their firms in a semi-autonomous manner; the New Rectification Campaign in 1957, directed against bureaucratic tendencies among cadres of the Party and the State.

The basic concept behind all these campaigns was essentially the same: that the fundamental human values, people's thoughts and motivations, are the crucial factor in the functioning of society; that even a political revolution, in which state power has been captured, and an economic revolution, in which all major productive assets are collectively owned, are not enough to insure the success of the revolution unless there is also a revolution in men's minds. Hence the object of these campaigns was to construct a new morality—a new set of rules of human conduct in tune with the new collectivist society, based on the dictatorship of the proletariat. The old morality is held to be derived from the old bourgeois society of private ownership, and the private interest of the individual to be its fundamental attribute. The new morality must be related to the new collectivist society; its fundamental attribute is to be the exaltation of the public interest over private interest, and of proletarian values over bourgeois values. Mao holds that the old ideas will not go away by themselves, but must be deliberately driven out, and new ones deliberately inculcated. The Cultural Revolution is no exception; its only difference is in its intensity and scale of operation, for it was not confined to selected groups, such as intellectuals or party cadres, but was directed at all those in positions of authority in every field. It may therefore be regarded as an enormous extension of previous attempts, but not as their culmination, for it is seen as a continuing process, which will be necessary for every successive generation, to insure the correct ideological orientation of future leaders; "correct," of course, means conforming with the basic tenets of the thought of Mao Tse-tung.

The techniques used in previous mass campaigns have included intense propaganda advocating the study of Mao's thought, widespread mass rallies involving literally millions of people, mass denunciations and public humiliations of the worst offenders, and public confessions and self-criticism by those acknowledging their mistakes and undertaking to reform themselves. In these campaigns there has been relatively little bloodletting, imprisonment, or even dismissal from office, the main pressure being social and psychological, but of so intense a nature as to provoke suicide in a few cases. The language used is—to non-Chinese ears—highly colored, with the accent on struggle and dramatic effects, with much use of military metaphor and Chinese symbolism, too often taken at their face value by Western correspondents. In the early stages the Cultural Revolution employed similar techniques, except that its scale of operation was much vaster than that of previous campaigns, and that a new extra-Party youth organization, the Red Guards, came into existence to spearhead it.

CHINA DOES NOT "CHANGE ITS COLOR"

Although the Cultural Revolution is in the mainstream of the tradition of the Chinese Communist Party under Mao's leadership, a most important factor affecting its timing and intensity has been the emergence in Russia of what the Chinese have called "revisionism." This is not the place to enter into the ideological dispute between the two Communist Parties (some points of which were noted in the previous chapter). It will be sufficient to emphasize Mao's theory that classes continue to exist under socialism, and will continue to exist until the classless communist society is achieved, and the traditional divisions of labor are abolished—a theory which is the subject of a well-known essay by Mao, first published, significantly, in 1957, after the emergence of Khrushchev in the Soviet Union.[2] These are not classes in the old Marxist sense of direct relation to the ownership of property, that is, landlords, capitalists, workers, and peasants; but functional classes of workers, managers, peasants, party and State cadres, intellectuals, academics and other brain workers, soldiers, and so forth. Contradictions still exist among these classes, and may develop into sharp antagonisms unless carefully handled. According to Mao, a particularly dangerous contradiction exists between the masses and those in positions of authority over them, that is, between the workers and peasants, on the one hand, and the managers, administrators, State and Party cadres, and those in charge of educational cultural institutions, on the other. Unless energetic preventive steps are taken, this contradiction can develop into a fundamental antagonism between rulers and ruled, such that a privileged bureaucratic and technocratic class emerges with interests of its own, divergent from those of the common people. If this is allowed to happen, and especially if this privileged group still retains substantial remnants of the ideology of the old bourgeois society, the stage is set for revisionism, that is, for revision of the basic Marxist-Leninist tenets of revolutionary socialism, both internally, and externally in relation to the imperialists. In short those in privileged positions of power will be more interested in keeping the status quo, both internally and externally, than in pressing on with revolutionary development both at home and abroad.

The Chinese Communist Party leaders believe that this happened in Russia after the death of Stalin, particularly with the emergence of Khrushchev, and that this happened primarily because Stalin did not acknowledge the existence of classes under socialism, and took no steps to resolve these contradictions; he merely attempted to eliminate opposition by purges. The only way to prevent the emergence of such a bureaucracy—which arises both within and without the Party—is, Mao believes, by the thoroughgoing practice of democratic centralism, described in his slogan of "From the masses to the masses," and not by merely paying lip service to it. This means preventing the emergence of a style of life of the upper echelons too far removed from the masses: not only in dress, income, and other outward manifestations, but also in work, especially in attitudes toward physical labor and the giving of orders. It is clear from his writings that Mao holds that in socialist society the proletariat cannot and should not be led by a group which elevates itself much above the common people in any respect, for then this category will revert to bourgeois traits and attitudes; rather, the leaders of the proletariat should be leaders from within, who should live as close as possible to the lives of the common people. Only in this way can the people be effectively mobilized, and their enthusiasm and initiative fully aroused. It is also abundantly clear that what Mao and other Party leaders label "revisionism" has made a deep impression on them, and strongly reinforced their traditional thinking on the subject.

Further, having decided that the Russian "revisionist" policy of peaceful coexistence has resulted in capitulation as far as militant resistance to imperialism is concerned—by implicit agreement to keep the status quo in world affairs—Mao and his supporters have concluded that China may well be on its own in any future conflict with the United States. Military support was promised to North Vietnam if its leaders requested it from China. In 1966 bombs were already dropping a few miles from China's Southwestern borders. It has been economically blockaded for years and menaced by a ring of United States military bases to the east and southeast, and has been officially branded as "enemy number one" by the United States. In these circumstances, and for good reasons, China felt that the probability of invasion, or at the very least bombing attacks by the United States, was very high. Consequently this was an additional reason for heightening revolutionary consciousness at home, rooting out revisionism—which in this context means sympathy with the Soviet Union's "soft line" to the United States—and uniting the nation in its determination to fight United States imperialism should the need arise. China now sees herself as the major repository of revolutionary socialism, and one of the objectives of the Cultural Revolution was to insure no backsliding in this respect, or in Chinese terminology, to insure that China does not "change its color."

PRE-LIBERATION

What has been described so far must be seen against the background of the construction of socialism in China, and the problems that have to be faced. As was emphasized in Chapter 1, notwithstanding its 2,500 years or so of civilization, China was, at the time of the Communist victory ("Liberation," as the Chinese call it), a very backward country. It was semifeudal, with five-sixths of the population living in the countryside, under an oppressive landlord class. The overwhelming majority of the population were peasants, mostly very poor and illiterate, riddled with the superstitions and value systems characteristic of a semifeudal social system. Most of the educated people in the countryside were drawn from the ranks of the landlord class and the middle and rich peasants. (Mao himself came from a family whose members probably began as poor peasants, but who managed to rise to the level of middle peasants; hence he was able to receive an education and become a schoolteacher in his early days.)

In the cities the ranks of the relatively small industrial and commercial proletariat would have included substantial numbers of educated people, but most of those in positions of authority, possessed of administering and organizational skills, would be drawn from the national bourgeoisie and comprador class, or from the scholar class recruited into government administration. This last category had traditionally held very powerful positions in Chinese society, for civil administration was in their hands; they were the product of a very conservative and élitist educational system, which during long and arduous years of Chinese classical education inculcated in them bourgeois values and a contempt for physical labor or technical or practical work, to an even greater extent than has been the case in Western countries at similar stages of development.

Thus, at the time of Liberation China exhibited the basic problem of all backward countries attempting to construct a socialist society, that is, an acute shortage of cadres to engage in the task. It is one thing to recruit sufficient numbers of dedicated leaders into a communist party from the ranks of peasants, workers, and intellectuals, to lead a predominantly peasant revolution to victory after a struggle lasting a quarter of a century—a tremendous and historic achievement in itself. It is quite another to produce sufficient numbers to engage in the task of socialist construction, to organize, inspire, and lead peasants into new collective units such as cooperatives and communes, to set up and manage new state-owned factories, to extend and run the transport system, organize public health services, administer towns and cities, build up an educational system, and all the myriads of other tasks which require levels of education, skill, and competence sadly lacking in a backward society. So, once the revolution seizes power, and hard-core counterrevolutionaries have been executed or imprisoned, practically everyone who has the least competence is pressed into service.

The dramatis personae may not have changed, however. The vast majority of former Chinese landlords continued to exist—not as landlords, it is true, but as peasants or workers on the communes in many cases; and those who managed to salvage part of their wealth, in the form of objets d'art and jewelry, migrated to the cities and lived off their capital, or the interest on it. Municipal land had not, in the middle of 1966, been nationalized, and many landlords still drew rent from their property, although at controlled rates. Former middle and rich peasants still existed, many living and working in the communes; of the older generation of peasants, they were the most articulate and educated, and could often sway the others even if they themselves did not achieve positions of authority. The great mass of former peasants still existed, of course, but as members of new collective forms of organization which were barely ten years old; they had responded astonishingly well to the new attitudes demanded of them, they were better off than before, but especially among the older ones the individual traditions and the superstitions of the old society kept a strong hold.

Most of the former capitalists still existed, and received five percent per annum on their investments in industrial and commercial enterprises taken over by the State; many also received handsome salaries as managers (subject of course to State control), a practice which dated back to the earlier period when there was no one else capable of running these enterprises. The old scholar class still existed, controlling educational institutions and administering some of the various organs of state.

In all of this it must be remembered that the first generation educated completely under the regime of the new society was just reaching maturity; it is from this generation that the Red Guards were recruited.

An additional factor is important. For a century prior to Liberation, China was a semicolony. Parts of its coastal cities had been ceded to various European imperialists in the form of trading concessions, and much of Chinese trade and cultural administration was in their hands. China suffered foreign invasions of one kind or another on no less than six occasions following the Opium Wars of 1840, and on the last occasion the Japanese occupied as much as one-third of Chinese territory for the best part of a decade. The significance of China's semicolonial situation was twofold. First, traditional Chinese society was breaking down under the impact of the Western incursions, for these were not only economic, political, and military, but also ideological and cultural; and the view was widespread that, in order to survive, China would have to adopt many Western techniques and ideas. One concomitant of this was the beginning of a sense of inferiority and a lack of confidence which, in such situations, often exist side by side with anti-imperialist feelings. Second, and more important, in its later stages, especially during the anti-Japanese war, the Revolution assumed in part the nationalist character of a patriotic war to unite the nation and throw out the foreign invaders. This meant that when the Communist leadership had demonstrated its ability, integrity, and superiority over the discredited and corrupt Kuomintang—especially in the struggle against the Japanese—many people, especially intellectuals, cast their lot with the Revolution, although ideologically they were far from convinced Communists. They had concluded that the Revolution was the only hope if China was to "stand up" and once more become a strong, proud nation; in short, their motivation was nationalistic and patriotic rather than revolutionary. The same is true of many scholars and others who returned to China in the early years of Liberation, often after spending a considerable number of years in Western educational institutions; this is especially true of scientists, many of whom were educated in the United States and the United Kingdom. A substantial proportion of these expatriates returned, not because they were Communists, but partly because of patriotism and national pride, and partly because for the first time in this century there existed in China a stable government that wanted to foster science and technology, and offered them good prospects. With them they brought not only their expertise but often many of the values acquired from Western education, which is not notable for its inculcation of socialist values.

THOUGHT REFORM CAMPAIGNS

These, then, are the basic reasons for the series of Thought Reform Campaigns, of which the Cultural Revolution is the latest and the most spectacular example. The word "culture" is used in a very wide sense; one of the clearest expressions of the nature and purpose of the Cultural Revolution appeared in an editorial in the army newspaper:

> Conducted mainly in the ideological field, fundamentally it is a great revolution to destroy the thousands-of-years-old concept of private ownership and establish the socialist concept of public ownership . . . Ideas, culture, customs, habits, political views, legal concepts, views on art and so on are all ideological forms in society, which generally go under the name of culture. Why must we carry

out a cultural revolution in the period of socialism? The reason is that the economic base of society has undergone fundamental change. It is a fundamental principle of Marxism-Leninism, of Mao Tse-tung's thought, that the mental springs from the material, and social consciousness arises out of social being, out of the social economic base and the social system of ownership. Social consciousness is secondary; at the same time it has a tremendous influence and impact on social being. In China, the socialist transformation of the ownership of the means of production has already been effected and the socialist economic system of public ownership has been established. Since the economic base has changed, the ideological superstructure must change accordingly to keep step with it. Otherwise it will obstruct the forces from developing, lead to the loss of the already-won fruits of the revolution, and give rise to revisionist rule and the restoration of capitalism, causing our country to go back on to the old colonial or semi-colonial and feudal or semi-feudal road . . .[3]

The word "cultural" is, according to popular Western usage, something of a misnomer, but a definition adopted by Western anthropologists fits the Chinese usage admirably: ". . . the essential core of culture consists of traditional (i.e., historically derived and selected) ideas and especially their attached values . . ."[4] One of the first salvos was fired by Mao Tse-tung in 1964, when, as mentioned in Chapter 4, he claimed that in the preceding fifteen years, literary and artistic circles, with some exceptions, had not carried out the policies of the Party, had acted as high and mighty bureaucrats, had not gone to the workers, peasants, and soldiers, and had not reflected socialist revolution and socialist construction. Indeed, in recent years they had slid to the very edge of "revisionism."[5] In September 1965, Mao pointed out that reactionary bourgeois academic authorities should be criticized. As a result, in November of the same year the Shanghai Committee of the Communist Party published in its newspaper a major criticism of literary material for which the Peking Committee of the Party had been responsible. This led eventually, in June 1966, to the dismissal of certain officers of the Peking Party, to its reorganization, and to the dismissal of the editorial board of its newspapers and journals. *Peking Review* declared:

The overthrown bourgeoisie, in their plots for restoration and subversion, always give first place to ideology, take hold of ideology and the superstructure. The representatives of the bourgeoisie, by using their position and power, usurped and controlled the leadership of a number of departments, did all they could to spread bourgeois and revisionist poison through the media of literature, the theatre, films, music, the arts, the press, periodicals, the radio, publications and academic research and in schools, etc., in an attempt to corrupt people's minds and perpetrate "peaceful evolution" as ideological preparation and preparation of public opinion for capitalist restoration.[6]

The power struggle in the Party had begun, between those who wanted to continue and expand the ideological revolution, of which the previous Thought Reform Campaigns had been in fact a part, and those who opposed it. The initial battle was thus joined on the cultural front. At about the same time the struggle on the educational front at Peking University came into the open; the following account of this struggle is by a regular visitor to China, Lee Tsung-ying, Editor of the Hong Kong journal *Eastern Horizon*:

In the wake of the reorganization of the Peking Party Committee the President of Peking University, Lu Ping, and his lieutenants were toppled by a single issue of *tatzupao** put up by a group of philosophy students who had been at loggerheads with Lu for the preceding seven months or so. Early in 1966, during the Socialist Education Movement, these students and some others came to the conclusion that University authority had been following a policy which they believed to be bourgeois and reactionary. They pointed out, for instance, that the University had been persistently discriminating against students of worker or peasant family origins and against demobilized PLA (People's Liberation Army) men who had enrolled for higher studies by expelling them on all sorts of pretexts, instead of rendering positive assistance to those who were backward in their lessons to enable them to catch up; had been allowing ordinary academic subjects to squeeze out political study, especially the study of Chairman Mao's works; and had been discouraging students from doing manual work. They accused Lu of deliberately training the coming generation in the bourgeois rather

---

* "*Tatzupao*": big character poster.

than the proletarian tradition. Instead of carefully considering the criticisms, Lu and his followers put heavy pressure to bear on the group of students, labelling them as anti-socialist or anti-Party elements. For seven months, vigorous exchanges of accusations and counter-accusations went on between the University authority and the students.

After the cultural revolution had been launched, the students began to see things in a much clearer light and became more firmly convinced that they had been right. So seven of them (many others had been sent to the countryside to do manual work) put up on May 25 a *tatzupao* accusing Lu and his lieutenants of opposing and suppressing the mass revolutionary movement in order to protect their superiors in the Peking Party Committee and themselves. The poster came to Chairman Mao's notice on June 1, and he requested the Central People's Broadcasting Station to release it on the very same day.[7]

The next morning, the walls of Peking University were covered with big posters, and a little later they appeared on the walls of thousands of schools and educational institutions all over the country. The reorganized Peking Party Committee dissolved the Peking University Party Committee, and dismissed Lu Ping and some of his colleagues. There was resistance to the new movement from within the Party, and the customary Party practice of sending work teams to various schools and institutes was tried. Evidently these teams resemble "trouble shooting" cadres of leading Party members who are sent to remedy difficulties. This was, however, a new situation. The teams were not accustomed to such tasks in educational institutions; probably they failed to see the significance of the movement, which was new, and not unnaturally tended to side with the Establishment against the revolt of the students and some of the younger teachers. Consequently the teams attempted to control the cultural revolutionaries, to restrict their activities, and in some cases even instigated other groups to oppose them. Lee Tsung-ying points out that this opposition led to a detailed declaration of official Party policy on the whole question of the objectives and methods of the new movement:

> This opposition to the new movement led to the holding of the Eleventh Plenary Session of the Eighth Central Committee of the Chinese Communist Party, during which a decision concerning the.

cultural revolution was adopted on August 8. It has become commonly known as the Sixteen Points and was reported to have been drafted under Mao's personal guidance. It exhorts cadres at various echelons to put daring above everything else, to support the putting up of big-character posters and the holding of great debates, to trust the masses, to rely on them, respect their initiative and encourage them to criticize the shortcomings and errors in the work of those holding responsible positions. It prescribes that in the cultural revolution the only method is for the masses to liberate themselves, and any method of doing things in their stead must not be used. This was later known as the proletarian line represented by Chairman Mao Tse-tung.

The decision specifies that, "at present, our objective is to struggle against and overthrow those persons in authority who are taking the capitalist road, to criticize and repudiate the reactionary bourgeois academic 'authorities' and the ideology of the bourgeoisie and all other exploiting classes, and to transform education, literature, and art and all other parts of the superstructure not in correspondence with the socialist economic base, so as to facilitate the consolidation and development of the socialist system."

Work teams were withdrawn and the direction of the cultural revolution was left in the hands of the Committee for Cultural Revolution whose members had been democratically elected in each school or institute.

Ten days later, Chairman Mao joined one million people from the revolutionary masses of Peking and many other parts of the country in a mammoth rally celebrating the birth of the cultural revolution. It was at this meeting that the Red Guards were first made known to the outside world when a detachment of them ascended the rostrum of the Tien An Men Gate and Mao himself put on their armband.[8]

Clearly, Mao and his supporters were using the Red Guards as the spearhead of the Revolution, but it seems unlikely that, initially, they were an official creation at all. To begin with, they were clandestine organizations of young students, frowned on by authority, who could not reconcile the principles of socialism, under which they had been brought up, with the principles and practices of the education they were receiving, and with some of the things they knew still existed in Chinese society. Apparently the first group originated in a middle secondary school which was a subsidiary of, or "feeder" for, Tsinghua University. Undoubtedly influenced by the ferment going on in Peking University, the young rebels formed themselves into a group and called themselves the "Red Guards" (the name was taken from a civilian organization which sprang up in the early days of the Revolution in Hunan Province in 1926). Similar groups came into existence in other schools and universities in the Peking area, and then in adjacent cities—Tientsin, for example. Originally "underground" for several months, the movement spread like wildfire when Mao gave it his blessing. When a Tientsin group announced their intention to march to Peking to demonstrate, Mao gave instructions to put a train at their disposal. From then on the movement mushroomed all over China; the astonishing rapidity and scale of its development must have surprised Mao and his supporters within the Party, and naturally they capitalized on it. Within three months, some fifteen to twenty million young people had formed themselves into Red Guards, organized on the basis of their educational institutions; they were mainly students of middle schools and higher educational institutions, aged between ten and about twenty, with a sprinkling of young teachers. The only conditions for membership—which they controlled themselves—were militant support for Mao's Proletarian Cultural Revolution, and a proletarian class background—from families of workers, peasants, "martyrs of the revolution," People's Liberation Army men, and so on. Their sole distinguishing characteristic was the red armband they wore with the Red Guard inscription, and they were of course unarmed. They carried the "little red book" of quotations from Mao which they waved and read from at the slightest provocation.

They were offered free rail transport anywhere in China, free food, and free accommodation in middle schools, universities, and so forth (which did not reopen after the summer vacation). At a mass rally of over one million in Peking in August 1966, they were reviewed by Mao, and enjoined by various leaders of the Central Committee to be the standard-bearers of the Revolution, to pay attention to State affairs, to criticize everyone in authority, to propagate the Cultural Revolution in society at large—to destroy old ideas, culture, customs, and habits, and foster new ones, to integrate themselves with peasants and workers, to eschew violence "which can only touch skins" and concentrate on reason "which touches souls," to model themselves on the exemplary code of conduct adopted by the People's Liberation Army men in pre-revolutionary days. All this, of course, to be in conformity with Mao's thought, which they must study and apply "in a creative way." [9]

Millions more came to Peking to be reviewed by Mao in similar circumstances. This continued till mid-November, by which time an estimated nine to ten million had come to Peking. At any one time between August and November, there were estimated to be two million Red Guards there—an increase of fifty percent in the Peking population. Thousands of extra buses were brought from other cities, temporary latrines and water pipes were erected in the side streets, and millions of square yards of temporary "walls" of matting were erected to contain the profusion of big character posters that overflowed brick walls. In November, the young people were exhorted not to come to Peking any more, but to fan out to the other cities and the countryside; and in late December it was stated that no more travel passes would be issued except for return to the home base. Emphasis was then placed on walking—in emulation of the Long March—to "temper" the young people, and marchers were a common sight, walking in small groups, with packs on their backs, always carrying red flags, sometimes carrying musical instruments and singing revolutionary songs. They did propaganda work and manual labor in the villages and on construction sites along the route; many of them walked thousands of miles. Especially favored were routes which included places of significance in the history of the Revolution—what in this book we call "revolutionary shrines." During the early stages, in July and August, there was some violence. Houses of those suspected of "taking the capitalist road" were ransacked. Some places of religion and worship were desecrated. Some people were beaten up. These incidents were of course singled out by the Western press, but they must be seen in the perspective of the enormous size of the Chinese population which exceeds that of the United States, the Soviet Union, and the whole of Western Europe. The Red Guards claimed to have discovered caches of gold bars, detailed lists of landholdings by former landlords, and even radio transmitters.

But the early outbreaks of violence were soon brought under control, and serious resistance did not materialize until early in 1967. To the foreign observer in November and December 1966, who could not avoid seeing and being in close contact with literally millions of these teen-agers wherever he went in China, they appeared very disciplined, well-behaved, and incredibly patient, waiting hours and even days for the buses and trains of an acutely over-strained public transport system.

Certainly, an outstanding feature was the big-character poster. It was almost as though all of the letters to the editors of all of the newspapers in a Western country were simultaneously on display on the walls of all the public buildings, ignoring the laws of libel. Millions of these posters went up criticizing everybody in authority—even a few criticizing Mao and his supporters. Naturally many were stupid and contained much inaccurate information, and the Western press was not slow to report the most sensational. Almost certainly the great majority of the accusations and counter-accusations were spontaneous, but there was probably an element of manipulation too, especially in attacks on the "heavies" (VIP's). The foreigner without inside knowledge of the power struggle can only be ignorant of the mechanics, and of the cases in which people were seized, denounced, and publicly humiliated; certainly it all appears contrary to the Sixteen-Point Program of the Central Committee, which stated:

The strictest care should be taken to distinguish between the anti-Party, anti-socialist Rightists and those who support the Party and socialism but have said or done something wrong or have written some bad articles or other works . . . The method to be used in debates is to present the facts, reason things out, and persuade through reasoning. Any method of forcing a minority holding different views to submit is impermissible. The minority should be protected, because sometimes the truth is with the minority . . . In the course of the movement, with the exception of cases of active counter-revolutionaries where there is clear evidence of crimes . . . which should be handled in accordance with the law, no measures should be taken against students at universities, colleges, middle schools and primary schools because of problems that arise in the movement. To prevent the struggle from being diverted from its main target, it is not allowed, under whatever pretext, to incite the masses or the students to struggle against each other. Even proven Rightists should be dealt with on the merits of each case at a later stage of the movement.

In the light of these statements, it appears that up to the end of 1966 the situation had sometimes gotten out of hand, probably as a result of much fiercer opposition than anticipated. It is fair to point out that they also noted:

> Since the cultural revolution is a revolution, it inevitably meets with resistance. This resistance comes chiefly from those in authority who have wormed their way into the Party and are taking the capitalist road. It also comes from the force of habits from the old society. At present, this resistance is still fairly strong and stubborn. But after all, the great proletarian cultural revolution is an irresistible general trend. There is abundant evidence that such resistance will be quickly broken down once the masses become fully aroused.
>
> Because the resistance is fairly strong, there will be reversals and even repeated reversals in this struggle. There is no harm in this. It tempers the proletariat and other working people, and especially the younger generation, teaches them lessons and gives them experience, and helps them to understand that the revolutionary road zigzags and does not run smoothly.
>
> The outcome of this great cultural revolution will be determined by whether or not the Party leadership dares boldly to arouse the masses.[10]

Two further incidents are of importance in understanding the prelude to the Cultural Revolution: the struggle at the top over the *Circular of the Central Committee of May 16, 1966,* and the balance of power in the Central Committee Standing Committee and in the Central Committee itself later in 1966. The outcome was the Sixteen-Point Program of the Central Committee of August 8, 1966; at that time it was the report of a minority group.

We have seen that largely as a result of the New Economic Policy of 1960–1964, there had been the growth of a privileged stratum of factory managers and technocrats, closely linked to the Party committees of the provinces. Supporting them were a large number of intellectuals whose cultural interests were in an élitist tradition, with some leaning toward the West. The shift of emphasis to markets in agriculture and wholesaling, the reemergence of "expertness" rather than "redness," was followed by a shift in political power against Mao Tse-tung. Political leaders like Tao Chu, former First Secretary of the Center South Bureau (embracing 200 million Chinese citizens), and Li Ching-chuan, "local patriot" of the enormously rich and powerful Szechuan Province, not only built up semiautonomous "feudal kingdoms," but also supported Mao's opponents in the central Party organization—Teng Hsiao-ping, Liu Shao-chi, Peng Chen. In Peking, control of the press, and the Propaganda Department of the Central Party apparatus, enabled Mao's opponents to refuse to publish criticisms of themselves, and to restrict printing and distribution of Mao's own works —hence the distribution on a mass scale of the "little red book" of quotations after the Cultural Revolution began. The official ideology of the Chinese Revolution remained Maoist, although State organizations were governed by different rules and a different ethos. There was, in essence, a struggle between two wings of the Party and the bureaucracy, between that section represented by the charismatic figure of Mao, creator of the Chinese Revolution, and the administrative pragmatists running the country.

The first contest was in February–May 1966. An "Outline Report on the Current Academic Situation" was issued on February 12, 1966, by the Group of Five in Charge of the Cultural Revolution. It was proposed largely by Peng Chen, and later repudiated by one of the five, Kang Sheng, and by Mao. The report, which contained the philosophy of "opening wide" the debate, and of "everyone is equal before the truth," was fully repudiated by the Mao group in the *Circular of the Central Committee of May 16, 1966*.[11] The repudiation, which was not made public until 1967, accused the five of using hypocritical language, of meeting class struggle in the ideological campaign, and of criticizing the Left. This incident marked the first clear ascendancy of the Mao group to actual control of the day-to-day affairs of the Central Committee, of propaganda and economic policy; it was underlined by the decisions taken by the Central Committee concerning the Cultural Revolution on August 8, 1966.

Mao Tse-tung had said repeatedly after April 1965: "Marxism consists of thousands of truths, but they all boil down to one sentence, 'It is right to rebel'—and from this truth there follows resistance, struggle, the fight for socialism." It is not hard to see why the proletarian headquarters headed by Mao were so vociferous about "daring to rebel" and "bombarding the headquarters"— they after all were the minority group in the Party Central Committee and the Standing Committee. Of seven members of the former Standing Committee, Liu Shao-chi, Teng Hsiao-ping, Chu Teh, and Chen Yun were "rightists"; only three stood with the "proletarian-revolutionary line," Mai, Lin Piao, and Chou En-lai. The task facing the latter group had to be nothing less than the replacement from top to bottom of those in authority, from Peking to the "alley committees," and at all levels (factories, communes, counties, and other provinces of the Party apparatus), by revolutionary committees.

Notes

1. Stuart Schram, *Mao Tse-Tung* (London: Penguin, 1966).
2. Mao Tse-tung, *On the Correct Handling of Contradictions Among the People* (Peking: Foreign Languages Press, 1967).
3. *Liberation Army Daily*, November 3, 1966.
4. A *Dictionary of the Social Sciences* (London: Tavistock, 1964), p. 165.
5. *Chinese Literature*, No. 10, 1966.
6. *Peking Review*, June 10, 1966.
7. *Eastern Horizon*, January 1967.
8. *Ibid.*
9. *Peking Review*, September 9, 1966.
10. *Peking Review*, August 12, 1966.
11. See *Circular of the Central Committee of May 16, 1966: A Great Historic Document* (Peking: 1967).

Chapter 6

THE CULTURAL REVOLUTION
AFTER 1966

In summing up the experience of the Paris Commune, Karl Marx said that the chief mistake was in the proletariat taking over the bourgeois state machine without proceeding to destroy it. This was also the chief theme of the Cultural Revolution as it developed in 1967 and 1968. Criticism was extended in 1968 from "persons like Khrushchev" to the idea that the "rightist" policies of the followers of the Liu Shao-chi group in economics and politics were counterrevolutionary. Followers of Mao were urged to treat the struggle against Party functionaries and organizations as a class struggle and were mobilized to destroy the Party organs of power where they opposed the program of Mao. As *Red Flag* put it early in 1967: "Proletarian revolutionaries must fully understand that the struggle to seize power, and counter-seize power, between us and the handful of persons within the Party who are in authority and taking the capitalist road, is a life-and-death struggle between the proletariat and the bourgeoisie." [1]

THE STRUGGLES OF 1967

This new level, and new version, of struggle began in Shanghai. The Party center, the Cultural Revolution group, under the Central Committee in Peking, was proposing Paris Commune-style organs of power, in cities and provinces. Its program was put into action in Harbin and in Shanghai in January 1967.

In Shanghai on January 5, 1967, a "Message to All Shanghai People" was published in the Shanghai newspaper *Wenhui Bao*. It read: "We of the revolutionary rebel group clearly understand, that if the great proletarian revolution is not carried out, we will lose our orientation in production, and slide back in the direction

117

of capitalism . . . we workers of the revolutionary rebel group must become models in 'taking firm hold of revolution and promoting production.' " [2] This was followed by an "Urgent Notice," issued by the Workers Revolutionary Rebel General Headquarters, and thirty-one other revolutionary organizations, to all Shanghai citizens on January 9, 1967.[3]

The "Urgent Notice" instructed supporters to prevent the sudden payment of bonuses by factory chiefs, who sought to build up support by this method, and to freeze all factory assets. It recalled all people about to travel, and ordered them to return to work. It ordered the property of all capitalists confiscated but forbade unauthorized confiscations. And it announced the seizure of power from the Municipal Party Committee. The revolutionary rebels then proceeded to introduce "extensive proletarian democracy," or government by the mass meeting, in organs of administration and in the factories. Other provinces and capital cities followed the Shanghai model during 1967, sometimes incurring violence and fighting (for instance, at Wuhan, the local military commander arrested two leading Peking supporters of Mao who then were freed by gunboat; in Canton, there was an armed revolt and armed clashes between rival groups).

Throughout 1967 Mao issued a series of very important "instructions" covering political and economic affairs. These became a guideline for groups rising in revolt, in cities and provinces, and extending the Revolution into factories and into the economic field. A struggle for the redress of economic grievances began when factory leaders fought back by the tactic of "economism," that is, of immediately issuing bonuses, clothing, and other benefits in order to win support. This had serious repercussions on the economy; some examples were given to the authors:

(1) The Vice-President of the Revolutionary Committee of the Shanghai docks said:

> The height of the struggle here was the period December 1966– January 1967 and it took us twenty days to drive our opponents out. Our main target was the power of the capitalist roaders, but they had much power and the means to protect themselves. They instigated the masses against the cadres, and the cadres against each other. Most of the character posters put up at first were attacks on

ordinary workers; few were about the people in power, although they allowed free debate. A work team sent here by the Party Municipal Committee branded many people as "sham Left." This work team shifted the target from those in power to participants in the mass struggle, through the tactic of "hitting hard at the majority to protect a few." They demanded that all hand in a written self-criticism, and they distributed Liu Shao-chi's works to help people to write it. Our difficulty was the protection of the work teams by the Party, since the Party leaders were not then exposed. This disoriented many workers. We decided to organize into groups, but the work team also organized groups. With the collaboration of the work teams and two leaders of the Municipal Committee, a new tactic—"economism"—was launched in December 1966. This was the payment of large sums of money to dock workers. Character posters were put up, saying that each loader would receive one cotton-padded coat. This misled some people— the coat offer was a bribe. Another trick was the circulation of a faked document, allegedly from the Central Committee, stipulating new wage standards—for example, raising the stipulated wages of a veteran worker from 80–90 *yuan* a month to 96–120 *yuan*. The leaders on the docks also distributed back pay indiscriminately. The reason for these techniques being adopted here, and for the first time in Shanghai, is that this is the biggest port. Raw materials and agricultural imports and exports go through here. If the port stops working, there is no coal for power plants, while products for abroad and other places in China would be stopped. Factories would have to close down. All of this was to put pressure on the Central Committee. We must say that the "economism" tactic was partly successful. Many veteran workers, however, knew, from their past experience, that bribery would be used. Some stayed at their posts when replacements failed to arrive, and goods destined for Vietnam were given top priority.

(2) At the Shanghai Diesel Pumps and Motors Plant, leading cadres of the factory Revolutionary Committee recalled:

During the Cultural Revolution we caught out the Director, Chu Bi-yen. He was a traitor—a Kuomintang agent. The Vice-Director was a former capitalist. The head of the design office had been a colonel of the Kuomintang Army. The head of the testing office was previously chief of the Three Principles League here, and had four pistols when we searched his belongings. A deputy engineer had secret title deeds of land he had previously owned, and an account describing where "his" land was. When the struggle began and we arrested these people, we frightened the State organs. The Central Industrial Ministry and the East China Bureau of the Party sent work teams here. Three times they came here. The second delegation was of higher station, but was driven out. The last delegation was of even higher status, containing a minister and members of the Economic Commission of the East China Bureau and leaders of the Shanghai Municipal Party Committee. The plant was thick with black limousines. They all praised the director, said the Municipal Party Committee would justly judge him, and falsely branded the "red rebels" here as pawns of a black gang of counterrevolutionaries. Many workers cherish the Party. Our enemies utilized this, and said: "The Municipal Committee and the Bureau of the East China Party are organs of the Central Committee and you should trust these organs." But our investigations were in conflict with this, and we drove the work team out for the third time. We sent cadres to Peking on foot, to bring charges against them before the Cultural Revolution Group of the Central Committee. A meeting was organized at the factory. Our well-organized opponents turned up to get the meeting over quickly, and they even took the director and the secretary to a boat on the river so that they could not be questioned and criticized. Eventually the revolutionaries in the plant were successful and set up a Revolutionary Committee in August 1967. We have learned that there is a need to be ever watchful for capitalist restoration.

Whatever one thinks of these examples, two things are clear. One is the sharpness of the struggle, with its ensuing interruption of production. The other is the way that a struggle within the Party, over "two lines" of policy, rapidly became a struggle over "two roads," with the red rebels around Mao accusing their opponents of promoting bourgeois ideas, and a longer life for capitalism. A struggle between the charismatic leaders and pragmatic leaders soon attained the character of a life-and-death struggle.

During 1967 Mao issued crucial "instructions," in addition to the Sixteen-Point Program of August 1966. Among the most important were:

(1) "Fight self, fight self-interest."
(2) "The veteran cadres made contributions in the past, but

they must not rest on their laurels. They should strive to temper themselves in the Great Proletarian Cultural Revolution and make new contributions."

(3) "The Great Proletarian Cultural Revolution is a great revolution that touches people to their very souls and aims at solving the problems of their world outlook."

The stage was set, by the end of 1967, for taking the Cultural Revolution even further, by setting up new forms of organization in every enterprise, university, and State organ. At the same time the ideological platform of Mao and the critique of Liu Shao-chi's program had crystallized by the end of 1967, and criticism was stepped up in 1968.

THE DEVELOPMENTS OF 1968

Discussions by one of the authors with revolutionary committees, at the factory, county, commune, and provincial levels in 1968, revealed this common theme: if things had gone on as they were, China would have followed the Soviet road—of material incentives, of a new privileged stratum, of a revision of Marxism, of a "selling-out" of the world revolution. Hence the common chorus of opinion: "Chairman Mao acted just in time." It is also significant that many members of revolutionary committees were young people who shouted exuberantly: "We are now the masters of the State!" Others were former beggars, pedicab drivers, and exploited apprentices—victims of the old regime, who revealed what can only be described as a class hatred of "bosses," "bureaucrats," "technocrats," and "Party apparatchiks," who they claimed were usurping power. Thus the difference over policy—over "two lines"—had quickly turned into the struggle over "two roads," capitalism or socialism.

By April 1968, the Cultural Revolution in China had entered a new stage. Not only had the proletarian headquarters around Mao Tse-tung seized power in twenty-three out of twenty-seven regional governments, but an attempt was being made to run a modern economy on "moral incentives" and "mobilization of the masses" with profound effects on attitudes, incentives organization, production, and efficiency. The latest phase was featured, above all, by the overthrow of an élite group of party bureaucrats, managers, technocrats, and "academic despots," and by the growing recognition that economic development depends not only on machinery and investment, but on the human factor, on what people believe and what people do—a recognition followed by entirely new ways of motivating producers and the myriads of decision-makers. It was argued that the Cultural Revolution was not just another power struggle, or a disagreement about economic policy alone, but that it went far deeper. A vice-minister said to one of the authors in an interview:

> The Cultural Revolution is not just a power struggle. It would be easy just to destroy the opposition. But this would not get to the root of the matter. Stalin solved nothing with his purges and reshuffles of the technocracy. What we are after is a process by which people give up selfishness. Some of us don't understand fully what is involved in such a process. Partly it is through reading and the mass meetings, through a person's contact with others. Partly it is through relying on one's own efforts. I am convinced that had Lenin lived he would not have single-mindedly pursued a line of material incentives, but would have promoted a full play of enthusiastic exchange of ideas, experience, and emotions in the collective.

In other words, Maoists did *not* see the Cultural Revolution as a zigzag stage in the policy and tactics between Left and Right, or as an opportunity for the Left to push ahead to a new advance. The issue between them and the Liu Shao-shih group was seen as being *over the whole nature and raison d'être of the socialist revolution.*

What Mao proposed in 1967–1968 was a new way of running a society. He set out to break down the gulf between the élite group and the masses, to spread a new outlook in the centers of decision-making, to motivate decisions differently, and to substitute for the "invisible hand" of the price mechanism the visible bond of Mao Tse-tung's thought; Mao preaches a socialist morality, a collective selfless attitude, and a concern for world revolution, as against an individualistic, competitive morality.

Crucial to all of this in 1968 was the establishment of new

organs of power in the economy, new "latest instructions" from Mao, and further ideological struggle.

The new year, 1968, opened with the spread of the "three-in-one" revolutionary committee. By April this parallel form of government was operating in a majority of factories and provinces; it comprised revolutionary cadres, representatives of the army, and delegates elected from mass meetings. Revolutionary committees began immediately to fulfill the State plans, "grasp revolution and promote production," and replace financial incentives by moral incentives; study classes for workers became an integral part of factory life.

Education reform in general proceeded apace. High schools and universities had been storm centers of the Cultural Revolution. From July 1968 great attention was paid to them. A "latest instruction" from Mao personally read: "It is essential to shorten the length of schooling, revolutionize education, put proletarian politics in command and take the road of the Shanghai Machine Tools Plant in training technicians from among the workers. Students should be selected from among workers and peasants with practical experience, and they should return to production after a few years' study" (July 1968). New "instructions" from Mao on education reform were issued in September 1968, while many examples of successful experiments were publicized in the press during September–October 1968.[4]

Two further aspects of the Cultural Revolution emerged in the second half of 1968. Both appeared to temper the role of the students and youth, and to switch the emphasis from rebellion to constructive politics. These were the launching of the stage of struggle-criticism-transformation, and the increasing role given to the working class in political reorganization and the administration of production.

The idea of struggle-criticism-transformation was summed up in a "latest instruction" of September 1968. "The struggle-criticism-transformation in a factory, on the whole, goes through the following stages: establishing a revolutionary committee based on the "three-in-one" combination, mass criticism and repudiation, purifying the class ranks, rectifying the Party organization, simplifying organizational structure, changing irrational rules and regulations and sending people who work in offices to grass-roots levels."

The aim of struggle-criticism-transformation appeared to be twofold. First, to consolidate the power of the "three-in-one" revolutionary committees, and to ratify the method of study classes as a way of implementing the injunction to "fight self, repudiate revisionism." Second, to follow through Mao's instruction issued early in 1968 that "the most fundamental principle in the reform of state organs is that they must keep in contact with the masses" and the earlier injunction "to grasp revolution and promote production." Struggle-criticism-transformation was, as it were, the tactic for the "stabilization period" after the first fury of the Cultural Revolution had spent itself, and owed its theoretical beginning to the first "stabilization period" of August 1966 and the Sixteen-Point Program. In fact, struggle-criticism-transformation aimed to achieve one of the goals of the Sixteen-Point Program —to transform all parts of the superstructure[5] "not in conformity with the socialist economic base," and to consolidate that economic base by curbing capitalist attitudes and tendencies.

The emphasis on "the working class exercising leadership" co-incided with the final stages of the process of establishing revolutionary committees in all provinces of China. It was argued that "in order to do the work of struggle-criticism-transformation conscientiously, and without losing any time, it is imperative to persist in leadership by the working class." [6]

Mao furnished new "latest instructions." The first, in August 1968, demanded that Chinese revolutionaries "bring into full play the leading role of the working class in the great cultural revolution and in all fields of work. On its part the working class should always raise its political consciousness in the course of struggle." On October 15, another followed: "Our power, who gives it to us? The working class gives it, the poor and lower-middle peasants give it, and the mass of labouring people who comprise over 90 per cent of the population give it."

The significance of these two "instructions" appeared to lie in the reduced role given to students and youth in the Cultural Revolution and a shift from rebellion to consolidation, with emphasis on promoting production, reform of State organs, and disciplined proletarian organization of output. This is evident in the instruction of September 1968: "In carrying out the cultural revolution in education, it is essential to have working class leadership . . . the workers' propaganda teams should stay in the schools and take part in fulfilling the tasks of criticism." This indicated a shift to discipline in place of the earlier student desire to rebel.

How absolute was the right to rebel in 1968 in China? Without question, millions were involved in the overthrow of the rule of provincial authorities, factory directors, technocrats, "academic despots," and "bourgeois intellectuals." Clearly, too, Mao's forces sought to contain the rebellion of anarchists on the one side and of "rightists" or "capitalist roaders" on the other. In Maoist political articles, constant references were made to those "who disregard revolutionary discipline and the interests of the people, party and nation" [7] and dissidents were warned that "If the anarchist trend continues, the proletarian dictatorships will be so weakened that production and the revolution will recede." [8]

Moreover, the efforts of those elements (ex-landlords and Party officials) opposed to Mao had been thwarted, and their exclusion from decision-making was clearly to continue, as can be seen from the "instruction" issued by Mao on April 8, 1968, concerning the raison d'être of the Cultural Revolution: "The great cultural revolution is in essence a great political revolution under the conditions of socialism made by the proletariat against the bourgeoisie and all other exploiting classes; it is a continuation of the prolonged struggle between the Chinese Communist Party and the masses of revolutionary people under its leadership on the one hand and the Kuomintang reactionaries on the other . . ." What was the essential message of this statement? Surely that in the transition period between capitalism and socialism, and also between socialism and communism, the issue of "who will win" is never definitely decided. Here we have a restatement of the Maoist claim that the struggle between "two lines" gives way to the struggle between "two roads"—capitalism and socialism.

This interpretation had been foreshadowed eight months before in an important article, "Along the Socialist or the Capitalist Road," dated August 15, 1967; its main conclusion was that "The essence of this struggle has been the question of which road China should take. Its focal point has always been a matter of political power, a question of which class should exercise dictatorship."[9]

This is a significant programmatic document of the Cultural Revolution. It strongly criticized the growth of rich peasants, and of a bourgeoisie in the towns, and quoted Mao's statement: "What will happen if our country fails to establish a socialist economy? It will turn into a country like Yugoslavia, in fact a bourgeois state and the dictatorship of the proletariat will turn into a dictatorship of the bourgeoisie."

Since, in the Chinese view, the Yugoslav economy had already become a system of "bourgeois cooperatives" under the control of a new capitalist group, the message was clear: the Cultural Revolution had moved from the superstructure (culture, literature) to the economy and the political power which derives from the organization of the economic system. The April 8, 1968, "instruction" put the utmost emphasis on this point.

This was perhaps the strongest attack on Mao's opponents, but it was also general. The trend in polemics was that the more sweeping the charge, the stronger the language; in fact, in mid-1968 the charges against the policies of the opposition to Mao were more detailed and more significant than the line taken the previous year, in "Along the Socialist or the Capitalist Road." The main points were:

(1) The "rightists" had made a fetish out of physical investment and technology, underestimating the dependence of these things on extratechnical factors—ideology, enthusiasm, the human factor. Maoists, on the other hand, hold that "the people and the people alone make history" and that "the spirit can be transformed into a material force."

(2) Managers and technicians had acted as executives of a social stratum entrenched in the Party. Their power must be limited, and then finally ended, in order to carry through the social aims of the revolutionaries. Revolutionary committees must replace managers and technicians in factories, and should also replace the Party apparatus in State organs and political structures (provinces, municipalities).

(3) The men on the shop floor had no rights of control or

participation worth mentioning. They must either seize these rights or go under.

(4) The Cultural Revolution expresses a sharpening contradiction between the growing social character of production in China and the antisocial mechanisms of decision-making, bonuses, the award of prizes, private plots in agriculture, and so forth. Thus a new superstructure must be established which is more in conformity with the needs of the economic base. This demands a reversal of trends, which may have to be achieved by undemocratic methods or by force. After all, a keystone of Mao's thought is that all societies rest on force, that "In order to abolish the gun, it is necessary to take up the gun."

(5) After the seizure of economic and political power the main task of revolutionary committees is to "study and apply Chairman Mao's thought"—more specifically, to find the slogans, aims, and solutions which will lead the masses toward aims which will transcend the previous ones. Foremost among these is "to serve the people," "fight self," and "produce for the world revolution in order to help peoples struggling for revolution—that is our internationalist duty."

Notes

1. "On the Proletarian Revolutionaries' Struggle to Seize Power," editorial statement, *Red Flag*, No. 3, 1967.
2. "Take Firm Hold of the Revolution: Message to All Shanghai People," *The Great Proletarian Cultural Revolution in China: 10* (Peking: 1968), pp. 6–7.
3. "Urgent Notice," *The Great Proletarian Cultural Revolution in China: 10*, pp. 13–19.
4. "The Revolution in Education in Colleges of Science and Engineering as Reflected in the Struggle Between the Two Lines at the Shanghai Institute of Mechanical Engineering," *Peking Review*, September 13, 1968, pp. 13–18; "7 May School Provides New Experience in Revolutionising Organisations," *Peking Review*, October 11, 1968, pp. 11–13; and "Workers' Mao Tse-Tung Thought

Propaganda Teams in Colleges and Schools," *Peking Review*, October 25, 1968, pp. 13–17.

5. "Advance Courageously Along the Road to Victory," editorial statement of *Jen-Min Jih-Pao* and *Honqui* in *Peking Review*, October 4, 1968, pp. 18–20.

6. Yao Wen-yuan, "The Working Class Must Exercise Leadership in Everything," *Peking Review*, August 30, 1968, pp. 3–8.

7. *Hupeh Daily*, February 13, 1968.

8. *Anwei Daily*, February 13, 1968.

9. The English version is in *Along the Socialist or the Capitalist Road* (Peking: 1968).

Chapter 7

PLANNING AND FINANCIAL POLICY

The Chinese system of planning, in its formal aspect, flows from a system of central industrial ministries, some of which directly control important individual enterprises (notably in transport and defense). In practice, however, the keystone of the system of planning has been the provincial governments and provincial bureaus of the ministries to which most enterprises and communes were responsible initially, although they were ultimately responsible to the Communist Party authority at this level. Until the Cultural Revolution, the *provincial Party committees* had the power to set economic targets, wage policy, and plans; and they enjoyed considerable freedom in setting them in accord with local conditions. Following the Cultural Revolution, the *provincial revolutionary committees*, composed of the "three-in-one" combination of representatives of the masses, the army, and revolutionary cadres, took over these functions. The provincial revolutionary committees were established progressively between January 1967 and September 1968 (see table). They are, at least in theory, under the Central Committee of the Chinese Communist Party; in actuality, supreme power has been invested in the Cultural Revolution Group of the Central Committee, headed by Mao, Chiang Ching, Chou En-lai, Chen Ta, and Kang Shen.

Under the provincial bureaus are the political organs which supervise social, economic, and political affairs; next, the prefectures; next, the counties and municipalities (large cities); and next, the communes.

Provincial Revolutionary Committees: Dates Established

Heilungkiang	Jan. 1967	Kirin	March 6, 1968
Shantung	Feb. 3, 1967	Kiangsu	March 23, 1968
Shanghai	Feb. 25, 1967	Chekiang	March 24, 1968

Provincial Revolutionary Committees (cont.)

Kweichow	Feb. 13, 1967	Hunan	April 8, 1968
Shansi	March 23, 1967	Hingsia Hui	
Peking	April 25, 1967	Autonomous	
Chinghai	Aug. 12, 1967	Region	April 10, 1968
Inner Mongolia		Anhwei	April 18, 1968
Autonomous		Shensi	May 1, 1968
Region	Nov. 1, 1967	Szechuan	May 3, 1968
Tientsin	Dec. 6, 1967	Liaoning	May 10, 1968
Kiangsi	Jan. 6, 1968	Kuangsi	
Kansu	Jan. 1968	Yunnan	Aug. 16, 1968
Honan	Jan. 27, 1968	Fukien	Aug. 19, 1968
Hopei	Feb. 4, 1968	Tibet	Sept. 6, 1968
Hupeh	Feb. 5, 1968	Sinkiang	Sept. 6, 1968
Kwangtung	Feb. 21, 1968		

Kwangtung Province, for example, with a population of 40 million, has 119 counties and municipalities, and 1,600 communes. Within the communes are the "alley" or "neighborhood" committees—citizens' groups, based on blocks or streets. Where a factory is being built, it is very common for these committees to be brought into its construction; they supply extra voluntary labor, help to repair damaged roads, operate canteens, and so on. The Chinese secret in plan execution can be described as *thorough organization at all levels.*

COMMUNES AND THE STATE

In theory, most communes are controlled (in the sense of being responsible to a higher authority) by the county revolutionary committee, but, in practice, the commune, which is not a State unit of ownership, but a cooperative, has a large degree of autonomy in its financial affairs. (For the commune, the "state" is usually the county or, in the case of the communes near the large cities, the municipal revolutionary committee.) Deliveries, output targets, and other matters are decided, in part, by consultation with the county, which accepts deliveries of crops and supplies chemical fertilizer and some machinery. The "state" sets prices and receives six to seven percent of total revenue from crop sales. For example, Red Star Commune near Peking is one of seven communes controlled by a county of Hopei Province; Clay Hill Commune near Peking is under the Peking Municipal Committee and sends many of its products to a marketing and supply cooperative; this is also the case with Tashi Commune in Panyi County in Kwangtung.

These cooperative marketing organizations are a result of an earlier period when the State, local organs, and private households invested jointly in a marketing organization. They continue to function side by side with the system of direct deliveries to the "state," and operate their own wholesale and retail stores in country areas.

Red Star Commune, which needs expensive machinery, gets it free of charge, directly from the Peking Municipal Committee, which purchases it from a corporation supplying machinery. The country communes, most of which are at a lower level of economic development, need fewer fixed capital items and usually buy small items from agricultural cooperatives. This is the case with Yueh Kechuang Commune in Tsun Hua County, Hopei Province, which sells its above-quota output to an agricultural cooperative marketing organization.

It should be stressed, however, that decisions about how to run commune activities and about income distribution are made either by the commune itself, or by the brigades which are the main "unit of account" in communes, and which correspond closely to the original village work force. Wages, previously allocated by the brigade on a work-points system, are now arrived at by discussion. The *team* cultivates the fields but a brigade is in charge of a piggery or a duck farm or a dairy. Industrial units such as small commune factories are owned and controlled by the commune as a whole; and a manager, elected for two years, runs the day-to-day affairs of the commune. Our impression was that communes do have a fair amount of autonomy in relation to the "state," but that factories have much less.

FACTORIES AND THE STATE

The controlling authority in relation to factories varies enormously, depending on the nature and importance of the production. The Shanghai Diesel Pumps and Motors Plant, with 7,000 workers, is under the Eighth Central Ministry of Machine Building; factories producing consumer goods may be under the provincial bureaus of the Ministry of Light Industry, or their affairs may be determined largely by the Ministry of Internal Trade operating through a State trading corporation.

All profits of factories are transferred to the State; the enterprise also pays certain taxes, but output plans are decided by consultation with the next highest authority, which varies with the particular case. Peking Steel and Alloy Works contracted directly with other enterprises; the Anshan Iron and Steel Mill and the Shanghai Diesel Plant were under direct supervision by the central ministries; the Pearl River Paper Mill, the Peking No. 2 Textile Mill, the Shanghai State Silk Mill, and the Wuhan Ceramics Plant, all dealt with State trading corporations attached to the provincial bureaus of the Ministry of Light Industry; others dealt with State trading corporations attached to the Ministry of Internal Trade.

During the Great Leap Forward, the Communist Party committees, at local and enterprise levels, were the most powerful organs of supervision, and they put the emphasis on "redness" rather than "expertness." As we saw in Chapter 3, this policy changed after 1959 and the manager emerged as the recognized authority in the enterprise. In every factory we visited we heard of the great powers of the management and technical staff between 1960 and 1965. The Cultural Revolution had, as one of its essential features, the struggle against managerial authority, the restoration of "redness" in factory affairs, the ending of the system of material incentives, and the managers' attempts to put "profits in command" within the factory. Formerly, decisions on production and bonuses were made by factory directors and technical specialists. Today these decisions are made by the factory "three-in-one" revolutionary committees. These are organized in various ways. In some committees, army representatives are "full-time"; in others, army representatives are just workers who are also reservists. In some factories, the personnel of the revolutionary committee is stable; in others, turnover is rapid.

The antitechnocracy attitude of such committees is well illustrated by the 555 Clock Factory in Shanghai. Under its system, only two members of the revolutionary committee are on duty at a time; the rest are in the workshop. The two on duty in the office are rotated to guard against the tendency toward bureaucracy of permanent office workers. Similar measures have been carried out in other enterprises, along with a certain amount of devolution of authority to workers on the shop floor.

WHOLESALE AND RETAIL TRADE

A considerable amount of flexibility has been imparted to the planning system by the consultation process, and by the direct contracting arranged through the State trading corporations,[1] which are attached to the provincial bureaus of the ministries concerned. As a result, the planning system, although of the "vertical" kind associated with what some Western economists like to call a "command economy," has operated since 1955 without the bureaucratic muddle associated with the "command system" of the Soviet Union and Eastern Europe.

In general, when the economic plans for a particular industry in the province have been worked out, representatives of all the enterprises concerned, and of the State trading corporation involved, come together to work out details. Each factory then shops around for the supplies it will need, and makes suggestions as to its actual output possibilities. When a "fit" between the supply of raw materials and the final output targets has been achieved on paper, the regional industry bureau gives approval, and draws up contracts with precise specifications and delivery dates.[1] In light industry, the State trading corporations accept all orders from retail and wholesale agents and channel them to the factory. This avoids the problem of a large number of firms telephoning the plant to place orders, and allows direct contracting between plants and wholesale purchasing stations—a method the Russians also found desirable during their great flurry over economic reform in 1964.

The plant managers we talked to were somewhat vague concerning what happens after products leave a factory and the exact link between supply plans and demand plans. A visit to Department

Store No. 1 in Shanghai enabled us to ask questions about the consumption and retail side. This store has more than 40,000 kinds of goods on sale and more than 51,000 square feet of floor space. It employs 2,000 shop assistants and staff members. The retail stores are invited to exhibitions of different goods, which shop assistants attend to put forward ideas on what they think customers will want. Where a factory produces something new, the store will set up a special experimental counter to receive suggestions from customers. Such suggestions are meticulously recorded, and go to the wholesale purchasing agencies and, in the case of a big retail store, directly to the factories. In large cities there are purchasing and supply stations for each important category of product—for textiles, ceramics, and so forth; a station's job is to distribute products made in the province to local shops and to other areas.

Mark-ups produce a difference between wholesale and retail prices. China's mark-ups vary with various goods. A store's plan for profits and costs is submitted to the bureau of commerce of the municipality. The policy in recent times has been to use the shop assistants as key informants on changing tastes and demands; in country areas, they go occasionally to live with the peasants for this purpose.

This system works fairly well in a country where the number of lines for individual commodities is fairly specialized and homogeneous, and fluctuations over a wide variety and quality of products are not a source of difficulty. An attempt is made to keep mark-ups and prices stable but substantial fluctuations in demand are handled by variable mark-ups and/or sales tax margins at the selling stage. Decisive units in matching supply and demand are the supply and purchasing stations operated by the State trading corporations.

WAGES AND SALARY POLICY

The provincial government classifies the categories of work within each industry through regional bureaus of ministries, but the central Labor Ministry has a final say in the pattern adopted. In some periods (for instance, 1961–1964) the provincial government also specified piecework rates in certain industries, as well as time rates. In non-State enterprises (such as communes), wages are not regulated by government agencies.

Control over stipulated wages, especially in the absence of bonuses and prizes, together with the regulation of prices, helps to guide the budgetary needs of the State. When wages are fixed, and assuming technological conditions are given, cost will be given and prices can be derived from known costs. Moreover, the centrally fixed wages constitute income; and the profit-wage relations of enterprises do not depend on market conditions. These conditions enable accurate planning of government income from taxes on enterprises and from transferred profits. Wages are paid monthly —generally to industrial and clerical workers, and those in administration, education, and so forth, in the cities. Peasants do not receive a wage or salary income, but a share in the collective income of the commune.

Policy has been, and continues to be, to keep wages relatively low and to provide employment for all who can work. Already there is a substantial proportion of families with two or three workers, and an increasing proportion of married women in employment, especially among the young. There are now three and a half times as many workers (in contradistinction to peasants) as in 1949.

This policy does not mean that wages have not risen; since 1952 average money wages have risen by 50 percent, as compared with price increases of 18 percent. It means, however, that average money wages are allowed to rise by only a few percent each year, and only in such a way as to diminish the wage and salary spread. In the very early years of the new regime the wage and salary structure was influenced by the Soviet pattern, by the pattern surviving from the old regime, and by the need to pay high rates to bourgeois managers of factories, whose skills were badly needed— indeed, many such managers were given a supplement which often doubled their nominal salary. (The Red Guards were interested in these supplements, and demanded their elimination. We were told that salary cuts had been imposed on the "tall poppies," and that Mao's salary had been reduced by twenty percent.) After 1955 a policy of low wage-spread was pursued for stipulated wages; substantial wage inequalities which resulted temporarily were due to the subsequently abolished bonuses, prizes, etc. The average wage for all workers in all trades and professions is now 65 *yuan* per month; the average for industrial workers is 70 *yuan*. The highest nonmangerial wage in industry is some 100 *yuan* for technicians; the lowest, for apprentices and the like, is some 40 *yuan*. Managers of small enterprises received 70–100 *yuan*; of big enterprises, 150–160 *yuan* (exclusive of supplements); but now members of revolutionary committees receive some 100 *yuan*. These wages, of course, must be considered in relation to prices. House rent (including utilities) takes 4–7 percent of family wage or salary, depending on the accommodation; this is fairly universal throughout the country. The following items were priced in Shanghai: food for one person, eating in a factory canteen, 12–15 *yuan* per month (much less of course for home cooking); padded cotton suit, 20 *yuan*; unpadded cotton suit, 10 *yuan*; cotton shoes, 3 *yuan*; leather shoes, 8–9 *yuan*; synthetic leather shoes, 3–5 *yuan*. To turn to luxuries—in Peking a watch costs 100 *yuan*; a radio set, 125 *yuan*; and a bicycle, 150 *yuan*.

Some economists have suggested that central wage and price control is a handy device for lowering real wages in order to help the accumulation of capital by the State.[2] However, such manipulation of real wages by price control is not really possible in China. The masses of citizens do not yet buy a very wide range of consumer goods and the State has been following a policy of supplying cloth, food, and fuel at very low prices. This policy would be difficult to reverse; nor can money wages in the communes be reduced easily or even held down with rises in productivity, since the brigade and not the State is in charge of wage setting.

THE PRICING SYSTEM

The function of prices in China is to serve the system of planning and to protect the standard of living. Prices are not related to "opportunity costs" or to world price levels. In the sphere of production, prices form part of the costing system, while in consumption industries, prices are subordinated to the planned structure of supply as a determining force on the market. In the sphere of income distribution, prices play a role. The government imposes a turnover tax to separate retail prices from producer prices, and so is in fact redistributing nominal money incomes. The Chinese approach to pricing has been to handle changes in supply and demand trends without disrupting activity inside factories. Tax rates and costing systems are kept stable, and ex-factory prices are altered only after careful consideration. Fluctuations in demand are handled by variable sales tax margins at the selling stage.

However, since prices are interdependent, administrative pricing has to be carried out on a fairly comprehensive scale. Usually price control is administered by provincial bureaus of commerce or by a municipal price commission which covers certain goods and services. Central price control bodies are also responsible for area pricing. Transport in China has always been poor; it has improved considerably, but it is still probably the weakest sector, as the streams of carts drawn by horse and donkey, and handcarts propelled by humans bear witness. In the past, industry was concentrated almost exclusively in the coastal cities, and the farther the customer from the coast, the higher the price of the industrial product. For the national minorities, situated thousands of miles inland, prices were prohibitive, even for essential industrial products such as kerosene and salt. Policy has been to try to remove these differences, and give better internal terms of trade for the remote areas. Already, for less bulky commodities such as medicines and watches there is a uniform price throughout the country; thus at the point of manufacture there will be a substantial profit, but at the remotest sale point there will be a loss, due to transport costs. The uniform price is set to achieve an overall result on country-wide production and distribution of the commodity in question; this may be a loss, a break-even point, a low or high profit, as policy dictates. Regional price differences for grain and cotton cloth have been reduced gradually, and soon unified prices will be possible in these cases.

For some commodities such as kerosene and salt, where regional price differences have not yet been eliminated, a ceiling price is stipulated; for instance, salt sells in Peking at 7–8 *yuan* per catty, but it may not be sold at more than 8–9 *yuan* elsewhere. Salt of course is a crucial item, and in the past peasants in remote areas were undoubtedly exploited by merchants and speculators; in some remote areas the price was so high that peasants could not afford the biological minimum, and this accounted for the prevalence of goiter in such places. The price of salt has dropped progressively. We were told that the uniform pricing policy already has resulted in a staff reduction of 50,000 at the pricing bureau, and has reduced mistakes and the dangers of manipulation.

TAXATION

There is no income tax. The main source of State revenue is from the transferred profits of State enterprises. The proportion between various sources of government income has been changing over time. In 1966 profits of State enterprises contributed nearly seventy percent of budget funds, and taxes on enterprises and communes about thirty percent; of the latter about two-thirds came from enterprises and one-third from communes. The distinction between "profits" and "taxes" is partly one of terminology because it could be argued that the pricing of commodities above cost constitutes an indirect tax similar to the Soviet turnover tax. The effect is the same, for the State revenue accrues from the difference between production and distribution costs, and selling price. The distinction between taxes and profits is partly historical, or else the tax is a precalculated amount—the minimum the State gets, regardless of the performance of the enterprise, which exists to guide the State's financial planning. The essential point is that there is no direct tax on personal incomes; even the five percent per annum, which the capitalists receive on their investments in enterprises taken over in 1956, is not taxed. There are still quite a number of big capitalists, each with fortunes of millions of *yuan*; legally, so far, these fortunes can be inherited without death duties, although the money cannot be taken out of China. The situation is under review, and partly as a result of the Cultural Revolution the payments of five percent per annum on previous investments may soon be abolished. The ideological pressure is such that quite a number of the children of capitalists have publicly renounced their inheritance.

PLANNING METHODOLOGY

We had difficulty finding out a great deal about planning techniques and their adequacy. Where excess capacity existed, it was usually denied that such capacity resulted from bad forecasting or balancing or from marketing problems (plans are fairly realistic and unsold stocks can be readily cleared by a price cut from the center); and claimed that it resulted from transport bottlenecks, raw materials shortages, or labor problems.

We were told that input-output techniques were studied after 1959, in order to give concrete meaning to the "socialist law of balanced and proportionate growth" but that, in the main, the well-known system of "material balance" * is used. Chinese economists stated that planning techniques as such are more useful for regional administrations than for the center, as balancing and target-setting take place in the regions. They also said that because of the relative smallness of the industrial sector, there is no need yet for "optimizing" techniques, and that the main objectives were still the balancing of sectors and the security of and discipline in plan execution. In international trade no "coefficients of effectiveness" testing the foreign exchange return on domestic investment were used because policy stressed self-reliance, balancing of imports, and the paying off of all foreign debt (achieved in 1964). Soviet planning texts and books were criticized for neglecting the human factor in economic development, and for exaggerating the role of technical change and technocracy in the development of a socialist economy. For example, the *People's Daily* article of April 16, 1968, on "The Struggle Between Two Lines of Transformation

---

* "Material balance": an accounting device used in planning which sets supplies of important commodities (from output, imports, and running down of stocks) against demand (from consumers, exporters, and building up of stocks). It was used first in the Soviet Union during the 1920's. When a series of these balances are added together, they form an input-output table —a chessboard sort of table with entries made in vertical columns reflecting the "input" side (industrial branches appearing as producers) and horizontal columns (with the same industrial branches appearing as consumers).

of Capitalist Industry and Commerce" was held up as a promising start on a political economy of Chinese socialism. Chinese economists we spoke to did not know of any wide application of linear-programming techniques, but admitted to the value of a national economy balance of the type constructed in the Soviet Union. On the other hand, at the 1968 Spring Canton Fair, representatives of a company producing computers (which solve linear and non-linear differential equations of the 8th order) stated that computers are being used increasingly to streamline national planning, and in the steel industry.

It should be emphasized that in a country which is still economically underdeveloped strategy and discipline are as important as planning techniques. After an initial period of Soviet-type strategy emphasizing heavy industry, the Chinese policy shifted to one of getting the quickest returns to the most people. This included a policy of getting agriculture right first, then of developing light industry, education, and health. Heavy industry was developed, but Chinese planners warned against being hypnotized by large size, and making a fetish of mechanizing everything. Above all, efficient organization is stressed. The genius of the Chinese is their ability to respond to changing orders for new designs and models; they can meet unexpected demand quickly by subcontracting with small-scale factories, households, and communes to produce large quantities of light industrial goods. When they decide to build a plant, they check on cost, availabilities of supplies, and the period of recoupment on investment. If these are satisfactory, they bring in people at *every* level to see how they will contribute—the municipal organizations, the local councils, and the "alley" committees. Because of this, there is a smaller gap between "paper plans" and "follow-through" in China than in India and other developing countries.

CHINESE PLANNING: A SUMMARY

(1) The central programming of production is combined with a system of direct consultation and bargaining between enterprises —especially at the provincial level.

(2) There is no self-financing by enterprises from ploughed-back

profits and depreciation reserves: all profits are transferred to the State.

(3) Enterprise incentives are moral and ideological rather than financial. "Politics" and not "profits" are "in command."

(4) Wages are stipulated and not related to enterprise results.

(5) Some goods (such as cotton) and raw materials (coal) are rationed and subsidized. Prices are fairly uniform and are administered. Since profits are transferred to the State, there is a reduced need for fluctuating prices and taxes.

(6) Since wages and incomes are directly controlled, there is no need for personal income taxes.

Fundamental changes in the *formal* planning system have not been made by the Cultural Revolution. The main change is that, instead of factory managers consulting with provincial bureaus, now revolutionary committees are sent from the factory to consult with revolutionary committees of the provincial municipal government and its various agencies. These provincial revolutionary committees have been cut down in number of personnel since July 1968. However, some formal changes of planning organs are likely to occur because of the "instruction" in the text of the August 8, 1966, decision of the Central Committee of the Chinese Communist Party which states that "Our objective is the reformation of all superstructures that do not conform with a socialist economic base." The beginnings of change may be seen in the reduced reliance on industrial taxes, and in the criticism of budgets, which are heavy with taxes, as "neocapitalist" or hangovers of the New Economic Policy period of 1961–1964.

The really big change in the system of planning wrought by the Cultural Revolution lies in *motivation*, not in the formal system. Within the factories, all piecework, bonuses, prizes, and policies of "profits in command" have been abolished. Not only the profit motive is rejected, but even profit as a criterion of efficiency is rejected.

There is today much talk about the promotion of the human factor in economic development. Mao and his followers have embarked upon a gigantic experiment in motivation. They seek to make the system of planning work, not by appeals to self-interest and material incentives, but by moral incentives. While the formal planning system remains almost intact, the myriads of decision-makers are now being geared to a new kind of motivation. This leads us to Mao's attempt to break down the power of a senior élite group of industrial specialists, by rejecting financial rewards as the pivot on which the whole economic system used to turn, and replacing them with ideological and moral incentives.

Notes

1. Joan Robinson, review in *Coexistence*, 4, 1966, pp. 105–107.
2. John G. Gurley, "The Economic Development of Communist China," review of George N. Eckland, *Financing the Chinese Government Budget* (Stanford University, mimeographed).

Chapter 8

MORAL INCENTIVES

The success of most non-material incentives depends on the participant's outlook. Thus, non-material incentives by themselves may not work effectively *unless they are accompanied by effective political indoctrination and education.* Such propaganda is aimed at heightening personal awareness, putting a particular campaign or drive in proper perspective, and making its technical requisites clear . . . They rest on the grounds that greater productivity or product derives mainly from (1) the desire to excel and surpass other individuals and groups—an individual and group competitive motive; and (2) the inclination to do better because of one's strong and close identification with the group—*a social or co-operative drive, the opposite of alienation . . . The manner in which co-operative incentives appear to operate is not inconsistent with what contemporary social psychological theory prescribes for increasing productivity.* The success for operation of certain types of group decision making, criticism, and goal-oriented mass movements is predicated on fundamental psychological needs being met. The individual's need for affection, for a sense of being included in important affairs, and for feeling some control or influence over events which shape his life may be positively carried out through some or all of these co-operative incentives. (Italics added.)[1]

THE GROWTH OF MORAL INCENTIVES

In the Soviet Union and Eastern Europe it is now taken for granted that the spur of the collectivist interest is insufficient to build a socialist society. Any motivation that does not harness the personal advantage of the individual is dismissed as romanticism. The trend is to seek a shedding of "primitive" socialist ideals, and to realize industrialization through the use of the management techniques and material stimuli associated with the advanced technology originally developed by capitalism.

Such views have never assumed full command among Chinese Communists, despite the operation of joint State-private firms and the New Economic Policy period of 1961–1964. Had not Mao said in the pre-1945 articles, "Serve the People" and "In Memory of Norman Bethune," that an egotistical competitive morality is inferior to working selflessly for the common good? Had not Mao, writing in 1945, said that revolutionaries should "proceed in all cases from the interests of the people and not from one's self interest or from the interests of a small group"? [2]

And in 1949, Mao spoke of the danger to the Revolution of the "sugar-coated bullets" of the bourgeoisie—selfishness, bureaucratic arrogance—and urged cadres to "remain modest, prudent and free from arrogance in their style of work," and to "preserve the style of plain living and hard struggle." [3]

In the 1950's the case for moral or ideological incentives was again stressed. A major work, first published in the *People's Daily* on November 29, 1956, pointed out: "Once we have the right system, the main question is whether we can make the right use of it; whether we have the right policies and right methods and style of work. Without this, even under a good system it is still possible for people to commit serious mistakes and to use a good state apparatus to do evil things . . . the task of the communist party and the state is, by relying on the masses and the collective, to make timely re-adjustments in the various links of the economic and political systems." [4]

The publication of Mao Tse-tung's *On the Correct Handling of Contradictions Among the People*, in 1957, marked an even stronger swing toward harnessing moral incentives. In fact, it would be no exaggeration to say that the seeds of the Maoist position in the later Cultural Revolution are to be found in this work, notably in the analysis of the transition period to communism, and in the view that rebellion is justified if it serves the masses. Especially notable was the discussion of problems arising from "contradictions among the interests of the state, the interests of the collective and the interests of the individual, between democracy and centralising, between the leadership and the led"; [5] and the advocacy of a style of economic and political life which involved "stamping out bureaucracy, greatly improving ideological and political education and dealing with all contradictions properly." [6]

Moral incentives had reached their highest postwar peak in 1958 during the Great Leap Forward—a period, incidentally, when Maoism was in full control of the country's affairs. The Water Conservation Campaign was built on moral rather than material incentives; the idea of sharing things in common, irrespective of the individual's contribution, made progress in the communes. The August 1958 Resolution spoke of the need to promote "the social consciousness and morality of the whole people to a higher degree," to institute universal education and "to break down the differences between workers and peasants"; and later in 1958, shipbuilding workers in Shanghai abolished the systems of bonuses and piecework.[7] All of these became central motifs again during the Cultural Revolution.[8]

Despite the growth of spontaneous market forces and of capitalist farming after 1959, an undercurrent of the Maoist moral incentives policy remained. We referred earlier to the Learn from Lei Feng Movement and the Socialist Education Movement of 1963. In that year the Chinese Communists, in their "Proposal Concerning the General Line of the International Communist Movement," warned that "For decades or even longer periods after socialist industrialisation and agricultural collectivisation, it will be impossible to say that any socialist country will be free from . . . bourgeois hangers-on, parasites, speculators, swindlers, idlers, hooligans and embezzlers of state funds; or to say that a socialist country will no longer need to perform or to be able to relinquish the task laid down by Lenin of conquering this contagion, this plague, this ulcer that socialism has inherited from capitalism." [9] In 1964 the Learn from Tachai and Taching Campaigns were appeals to moral incentives, and in the same year an official publication criticized Soviet practice for "substituting material incentives for the socialist principle" and for "widening the gap between the incomes of a small minority and those of the peasant workers, peasants and ordinary intellectuals." [10] It went on to ask: "Is our society today thoroughly clean? No it is not. Classes and class struggle remain. We still have speculative activities by old and new bourgeois ele-

ments and desperate forays by embezzlers, grafters and degenerates
. . . the socialist revolution on the economic front is insufficient
by itself and cannot be consolidated. There must be a thorough socialist revolution on the political and ideological fronts." [11]

All of these developments indicate that despite contradiction
between the practice of certain segments of the population and
some State organs, and the ideology of the Revolution, a key component of that ideology—moral incentives—not only survived but
was able to burgeon in the Cultural Revolution launched in 1966.
This tremendous emphasis on moral incentives increasingly affected
not only management, industrialization, and organization, but the
nature of Chinese life itself, especially through Mao's "latest instructions," to which we have referred previously and to which we
shall return for a discussion of their *operational* role. Especially
important was the part played by the injunction to "fight self," as
a central component of the Cultural Revolution which, as Mao
said in March 1967, "touches people to their very souls and aims
at solving the problem of their world outlook."

Many of these "instructions" of 1967–1968 may seem trite to the
outside observer. But their enormous importance is obvious to any
visitor, as they appear on virtually every wall, machine, and loom
in the country. Moreover, "If this be madness, there is method in
it." It is not an idle boast when Peking publications speak of Mao's
"great strategic plan." The plain fact is that at each crucial point
in the struggles after 1964, he supplied advice to the revolutionaries
supporting his line. Following one upon another, these "instructions" constituted a coherent strategy of political attack, political
struggle, and political advance. The basis of the whole approach
is the view that revolution is not a thing or an institution: it is an
experience, an act of will. Mao rejects the view that there is an
inevitable historical movement from primitive communism through
slavery, feudalism, and capitalism to socialism and communism.
On the contrary, he holds that revolution and collectivism are *not*
inevitable, that centralist bureaucratic exercises in social engineering can emerge, and that a once socialist country can revert to
capitalism. To intervene in these developments, to remove them,
it is necessary to establish the idea of revolutionary activity in the
sense of audacious human will. As a key article written at the

height of the Cultural Revolution put it: "Man's social being determines his thinking. But thinking in turn plays a great active
role, or under certain conditions, a decisive role, in the development of the politics and economy of a given society . . . In what
does the old ideology of the exploiting classes lie? It lies essentially
in self-interest—the natural soil for the growing of capitalism. This
explains why it is necessary to start a great political and ideological
revolution. It is a revolution to remould people to their very souls,
to revolutionise their thinking. That is why in the course of this
revolution we must 'fight self.' " [12]

WHY MORAL INCENTIVES?

From the standpoint of economics, the Maoist emphasis on
moral incentives has been justified on a number of counts. Basically Mao denies that the growth of the economy is simply a
function of physical investment and technical progress. He claims
that there is a missing link in this equation—human motivation;
increasingly his strategy has been based on the promotion of the
human factor in economic development.

This diagnosis of growth is shared by a number of economists
in other countries. Colin Clark, for example, holds that "While
investment in capital is undoubtedly necessary for economic
growth, it is certainly not the controlling or predominant factor.
Economists are not yet in a position to analyse this matter fully;
but we can say that the principal factors in economic growth are
not physical—natural resources and invested capital—but human." [13] Earlier "growth models" which assumed that capital is
the leading factor in growth are being replaced, even in the West,
with the view that organization and skills are to be regarded as an
independent parameter which exerts a growing influence on the
rate of economic growth.[14]

Another rediscovery of Western economics in recent years is
"learning by doing" and its contribution to growth. This is most
certainly a proposition that is in the full Maoist tradition, but
even this has been embraced by serious Western students of economic development. According to two British economists, "Investment benefits productivity largely because it provides opportunities

for learning new methods," [15] while "Learning theories show economies of scale from learning, quite different from the indivisibilities etc. of traditional economic theory." [16]

All of this has tremendous implications for the *style* of economic management. Earlier industrialization was associated with a system of management which gave managers of enterprises extremely autocratic powers of control. Mao sees this and wants to avoid it. On the level of society as a whole, he considers that Eastern European countries have merely organized socialism as one giant industrial concern, with all power to the technocrats, or (as in Yugoslavia) to an alleged class of bureaucrat-capitalists.

China may be able to profit as a "late-comer" to industrialization by giving more scope to the new *kind* of industrialization—automation and cybernetics—which requires more self-management, and less of the technocratic control implied by the mass-production-line factory; but this remains to be seen. However, if the "new industrial revolution" is introduced into China, people will have been better prepared for it than has ever been the case previously.[17] For as even the Czech Academy of Science has noted: "Everything depends on whether socialism succeeds in working out a system of *civilisation regulators*, of means and rules for adjusting the economic, and also the social, political, psychological and cultural conditions for promoting man's creative abilities and directing his interests to socialism. Modelling economic motivation, moulding the socialist style of life, stimulating democratic initiative, cultivating the collective reason—all these forms of indirect management also imply developing the actual *subject* in society, unfolding and reinforcing the subjectivity of sectors of management that meet the needs of transition to the scientific and technological revolution." [18] It is hard to see Maoist strategists disagreeing with this diagnosis. And there is surely justification for the Maoist emphasis on a high proportion of moral incentives in the amalgam of material-moral stimuli on which any economy depends. For even the Czechs, arch advocates of financial reward and more inequality in income spreads, admit that:

> We have abolished capitalist property and thereby paralysed the former driving force of the economic self-movement. This negation, however, has not by itself created any higher stimuli and forms of

movement of the economic development, it has not brought into being a particular socialist system with a universal spirit of enterprise. The negation has merely transferred the direction of the whole economy to the centre which under these conditions had to succumb to bureaucratisation and subjectivism. Outside the centre this has led to a lack of interest and irresponsibility.[19]

In terms of the motivation of economic behavior, this is the crux of the matter, for self-interest and material gain *are* the driving force of the capitalist system. The same motivations cannot continue to be the driving force of a socialist system; they must be replaced by others. If they are not, a basic contradiction results, caused by the continued coexistence of motivation based on individual material advancement, operating within the framework of a collectivist ethos and institutions. In such a contradiction something must eventually give way—either the motivation of individual material advancement, or the collectivist ethos and institutions. The Czechs are here pointing out that no attempt has been made in their case to resolve this contradiction; the expedient adopted has been a bureaucratic direction from the top downward. Thus, socialism has become bureaucratized, inefficient, and inhuman—hence the lack of response and effort, and the development of dissident groups whose opposition takes the form of opposing both bureaucracy and socialism, which become equated.

In an attempt to get out of the morass, emphasis is placed on a return to the material incentives and individual interest and advancement of the previous social order. In the last analysis, Mao's argument boils down to this: one cannot have a stable socialist society operating with the motivations of a capitalist society; if the motivations are not changed sooner or later there will be a reversion to a form of capitalism, for the old values of the old society will reassert themselves, helped by influences from outside on both the élite and dissident groups.

Maoists then may be said to have challenged not only the *morality*, but also the economics and the psychology of monetary incentives as a motor driving the economy. From the *sociological* point of view, Maoist strategy also makes a good deal of sense, premised as it is on similar fears that have been expressed by anthropologists and sociologists about the consequences, in economically backward countries, of the emergence of a great gulf between senior élite groups of specialists and political leaders, and the mass of peasants. Many of the old assumptions of anthropology are being challenged by the "new" anthropology,[20] for instance, the explanation of economic backwardness in terms of values and psychological characteristics of the native population; the assumption that it is desirable to avoid rapid, disruptive changes;[21] and the assumption that the main process by which economic development occurs is diffusion from an industrial center.[22] Nor is Mao the only revolutionary thinker to have challenged the orthodox view that the historical jump from presocialist to socialist forms comes about only by an increase in social wealth as a result of the "rationalization" process imposed on laborers by industry; or to note that this "rational" method of developing society conflicts with the self-realization of the individual.[23]

The Maoist approach, like that of many sociologists, is to discover why the masses have lost the power to direct their own lives in society. Why, even in collectivist societies, is it possible for man to be separated from his product, as a result of the centralized political and bureaucratic control of production engendered by a technological society, in which life is regulated by machines? Mao uses moral incentives as an essentially practical way of getting people to take a more active part in deciding how their material creations are to be used, and how to arrange their social lives without subordinating the mass to the élite. Hence the continued emphasis on the line of "from the masses—to the masses" as the normal style of political work of all in positions of authority.

Sociologists also increasingly realize that "The ability of forms of life to adapt to a great variety of conditions, frequently under the greatest handicaps, in order to survive, grow and function, suggests a mode of creativity." [24] This means that "Moral problems may have potentially, at least, a practical or technological solution . . . moral rules develop where there are no clearly defined technological patterns of instrumental activity, where the usual rules of living break down, or where individuals and societies are left on their own to structure actions deemed proper." [25] Mao has had to build on the fractured society left by the Chinese Civil War; it is no wonder then, that he has analyzed the "nonantagonistic" contradictions between people, and between people and State, in the transition period to the socialist society he wishes to see emerge in China. If he permits the continuance of some older Chinese moral values, it may be because he realizes, as some sociologists do, that "To ignore the existing structure of value facts is to operate in a vacuum, and to do so would be to make decision illusory and unrealistic." [26] Thus he both recognizes the continuing influence of older moral incentives and the need to give them a new direction. As a recent Maoist article put it: "Confucius died more than 2000 years ago. But his thinking still stubbornly spreads to corrupt people's minds and influence public opinion in society . . . the proletariat must vigorously create revolutionary public opinion, launch a large scale ideological revolution in which hundreds of millions of people take part." [27]

The direction of change Mao seeks, then, is to promote moral incentives within the framework of Marxism-Leninism as he interprets it. These incentives are the utopian ones of Marxism-Leninism, which are being used to break down older values and reorient them. Thus, for example, the reference above to Confucian thought corrupting people's minds and influencing public opinion in society relates to the fact that the Confucian system was based on respect for and obedience to authority of the rulers, whether in the form of the head of the extended family, the emperor, or the officials or organs of the State. This has had a profound influence on the thinking of the Chinese people about the role of the State. As Hegel pointed out: "The morality of the State is not of the ethical kind in which one's own conviction bears sway; this latter is rather the peculiarity of the modern time, while the true Antique morality is based on the principle of abiding by one's duty to the State at large." [28] Related to this is the Chinese tradition that any group which isolates itself from the State and takes its own path is considered a conspiracy and is suppressed. For that reason the progressive minority cannot risk an experiment in the hope that others will follow if it is successful. The minority favoring a renewed system must seize power and impose its will on the majority by force.[29]

To combat this problem, Mao has often said that "the minority is sometimes right" and "it is right to rebel." This call to revolt issued to youth in the Cultural Revolution is, as Han Suyin points out, totally against the tradition of Confucian China, but Confucius was also repudiated in a previous period of cultural and political ferment, between 1890 and 1919.[30] This also explains Mao's apparent willingness to permit the shattering of the old Party apparatus during the Cultural Revolution, as well as the great stress he places on the new education system, under which contact between people—especially between intellectuals and peasants—should replace contact between people and State organs. On State organs, Mao said in April 1968 that "The most fundamental principle in the reform of state organs is that they must keep in contact with the masses." In 1968 the big campaign began to send youth and intellectuals to the countryside, and a series of Mao's latest "instructions" were issued to this effect, while at the same time other "directives" enjoined the working class to visit the schools.[31] This reduces people's *vertical* dependence on State and Party, and increases their *dependence* on each other in developing ideology and moral incentives.

This strategy may be seen from a number of different viewpoints. Some will see merely Mao's yearning for a return to the spirit and methods of the prewar period in the "red" base at Yenan. Others will see it as a way of bringing into national life the creative experience of the masses, and not merely the empiricism of planners and top officials. The Chinese are fond of quoting Lenin's point that "Practical experience is ten times more valuable than a conceited Communist who is ready at any time of the day or night to write theses. Less intellectualist and bureaucratic conceit, more study of what our practical experience reveals is what science can give us." [32] Mao rephrased this when he said in 1968 that "We communists seek not official posts, but revolution," just as in 1967 he said that "People do different types of work at various posts, but no matter how high-ranking an official anyone is, he should be like an ordinary worker among the people. It is absolutely impermissible for him to put on airs."

Assuming that such moral exhortations are intended to take on an operational character, the role of *consciousness* is understandable. It helps to show people that there is a "correct" solution to problems where practical experience is combined with correct theory. This also reflects the firmly held Chinese Communist belief that, in the Soviet Union, consciousness is not trusted—that individual, selfish material incentives have already replaced the "correct" policy of exchanging ideas and experiences in the collective. They believe there has been a Soviet counterrevolution in economic administration, and the restoration of a bureaucratic manipulation of the economy through selfishness campaigns. The Chinese operational principle of "fight self, fight self-interest" provides the counter strategy to the rising of a similar development in China. Hence the stress on the need to use moral incentives, not only to handle the contradictions that inevitably arise between the economic base and the superstructure, but also to release the "mind-forged manacles" which otherwise would retard the rapid expansion of the forces of production. What Maoists claim for their Great Proletarian Cultural Revolution is, essentially, that they have been able to overcome, by a principled combination of unity and struggle, the tendencies gravitating toward capitalism and/or bureaucratic management and control.

A final motivation for the moral factor stress is to show the relevance of socialist morality to other economically poor countries, to underline the practical possibilities of socialism here and now for Asia, Africa, and Latin America. As Gurley puts it:

> The Maoists have pulled the peasant from the muck of ignorance and poverty. Listen to us, the Maoists whisper,—"first enrich the people and you will enrich yourself." But the peasant with an eye on his private plot also has an ear for the song of the "revisionists": "first enrich yourself and you will then enrich the people." In which appeal, I wonder, lies the greater hope for the world's poor? [33]

The Maoist view, then, is that the role of consciousness, even in underdeveloped countries, permits individuals to leap across whole historical epochs of thought, even if not consistently, and to adopt, on the whole, the morality of communism. Such individuals in the revolutionary movements within the "third world" in fact constitute a "mass" which form enclaves within colonial and postcolonial societies. This line of thought also aims to break the hegemony of Soviet ideology over underdeveloped countries. From the Maoist viewpoint the Chinese Revolution broke more than a material structure of power; it also broke an intellectual stranglehold, which had impeded many revolutionaries and socialists from achieving a correct appraisal of the balance of social forces in their own countries, and led them to misdirect their political and organizational tactics. Mao Tse-tung consolidated creative Marxism by basing the Chinese Revolution on new assumptions. No longer could theorists of revolution in the West or the Soviet Union claim theoretical and practical preeminence.

FEATURES OF MORAL INCENTIVES

As shown in the previous chapter, Chinese economic strategy has sought a mixture of economic decentralization and ideological unity, the latter being exercised by the use of the "little red book" of quotations, the "three constantly read articles," Mao's poetry, and his "latest instructions." The centralizing force in this has been the Cultural Revolution Group around Mao, and the revolutionary committees which are under his strong influence.

Before ideological unity, however, there was ideological struggle. We have already emphasized the role played by Mao's work, *On the Correct Handling of Contradictions Among the People*, of 1957, as the most cogent analysis of the need for ideological struggle. Later, after 1965, Liu Shao-chi was opposed by the Maoists with the allegation that his theories and policies did not fit in with the "fight self" approach and a collectivist way of life. Putting it more crudely, the ideological fundamentalists supporting Chairman Mao Tse-tung, who were prepared to sacrifice specialization and large-scale market efficiency for the ideal of building a selfless nation, were opposed by hard-headed technocrats who had their supporters not only in the State organs, but within the Party itself.

Specifically, the criticism made of those aspects of Liu Shao-chi's approach which tended to block the "fight self" strategy were as follows:

(1) His "seventy points" charter for industry excluded workers' control and the hegemony of "politics in command," by putting material incentives first, or "bonuses in command," so that indus-

trialization would be achieved purely through running the economy by economic methods.

(2) In agriculture, his *"san zi yi bao"* policy had released the forces of kulakism and capitalism.

(3) In the agricultural brigades he put work points in command instead of voluntary public service.

(4) Like Bukharin, he argued that class struggle in China would die away as socialism in China won more victories.

(5) He denied that "political work is the life-blood of economic work," as taught by Mao.

(6) He upheld the maintenance of Party discipline and unity as an absolute principle, in opposition to the Maoist view that "the minority is often right."

A second feature of the drive for moral incentives, and one which follows from the criticisms of Liu Shao-chi, is the rejection of the notion that in each country, at every point of time, there is a "correct" amalgam of material and moral incentives. Rather, under the system of socialist social property, the responsibility of working communities and collectives is to participate in both the labor process and decision-making, in a way that is both positive and unified. People must have the right to self-management and the obligations stemming from it. One of these is the need for a "unified State plan"—the unity of a new right and a duty which ensures against economic and other relationships turning into a conflict of rights, and therefore also ensures against socialist society becoming a competitive commercialized market and smallholder community of the old type, which would be even more irresponsible as a result of being freed from the check put on it by the risk faced by the owner of private capital.

Many commentators have seen the "personality cult" as a main feature of moral incentives. Certainly there is a tremendous emphasis on Mao's contribution. The Peasant Revolts of 1921, 1925, and 1927, as well as many other activities, are attributed to him personally. The idea behind this seems to be somewhat as follows. The will to struggle already exists. Mao Tse-tung's thought can concentrate that will. But in order to concentrate it, there must exist an instrument, as well as people who analyze society, analyze reality, who see the road taken by the economy, the forces that direct the economy, and at the same time the masses' state of spirit, capacity, resolution, and combative will. Analysis, experiment, the drawing of conclusions, the organization of programs cannot be done without an instrument—of such a character that it is linked to the life of the masses. Such an instrument, say the Maoists, is Marxism and, in particular, Marxism in the current epoch as set out by Mao Tse-tung.

Here we come up against the problem of "charismatic bureaucracy" and its role. As Seligman notes:

The great man influences society only when society is ready for him. If society is not ready for him, he is called, not a great man, but a visionary or a failure. He is great because he visualizes more truly than anyone else the fundamental tendencies of the community in which his lot is cast, and because he expresses more successfully than others the real spirit of the age . . .

History is full of examples where nations, like individuals, have acted unselfishly and have followed the generous promptings of the higher life . . .

The content of the conception of morality is a social product; amid the complex social influences that are operated to produce it, the economic factors have been of chief significance . . . pure ethical or religious idealism has made itself felt only within the limitations of existing economic conditions.

Unless the social conditions, however, are ripe for change, the demands of the ethical reform will be fruitless.[34]

The "charismatic bureaucrat" is both a product of his times and an agent of change. But also, as Weber noted,[35] charisma tends to transform itself ("routinize itself," as Weber said) in order to serve as a durable base for a political order. The usual way this occurs is for charisma to attach itself to the office and not to the person, or for an hereditary line to develop. In either case, the charismatic bureaucracy is replaced by a legal-rational one.

Mao Tse-tung has attempted to counter this in two ways (apart from developing moral incentives which promote his own ideology). In the first place, by his big character poster entitled "Bombard the Headquarters," and his campaign against Liu Shao-chi, he has robbed the "office" of President of its charisma. Second, he has handled the Cultural Revolution in such a way that no personal struggle for succession will follow his death. The aim is to give the succession to a party interested in serving rather than ruling the people; authority has been given to the broad masses, not to the administration.

Nor can Mao's regime be regarded as a legal-rational bureaucracy in Marx's sense: "Bureaucracy is a circle no one can leave. Its hierarchy is a hierarchy of information. The top entrusts the lower circles with an insight into details, while the lower circles entrust the top with an insight into what is universal, and thus they both deceive each other." [36] No account of Chinese government or Party conduct resembles this picture.

ASSESSMENTS

A number of Western economists and sociologists reject the view that moral incentives can play a predominant role in a modern economy, pointing to the emergence of black markets and incentive-lags during periods of war, or arguing that people in underdeveloped countries are actually interested in the idea of maximum gains.[37] To a large extent this reflects the methodology of looking at Asian societies through the prism of a Western economic theory designed for a completely different institutional setting. (See the discussion in Chapter 12.) Surely it is a more commonsense view to say that a country like China sets up the institutions to achieve its own goals; that the functions capitalists perform in the West are absent; and that various new ways of managing the economy are being tried.

The other main source of doubt about the genuineness of the use of moral incentives emanates from the Soviet Union. Soviet theoreticians assess the Cultural Revolution in terms of Chinese tradition,[38] and little else. Their idea is that Mao has simply become the focus of age-old chiliastic religious fervor, based on the hope that a leader will appear to "raise his fist in the name of harmony and justice"—and that this has been the psychological background of countless Chinese uprisings. Maoism is not even explained as "petty-bourgeois" socialism of the peasant type, and is openly attacked as bringing less peasant democracy than did Sun Yat-sen.[39]

However, Marxism itself has always contained two elements. One of these is its appeal to the "jacquerie":* its romanticism and appeal to communal living, revolution, and brotherhood. This aspect of Marxism has always had a big impact on people living in predominantly precapitalist forms of society (Russia in 1917, China, Cuba). The second element is the emphasis on raising the level of productive forces through industrialization. The first of these two elements has been very strong at various times; certainly it is not an insignificant strand of Marxist-Leninist thought. One does not, therefore, need to explain the Cultural Revolution in terms of "Chinese tradition"; it is in the mainstream of Marxism itself.

There are two difficulties in analyzing the role of the moral factor, however. We have to distinguish what Maoists are trying to achieve by this method, and what they have actually implemented. This requires a close study of individual plants and institutions—at which we have aimed in this book. The second difficulty concerns the basis on which the myriads of moral incentives are constructed. To work effectively these incentives must provide a totality of experience, and people will have to come to "Maoist" conclusions for themselves, from their own existence. Moral incentives need to function as a technique for promoting creative effort. It is not a question, then, of teaching the people the Maoist ideology, but of the Chinese people learning a certain *way* of reasoning things out, and a way of fitting in their activities with society's goals.

Notes

1. Charles Hoffman in *An Economic Profile of Mainland China* (New York: Praeger, 1968), pp. 488, 491.

---

* "Jacquerie": French term for rising of the peasantry, especially in 1357–1358, in France.

2. Mao Tse-tung, "On Coalition Government," *Selected Works* (Peking: Foreign Languages Press, 1961), Vol. III, p. 315.
3. Mao Tse-tung, "Report to the Second Plenary Session of the 7th Central Committee of the C.P.C." March 5, 1949; reprinted in *Peking Review,* November 29, 1968.
4. *More on the Historical Experiences of the Dictatorship of the Proletariat* (Peking: 1957), p. 17.
5. Mao Tse-tung, *On the Correct Handling of Contradictions Among the People* (Peking: Foreign Languages Press, 1967), pp. 3–12.
6. *Ibid.,* pp. 45–46.
7. Reported in *Chieh Fang Ji Pai* (Shanghai), October 19, 1958; see *SCMP,* No. 1947.
8. Even the use of big character posters to air individual viewpoints and make suggestions and criticisms in factories, villages, and shops was not invented during the Cultural Revolution—but was part of the "mass line" in 1958 and 1959, and was described in M. Shapiro, "China's First Ten Years," *Marxism Today,* October 1959.
9. *A Proposal Concerning the General Use of the International Communist Movement,* March 30, 1963 (Peking: 1963), p. 37.
10. *On Khrushchev's Phoney Communism and Its Historical Lessons for the World,* July 14, 1964 (Peking: 1964), p. 27.
11. *Ibid.,* pp. 63–64.
12. "Fight Self, Repudiate Revisionism Is the Fundamental Principle of the Great Proletarian Cultural Revolution," *People's Daily,* October 6, 1967; reprinted in *Long Live Victory of the Great Cultural Revolution* (Peking: 1968), pp. 41–48.
13. Colin Clark, *Growthmanship: A Study in the Mythology of Investment* (London: Barrie and Rockliff, 1961), p. 13.
14. R. M. Solow, "Technical Change and the Aggregate Production Function," *Review of Economics and Statistics,* August 1957.
15. R. T. Hahn and R. C. O. Matthews, "The Theory of Economic Growth," *Survey of Economic Theory* (London: Royal Economic Society, 1967), p. 69.
16. *Ibid.,* p. 67.
17. This view is disputed by economists and sociologists in Eastern Europe and the Soviet Union. The Czechs argue that the "human factor" becomes crucial only "above a certain level of civilization." See Richta *et al., Civilisation at the Crossroads: Report of the Czechoslovak Academy of Sciences* (Sydney: 1968), p. 15 n. A

Russian writer holds that communes "possess only primitive means of production. Simple reproduction proceeds laboriously, labour productivity is extremely low, and economic activity and the entire life of the community bears the stamp of seclusion . . . History has not given us an example of communal forms of ownership, which are a survival of the clan system, being able to engender a socialist society." V. Afanasyev, *Scientific Communism* (Moscow: 1967), p. 174. This last is a rather obvious thrust at the Chinese communes and the Chinese "road" to socialism.

18. Richta *et al.*, *Civilization at the Crossroads*, p. 203.
19. R. Richta, "Models of Socialism," *Rude Pravo*, July 11, 1968.
20. K. Gough, "Anthropology—Child of Imperialism," *Monthly Review*, April 1968, p. 20.
21. Claude Levi-Strauss, *Structural Anthropology* (New York: Basic Books, 1963), Ch. 16.
22. *Ibid.*, pp. 330–333.
23. H. Marcuse, *Soviet Marxism: A Critical Analysis* (New York: Columbia University Press, 1961), p. 20.
24. Paul Kurtz, *Decision and the Condition of Man* (Seattle: University of Washington Press, 1965), p. 56.
25. *Ibid.*, p. 260.
26. *Ibid.*, p. 244.
27. Hsieh Sheng-wen, "Great Struggle in a Great Era," *Peking Review*, March 28, 1969.
28. G. W. F. Hegel, *Philosophy of History*, J. Sibree, trans. (New York: Wiley Book Company, 1944), p. 41.
29. L. Kyuzayhyon, *The Chinese Crisis, Causes and Character* (Moscow: 1967), p. 26.
30. Han Suyin, *China in the Year 2001* (New York: Basic Books, 1967), pp. 27, 165.
31. See the Appendix for "latest instructions" on the need for the educated to visit the countryside and the working class to visit the schools. By March 1969, 25 million people or 15 percent of the urban population had visited the countryside for ideological exchanges (*Australian Financial Review*, April 2, 1969). Incidentally, such appeals to educated youth to visit the Chinese masses, and to struggle to find ideas which would enable China to survive, were pursued by Mao's foremost Marxist forerunner, Li Ta-chao, in a series of articles in *New Youth*, in 1917–1920. Impressed by the Populist Movement in late nineteenth-century Russia, Li Ta-chao urged young intellectuals to go out and awaken

the laboring classes, claiming that the peasantry would be the base of revolution in China.

32. V. I. Lenin, "The Single Plan," *Pravda*, February 22, 1921; see *Selected Works* (New York: International Publishers, 1935–1938), Vol. II.

33. John G. Gurley, "The Economic Development of Communist China" (Stanford University, mimeographed).

34. E. R. A. Seligman, *The Economic Interpretation of History* (New York: Columbia University Press, 1902), pp. 31, 97, 126.

35. Max Weber, *The Theory of Social and Economic Organization*, T. Parsons, ed. (New York: Oxford, 1947), p. 328 ff. In fact Weber did not attempt to prove that newer or more recent eruptions of charisma will always be increasingly institutionalized along legal-rational lines. He merely assumed this to be true because it was the historical trend.

36. Karl Marx, "Critique of Hegel's Philosophy of the State," 1843, *Writings of the Young Marx on Philosophy and Society*, L. D. Easton and K. H. Guddat, eds. (Garden City, New York: Doubleday, 1967), pp. 185–186.

37. Harry G. Johnson, *Money, Trade and Economic Growth* (Cambridge: Harvard University Press, 1966), p. 157.

38. Kyuzayhyon, *The Chinese Crisis*, pp. 17–24.

39. *Ibid.*, p. 24.

Chapter 9

TECHNOLOGICAL POLICY

THE MILIEU OF TECHNOLOGY

Technological policy, in any society, is part of a set of economic control techniques. To establish the function of technology and the rationality of technological policy one must first identify the social goals. In other words, technology is *not* neutral, as often assumed in Western growth models.[1] It is worth exploring why this is so.

First, rapid technological advancement creates economic, social, and political conflicts. These may range from problems of employment to problems of a whole way of life in an industrial society.[2] Second, technological progress causes an intricate division of labor which may require elaborate organizational arrangements. This affects the location of power and affects politics. How are factories to be controlled and why? What power will executives have? What relations ought to exist between the State and industrial units which implement technological policy? The nature of these arrangements is not ideologically neutral. Third, ideology influences technological policy.

In the West, premature obsolescence fits in with a consumer-orientated investment policy which requires rapid turnover of product-mixes, and of the technology stock which supports it. In the Soviet Union the neglect of technological inputs in agriculture, as well as recent delays in the introduction of computer technology to planning, were ideologically conditioned to a high degree. China can hardly hope to evolve a "neutral" technological policy even if such a highly ideological society would like to do so.

The social milieu in which Chinese technology operates is that of an economy distinguished by social control and by the discipline of the unified State plan, to which is attached the "motor" of moral incentives to make the whole system work. It is a milieu utterly different from that of the markets, relative price movements, and self-financing corporations of the market economies of the Western world (and of Yugoslavia). Also China is a peasant society with strong regional rivalries and with decision-making decentralized at the provincial level.

The main features of Chinese technological policy are as follows:

(1) Investment in large industrial plants (outside the defense sector) is strictly limited—provinces are encouraged to become self-sufficient "base areas" in order to be able to meet any armed invasion.

(2) Small and medium plants are set up; these can rely on local financial and labor resources and raw materials to meet local (provincial) industrial needs,[3] thereby minimizing demands on the State.

(3) Small, self-reliant enterprises are promoted wherever possible, to be run by the "red masses" rather than by technocrats, and to be used as centers of education in politics and ideology. There is, therefore, a direct connection between features of current technological policy and the "redness" versus "expertness" controversy of the early 1960's. (See Chapter 3.) The Chinese appear to have abandoned the conception of a factory as a highly rationalized production unit: *the enterprise is not viewed as a purely economic unit where economic performance takes undisputed priority*.

(4) Many plants making final products are also encouraged to make their own machine tools, lathes, nuts, and bolts, and so forth.

(5) The policy of copying foreign machine design, noted also by foreign observers[4] in the pre-Cultural Revolution period, has been now identified with the technocratic bias of the Right-wing policy in economics, and is being steadily reversed.

(6) In most factories where workers have improved on a Soviet or Western design, they keep the old machines on display for

use in education about the merits of self-reliance, and the potential ability of the "lowly" to out-innovate the "expert."

(7) Attempts are being made to encourage mechanization of processes through modifications suggested by the workers themselves.

(8) Certain parts of production processes which can be handled mechanically are carried on by labor-intensive methods—particularly in packaging and assembling.

(9) In assembly work or in joining parts of various machines, the policy is to join parts into a single piece of equipment by welding or by screws. This prevents the need (inherent in much Soviet equipment) to scrap the whole piece if something goes wrong with one of the parts. Such was the case in the construction of China's 12,000-ton hydraulic press and the Shanghai diesel pumps (described below), but we found this approach operating in every plant.

(10) Much attention is paid to the construction of efficient marketing outlets, and arrangements are made (even to the extent of permitting a putting-out system) by which emergency orders or unexpected foreign demand in textiles, glassware, and other consumer goods can be met quickly.

(11) Where foreign machinery and technology *is* borrowed or hired, the most up-to-date is demanded to avoid a fast rate of obsolescence.

These points may be illustrated by reference to some factories visited.

THE PRACTICE

—In the Shanghai Diesel Pumps and Motors Plant, three out of the five workshops make all their own lathes. An enormous number of lathes and a variety of intricate screws and small spray heads are required in the production process. Many of these have been made from scrap iron and copper in the spare time of workers. A technical innovation of this plant is the use of wind-driven machinery to process the small oil-sprayer heads. Since the quality of the spray depends on the number of revolutions per minute of the lathe, the Chinese machine which makes 100,000 revolutions per minute is very creditable when compared with the American machines, formerly imported, which performed 40,000 revolutions per minute.

This plant has a number of other innovations to its credit: a completely automatic machine for polishing valves; a streamlined circular rotating assembly line; a series of automatic gougers which can handle more than one kind of iron cast. A new kind of automatic gouger for the second stage of processing the cast is highly effective, but took a year of experiment to get into full operation. A large reaming lathe, invented by women workers ("to refute the idea that they could not innovate"), enables more than one top of the cast to be processed. The assembly of different parts of the diesel engine is done by screwing with a pneumatic screwdriver which is an innovation of this plant, and now marketed as Dong Feng brand.

One of the final products of the factory is a brand new diesel locomotive engine, twelve-cylinder, with pump injection. In Workshop No. 4, which is mainly responsible for it all, machines are automatic or semi-automatic and all are made in the workshop itself. Once again there was a screw-tightening machine worked by an operator with a pneumatic screwdriver; the pump itself is joined by screws from five parts, whereas the Russian pumps, formerly imported, were in a single piece.

In the fifth workshop a number of automatic drilling machines make the threads of the plate, but also working are two Soviet lathes which, according to the Revolutionary Committee members of the plant, have been kept "for education purposes"; only two of these lathes were delivered, and according to the Chinese—"The Russians became difficult when they learned we had developed a diesel engine with twelve cylinders, and with a diameter of 135 centimeters."

—At the Shanghai Heavy Machine Building Plant, there is a justly famous 12,000-ton hydraulic forging press—one of the largest in the world. This press is lighter than 10,000-ton capacity presses abroad, largely because it was constructed with hollow columns (comprising three pieces put together with electric slack welding). This contrasts with the solid rods (columns) of overseas presses. This is a typical Chinese approach—to use lighter materials and to weld or screw the pieces. It is as if a definite reaction against Russian "gigantomania"—complex structures and heaviness—has set in among Chinese technologists: the same is to be observed with large lathes of all kinds, trucks, tractors, and mechanical ploughs. The result, in all plants we visited, is a continuous search for lightness, simple structures, and medium size.

—At the Shanghai Waitung Truck Factory, an important machine for treating the engine cast has been completely made from worn-out parts and scrap. A second ingenious but simple machine, which processes the cogwheel and has increased productivity 40 times over since 1964, was made by a worker entirely from scrap he collected. In this plant a lathe for processing the speedometer control cog made in the plant's workshop coexists with a large lathe from Changsha, and an "indigenous" (to the factory) automatic lathe for planing the teeth of cogwheels coexists with a more modern one from Tientsin. In both cases, however, it was admitted that the "import" from China's modern machine-building sector was more efficient. About fifty percent of the lathes in the factory have been made in the factory workshop; but this is claimed to be economical because much scrap was used in their production and the machines were made in the workers' spare time. The engines themselves are tested for four hours, using methane gas and not gasoline—a method originating during the Soviet gasoline embargo. This method is still used to economize on gasoline and release it for the defense sector, while the engines themselves can, if necessary, be converted into methane gas-run models instead of being run by petrol.

—At the 555 Clock Factory in Shanghai, in February 1968, one of the most advanced polishing techniques in the world was introduced: the firing of static electricity at frames as they go past on a transmission belt. This was operative by November 1967, after many experiments, and it was introduced after another three months of experimental work.

—At the Double Rhomb Clock Factory in Peking there are two items of interest. The first is a machine for stamping out the metal backing of the clock—a machine tool produced in 1967 by a small country town in Shantung Province, of which people in the factory had never heard. The second is a stove for heat-strengthening of small iron pieces in the clock. It is run on alcohol only and is made of iron plate, whereas Soviet and Swiss models, previously imported, were constructed of cast iron. The stove is more efficient and cheaper to operate. It is the innovation of the operator in this workshop and has since been popularized in other parts of China.

—At the Wuhan Steel Rolling Mill, because of the relative unavailability of small mobile cranes for unloading steel bars, the plant itself has manufactured some models of its own, including a crane on rails, with the tower low off the ground, which can lift five tons of bars into the wagons of the regular railway system, and a four-ton capacity crane on rubber wheels. This plant is alive with small carts, all with rubber wheels, carrying ingots from the delivery wagons to be piled for cranes to remove. The rest of the plant is almost a copybook example of the policy of "walking on two legs"—forming the small-scale, indigenous technique "leg." It has a relatively backward, labor-intensive technology by comparison with Anshan, where there are huge rollers and the thinning of iron into wire is all done by pressing a button. But it is this kind of small plant in the "heavy" field which constitutes a crucial cell in the strategy of "every province a self-sufficient base area."

—At the Wuhan Tractor Factory, about 55 percent of lathes and machines are supplied by the provincial bureaus of the Agricultural Equipment Ministry; about 45 percent are made in the factory itself. In the workshop which reams the case for the tractor's gearbox, about 80 percent of machines and lathes were produced in the plant. An innovation of 1966 is a machine which drills holes in the gearbox case, using twelve drills at a time. This replaced a machine which did one hole at a time. Whereas previously it took an hour to completely ream and drill the cast of the gearbox, it now takes one minute. To develop this machine a delegation was sent to a Shanghai tractor factory to "live in" and learn. They saw something similar to what they were seeking, and modified it to suit Wuhan conditions—the main difficulty being to get enough fluid pressure on twelve drills.

One of the final products of this plant is a light, strong, very maneuverable mechanical plough-cum-tractor, especially suited to hilly terrain. Of 6 or 8 horsepower, it is sold to communes for 2,000 *yuan* and is multi-purpose in character: it fills the function of a mechanical plough, but also can pull carts into town, while its diesel engine is detachable and can be used to drive water pumps (and film projectors) in remote country areas.

—At the Hsinua Printing Works, Changsha, there is a wide variation in machines which mold type. Machines with different levels of technology and sophistication are all working simultaneously. Four of the machines were mechanized to a fair degree and were made in Shanghai in 1957; four others work by hand and pedal. An old machine is also operating, but mainly "for education," as it can do only 40 pounds of type mold per eight-hour shift, while the Shanghai ones can do 170 pounds per shift.

THE THEORY

It remains to explain the tendencies we have described and to comment on their suitability for the Chinese milieu and to point out what is irrational in this context. As a starting point let us take up an important question: why have the Chinese been content to pursue a policy in which self-reliance, medium-scale technology, and "make your own lathes," are pursued at the cost of lower productivity?

In part, the answer is military and political. Provinces are being encouraged to become self-sufficient "base areas" in order to be able to meet any armed invasion. The policy of local self-reliance, of each factory making its own machine tools, emerged even more strongly in the wake of the Cultural Revolution. One reason is that it is easier for "reds" to manage self-contained small enterprises: large, specialized factories by their nature depend on "expertness," which may not be "redness." Chinese economists also approve of factory self-reliance as a way of cutting down on transport demands, and are reluctant to build a network of feeder industries whose products would have to be rationed among competing regional authorities.

Politically, too, the idea of "red" control forms part of the struggle against Liu Shao-chi who is alleged to have said in 1949 that "The state relies on staff members of state owned factories, particularly directors, engineers and technicians, as much as it relies on workers." [5] Nor is the Chinese strategy of self-reliant factories without *economic* sense. Their attitude toward production technique is that no equipment should be scrapped and no method rejected so long as the materials and the labor used with them cannot find a better use elsewhere. Many of the lathes built by the factories producing final goods were made out of scrap iron in the unpaid time of the workers. They are certainly less productive than the products of a specialized machine-building industry would be, but their economic cost to society (or social cost) is very low. Or, again, the Chinese see some noneconomic benefits in people "relying on their own efforts." In the jargon of the academic economist, the "social welfare function" is thereby enhanced.

The trend away from borrowed technology may have some effects on productivity—short-term benefits being sacrificed for the longer-run kind that the Chinese believe to be inherent in expanding the initiative of the "lowly." Against this, copying foreign designs has many pitfalls. As one prominent Japanese technologist pointed out, imitation retards the development of the capacity to design,[6] and development of technology of design is an essential step toward full industrialization. As he said: "One had better be careful about what one selects for copying. A case in point is an agricultural machine China began to produce a few years ago. It was copied from a machine that had been designed and produced by a small manufacturer in Japan. After a year or so the Chinese found that the machine was poorly designed— and that the Japanese manufacturer who had produced it had gone into bankruptcy." [7]

Many similar examples may be cited for other countries—for instance, for Yugoslavia,[8] which bought foreign design or gave contracts to foreign firms incapable of constructing machinery or factories suited to local conditions. We were told of other examples in China, including the tractor factory at Loyang, which produces a Russian model with a 60 horsepower heavy engine, very expensive and not generally suited to Chinese conditions.

The Chinese approach to power over decision-making in the factory reduces the factory, in concept, to a nonspecialized rational unit. However, their belief that technocracy breeds bureaucracy and a built-in tendency to copy foreign designs is a valid one. Experts certainly have this tendency, while the workers do not— they try to innovate and adapt to local conditions, as the examples of the Shanghai Diesel Plant and the 12,000-ton hydraulic press show. With a policy of mass initiative, workers are given a challenge so that, in Mao's terms, the moral can be transformed into a material factor.

TECHNOLOGICAL ACHIEVEMENTS

Every country has some technological triumphs of which it can boast. Since the Chinese ones are relatively unknown, we have selected a number of them for description:

(1) The 12,000-ton hydraulic free-forging press produced by the Shanghai Heavy Machine Building Plant is justly famous—if only for the difficulties that had to be overcome in its construction. The plant was appointed to produce the press without previous experience and without the workers having seen large foreign presses. The bottom crossbeam was so heavy that no crane in China could lift it (it was finally lifted by 100 small jacks); no sophisticated measuring equipment for fitting the columns through the beam was available. Today the press plays a crucial part in producing the massive forgings (up to 250 tons) for rolling mills, power shafts, and big generators.

(2) The construction of a number of 10,000-ton ocean-going vessels has been completed. One of these, the *Gaoyang*, was finished within 39 days of the laying of the keel. High-speed ship-building is a new development in China.

(3) While most Chinese steel production is by the open-hearth furnace technique, a beginning has been made on the liquid-oxygen converter method first developed in Austria in 1960. In May 1967 a pure-oxygen top-blown steel converter shop was opened in Shanghai. This converter can produce more steel than ten open-hearth furnaces of the same size. In the new Shanghai plant, loading, smelting, and pouring are all automatically controlled. All the equipment was designed, built, and installed by

Chinese engineers and workers; all the instruments, meters, and electronic devices were made in China.

(4) The development of high-precision instrument lathes is attaining importance, and these are now coming out of Siangtan and other places, including the Shanghai Instrument Lathe Plant. The cutter is of Chinese hard-alloy steel and replaces the diamond cutter of overseas machines, thereby drastically reducing costs of production.

(5) In 1967 China successfully perfected its first automatic stereo-camera. This has extensive use in industry, medicine, and journalism.

(6) China has developed a number of computer models for use in industry and national economic planning. The electronic analog computer, which solves linear and nonlinear differential equations of the 8th order, with standardized parts, was produced first in 1958, and since then has been produced in greater numbers. These computers, as we reported in Chapter 7, are being used to streamline economic planning—and can do up to 20×20 equations. Another model, DMJ-2, is used in research institutes and has some industrial applications. High-speed digital computers with solid-state components are also being produced.

(7) Chinese attempts to develop automobiles in the early 1960's were jibed at by overseas observers who thought the sedans looked "as heavy as a small dump truck." [9] The Chinese evidently have learned from their mistakes: at the 1968 Canton Fair they had on display four more pleasing models. One, made in Shanghai, similar to the Fiat, weighs something over .5 tons and uses 1.25 gallons of fuel per 62 miles. A second "Shanghai" sedan weighing 1.5 tons uses 2.5 gallons per 62 miles. The largest model, the Honqui, an automatic-transmission six-seater, looked heavier, but not as heavy as a truck.

(8) A number of products from the Shanghai Shaped Tube Works have been highly praised by foreign buyers. These include caterpillar steel for tractors, shaped flat steel for high-pressure containers, periodical section plough steel, carbon polished steel strip and carbon tool steel strip.

(9) Significant innovations in which China leads the world

appeared in 1966–1967, including in particular the development of synthetic benzene and of artificial insulin.

(10) A number of industrial oils, developed largely from the Taching Oil Field, have become available for the first time, although not yet in sufficient quantities to be available for export. Considering that in Chinese the word "gasoline" is rendered as "foreign oil", the availability of Chinese oils is of considerable importance to national pride. Aviation gasoline of various grades, jet fuels, light diesel oils, condenser oils, special precision instrument oils, aviation hydraulic fluids, and vacuum and diffusion pump oils are also available.

(11) A main attraction at the Canton Fair was a precision horizontal surface grinder model (No. MM7120) produced only in 1968 at Hangchow. This machine grinds planes, side-surface slots, and inclined surfaces of high-surface finish. Its structure is different from that of overseas designs: the moving speed is very slow while the life of the grinding stone is twice that of models in other countries.

(12) A number of pieces of electronic equipment have been developed in recent years. These include a transistorized multi-purpose oscilloscope, an electronic frequency counter, and a transistor curve tracer.[10]

Further, as mentioned in Chapter 8, the big drive to popularize Mao's "latest instructions" has helped to boost technological development. Especially notable are the improvements in the variety and quality of ordinary low-alloy steel production, bearing in mind that the production of low-alloy steel is a recent development in world steel making;[11] the development of controlled silicon rectifying transformers in printing and dyeing;[12] the production of artificial diamonds;[13] the completion of China's first methanol plant at the Wuching Chemical Works;[14] and a vibrating de-watering centrifuge plant for coal washing at the Lingshan Coal-Dressing Plant.[15]

MANPOWER AND SCIENCE

Chinese technological development, insofar as it has central direction, is affected by the activities of the State Scientific and

Technological Commission. There are some 1.3 million engineers and scientific workers in China; 112 institutes are under the Academy of Science; 600 research institutes are attached to the ministries; and there are numerous universities.[16] Military research is under central control, and two "clean" hydrogen bombs have been detonated in the last few years—a considerable technological feat. Observers on visits to China, however, are regaled more with the innovations of bench workers—the "lowly"—than with the results of expert industrial research in institutes. This is part of the twofold strategy of using intermediate techniques of production to provide quick returns, while building more modern plants, and of taking the scientific and medical revolution to peasants and workers. In January 1966, official organs announced that China's goal was to catch up in fundamental sciences in 20 or 30 years— a realistic, if cautious, estimate, which may be shortened by the confidence gained during the Cultural Revolution.

The *fulfillment* of the economic plans of the Chinese government requires an emphasis on applied research, and the quick diffusion of results on a massive scale. How far the drawing up of the economic plans by the central government is assisted by the latest scientific knowledge about dynamic programming is not quite clear. We do know that about a decade ago the input-output technique developed in Russia, and then in the United States, by Leontief, was being applied on a limited scale in Chinese economic planning,[17] while linear programming was popularized in 1959–1960: "In six months over 6,000 transport employees and workers learned linear programming. The masses sang in glory: linear programming what a treasure! There is an increase in efficiency with a decrease in time, which results in an emancipation of manual labour with a rise in production and education." [18]

TECHNOLOGY AND THE REVOLUTION IN EDUCATION

Deficiencies in Chinese technological and manpower policy have been connected with the whole approach to education. In 1966 one observer noted that "Another obstacle to the rapid development of Chinese scientific and technological self-sufficiency, appears to be the over-specialisation of Communist China's new engineers and technicians. In the interest of speed many of the new graduates of regular and special training classes have such narrow specialisation and limited experience, that they cannot be freely transferred from one function or field to another without retraining." [19]

Such criticisms were even more strongly voiced by students of universities and technical institutes after 1966. Complaints made to the authors centered on overspecialization in courses; remoteness from practice; mechanical copying of unsuitable foreign designs and methods; excess privileges for senior academics and research workers.

At the Tungchia Architectural University, Shanghai, student members of the Revolutionary Committee said:

> We charge many of the "colossi" who were in authority here with sheer incompetence. The University Vice-President, for example, was an expert in the field of plumbing and draining, and he wrote textbooks on this, including one called *Pumps and Pumping Stations*. After the Cultural Revolution, we put a pump before him and asked him to start it—he could not.
>
> Another professor was an expert on bridge building. In 1961 in Hunan they asked him to design a bridge. He took several months on the design, but when it was built, it could not be used—a waste of 400,000 *yuan*. After questioning later, it emerged that he had copied the design from a French journal; the design turned out to be purely hypothetical, and no such bridge had actually been built from it in France.
>
> Many theories taught here were obscure and pretentious. They were copied without understanding from abroad.
>
> The academic authorities encouraged only self-interest and had a contempt for the idea of helping the masses and serving the people. The Dean of the Faculty of Architecture would say to fresh students on their very first day: "We train you to become experts in architecture. What does this mean? It means that you become the director of an orchestra, not an ordinary mason. As an expert you should have artistic self-cultivation—you should have a philosopher's brain, the eyes of a painter, the ears of a musician, the voice of a singer, and the feelings of a poet."

The opinion of the revolutionary students of the Central China Engineering University was similar:

The arrangement of time for practical work here was inadequate and the courses were too theoretical and overlapping. The cogwheel appeared in no less than three courses. Soviet textbooks were used in most courses. There was no concept of integrating study with practice nor of examining indigenous methods which best suit Chinese conditions.

The beginnings of an educational reform emerged in the wake of the Cultural Revolution and the shift to the control of universities and institutes by Mao's supporters. The main elements of this reform appear to be as follows:

(1) The administration of universities and schools should be trimmed and bureaucracy should be cut back. Mao's "instructions" on this stated: "It is still necessary to have universities; here I refer mainly to colleges of science and engineering. However, it is essential to shorten the length of schooling, revolutionise education, put proletarian politics in command" (July 1968); and "The workers propaganda teams should stay permanently in the schools and take part in fulfilling all the tasks of struggle-criticism-transformation in the schools . . . In the countryside, the schools should be managed by the poor and lower-middle peasants—the most reliable ally of the working class" (September 1968). These injunctions followed his earlier appeal (January 1968) for all units to "do away with redundant or overlapping administrative structures," have "better troops and simpler administration" and "organize a revolutionarised leading group which is linked with the masses."

(2) All who enter colleges must come from working-class or poor-peasant backgrounds. Existing students should be reeducated by workers and peasants. As Mao said: "Students should be selected from among peasants and workers with practical experience, and they should return to production after a few years' study" (July 1968). He also said "The majority or the vast majority of the students trained in the old schools and colleges can integrate themselves with the workers, peasants and soldiers, and some have made inventions or innovations; they must, however, be re-educated by the workers, peasants and soldiers under the guidance of the correct line, and thoroughly change their old ideology" (September 1968). Another "instruction" states that "Cadres and other people in the cities should be persuaded to

send their sons and daughters who have finished junior or senior middle school, college or university to the countryside. It is very necessary for educated young people to be re-educated by the poor and lower-middle peasants" (December 1968). This appears to strike at the old Chinese tradition that scholars hold themselves to be high on the social ladder.

(3) Education must be very sharply technical, practical, and directly useful. Pure theory and humanities should be reduced in importance.

(4) All education must be amalgamated with practice. Students must go to the factories while studying. An earlier (1964) "instruction" by Mao was increasingly promoted during 1968: "It is necessary to maintain the system of cadre participation in collective productive labour. By taking part in collective productive labour, the cadres maintain extensive, constant and close ties with the working people."

(5) Students should return to rural areas for fairly long periods. Such a policy has some incidental advantages: it cuts down the intensity of intellectual and political debate occasioned by the presence of large numbers of young Red Guards in the cities, and forms part of the process of amalgamating theory and practice, by developing indigenous experts and providing job opportunities for them. To quote Mao again: "All people who have had some education ought to be very happy to work in the countryside if they get the chance. In our vast rural areas there is plenty of room for them to develop their talents to the full" (July 1968).

A number of practical steps have been taken to implement various aspects of the reform. One of these is the movement for agricultural or agronomic indigenous experts, whereby communes are encouraged to run agro-technical teams to advise on crop disease, seeds, and insecticides, rather than to rely on visiting experts.[20] Another is the experiment in training medical workers through "learning by doing." By studying at patients' bedsides rather than only in books, numbers of "lowly" ex-peasants and workers are learning simple medical and surgical techniques.[21] This provides a useful supply of medical technicians to the rural areas, shortages of which incidentally have plagued the Indian government for years in implementing programming to eradicate disease and to introduce widespread family planning.

A number of colleges and institutes which pursue close integration of theory and practice (and which make education strictly technical and "useful") are held up as examples, in the way that Tachai Brigade and Taching Oil Field were held up as examples in 1963. These include, in particular, the Shanghai Machine Tools Plant,[22] the Shanghai Institute of Mechanical Engineering,[23] the May 7 School in Heilungkiang Province,[24] and the Wukou Part-Time Tea Growing and Part-Time Study Middle School in Kiangsi Province.[25]

It is perhaps too early to draw definite conclusions as to the likely effects of these changes, but some may be indicated. In the short-run, they should boost innovation and productivity by the emphasis on productivity; in the long-run, however, they may reduce productivity by a neglect of pure theory. The continued emphasis on self-reliance, involving less dependence on foreign design, is good for morale, and should continue to be so for some time. The rural areas will be receiving a greater share in the benefits flowing from the nation's expenditure on education: this appears to be overdue and represents a lessening of the dominance of the urban areas.

Among the deleterious effects, some foreign experts have mentioned the disruption of the flow of graduates caused by the Cultural Revolution. However, others maintain that China will not suffer seriously from the three or four lost years because of the previous surplus of graduates relative to suitable job opportunities for them. The critics may be on stronger ground, however, when they refer to the zigzags in official policies about the role given to students and Red Guards in the Cultural Revolution,[26] for instance, the danger that chopping and changing on this question—and especially the line that "The working class must exercise leadership in everything"—may create cynicism among young people who were promised a greater share in power as students.

So far China has managed to develop an appropriate raw material supply system, and an end-product marketing and distribution network. Its main weakness continues to be the relatively small size of the transport network—in practice, railways, since the motorization of the economy would be too expensive at this stage of development. Other obstacles, of a resource availability sort, include the foreign exchange bottleneck in trying to finance imports of component parts. Yet China has shown in the past that even the foreign exchange expenditure for the imported equipment needed by nuclear weapons can be provided, even in crisis years.[27] As long as grain production expands and foreign exchange is not eaten up in grain imports, the balance of payments need not constitute a crucial bottleneck on growth.

The main problems appear to lie in technological *policy*. Here are some of the criticisms made by visitors about technological policy:

(1) Many machine models and diesel motors are replicas of overseas models, rather than of Chinese invention. It is hard to see why this should be criticized under all circumstances. In fact, while the Chinese undoubtedly copy some foreign models, this policy has been much less in evidence since 1963. Foreign models which are "copied" usually are modified, after trials, to suit Chinese conditions, while (as mentioned earlier) the Chinese have also achieved a number of world "firsts."

(2) The through-put of factories is small, and therefore of low productivity and irrational. This is an important issue which is discussed further in Chapter 11. Here we may note the fact that "optimum scale" is rarely achieved in any country because of the social, political, and defense arguments for protection of "infant" industries. The ideological, political, and defense arguments for self-reliant medium plants are very strong at this stage of China's economic development.

(3) The Chinese government tends to buy only the latest models from overseas. While this is an understandable attempt to

reduce the rate of obsolescence, it overlooks the fact that the newest models are not necessarily the best for China's needs.

(4) The parts industry is unorganized in the sense that there is no base of feeder industries for making parts and components.[28] In the short-run this may not matter, as self-reliance in individual factories will certainly ensure that components and parts are produced. However, without a more specialized sector producing parts, in the long-run no group of highly skilled technical people will grow up. Rather, a pool of practical, semi-skilled people will remain suited to China's level of industrialization, but unsuited to a highly sophisticated industrial system in which satellite parts plants are fully integrated into the industrial system as a whole.

Notes

1. Joan Robinson, *Exercises in Economic Analysis* (London: Macmillan, 1960), pp. 38–56, and N. Okishia, *Economic Journal,* September 1966, have stressed the importance of choosing the right kind of machines in the course of development of a socialist economy but both assume a constant proportion of the labor force is devoted to the consumer-goods sector.
2. Robinson, *Exercises in Economic Analysis,* Ch. 12.
3. Formal announcements that this strategy would be pursued were made during the Great Leap Forward (see Ch. 2) and by Hsinhua News Agency on October 11, 1966.
4. G. Uchida, "Technology in China," *Scientific American,* November 1966, p. 39.
5. Liu Shao-chi, "Speech to the Staff Members of State-Owned Enterprises in Tientsin," cited in *Quotations from President Liu Shao-chi* (Melbourne: Paul Flesch and Co., 1969).
6. Uchida, "Technology in China," *Scientific American,* p. 39.
7. *Ibid.*
8. E. Johnson, "Problems of Forced-Draught Industrialisation," *Proceedings of First Conference on Economic History,* M. Postan, ed. (Paris: 1960), pp. 483–484.
9. Uchida, "Technology in China," *Scientific American,* p. 39.

10. The catalog numbers in the Shanghai Exhibition are, respectively, SPM–10, E–312, and JT–1.
11. *Peking Review*, June 14, 1968, p. 27.
12. *Peking Review*, October 4, 1968, p. 37.
13. *Peking Review*, August 16, 1968, p. 27.
14. *Peking Review*, June 28, 1968, p. 29.
15. *Ibid.*
16. G. H. G. Oldham, "Science in China's Development," *Far East Trade and Development*, March 1968, pp. 223–227.
17. S. Labini, "Mathematics in China," *Monthly Review*, June 1959, p. 61.
18. *U.S. Joint Publications and Research Service* (Hong Kong), October 29, 1960, pp. 2, 4.
19. Yuan-li Wu, "The Third Five-Year Plan," *Current History*, September 1966, p. 163.
20. See "Indigenous Experts and the Revolution in Agricultural Education," *Peking Review*, December 20, 1968, pp. 3–8.
21. *Agence France Presse*, January 17, 1969.
22. *Peking Review*, No. 31, 1968.
23. "The Revolution in Colleges of Science and Engineering," *Peking Review*, September 13, 1968, pp. 13–16.
24. "What Kind of School Is the May 7," *Peking Review*, November 8, 1968, pp. 8–10; and "7 May School Provides New Experience in Revolutionary Organisations," *Peking Review*, October 11, 1968, pp. 23–25.
25. "A New Type of School Where Theory Accords with Practice," *Peking Review*, November 1, 1968, pp. 4–7.
26. *Agence France Presse*, January 17, 1969.
27. Yuan-li Wu, "The Third Five-Year Plan," *Current History*, p. 164.
28. Uchida, "Technology in China," *Scientific American*, p. 40.

Chapter 10

THE COMMUNES AND THE
CULTURAL REVOLUTION

There are some 70,000 communes in China, in which over one hundred million families live and work. A foreign visitor can hope to visit only a few of these and, spending a few hours at each, with the aid of an interpreter who sometimes has difficulty with the local dialect, can obtain only superficial impressions. A detailed account of the origin, structure, and functioning of the communes was given earlier and we do not intend to duplicate that here; rather, we want to give first-hand impressions.

Each visit to a commune begins with a brief account of the structure, achievements, and problems of the commune. The spokesman may be a member of the commune's revolutionary committee, the director of the commune, or the leader of one of the brigades. He may be quite well educated, or a former poor peasant who was illiterate at the time of the establishment of the Communist government, and who has been able to develop his leadership qualities. Communes vary enormously in size, from a few thousand people to as many as 50,000; they also vary enormously in wealth, those in the high rainfall and more fertile areas being several times better off than those on poor land with low rainfall. Those close to large cities have many advantages, not the least of which is a contract to supply vegetables to the city, and in some cases to supply easily made spare parts from the commune factory to industry in the city.

A commune is an economic, social, and political unit, collectively owned and run by the people who live there, which organizes agricultural and other production, but also caters to the educational, medical, welfare, and cultural needs of its inhabitants. Despite the differences in size, wealth, and location of communes, a number of common themes emerged from the talks given by their leaders, and from their leaders' replies to questions.

On almost every commune the authors were taken to see the reservoirs and the irrigation works that had been constructed. In most cases these had been built in 1958–1959, or after 1965, when moral incentives and unpaid labor effort were at a peak. Time after time, Chinese cadres claimed that without the Great Leap Forward there would have been no commune, and without the commune, which allowed the cooperatives to pool their resources and to deal with a large catchment area, there would have been no reservoirs. It was the construction of these reservoirs, sometimes large, sometimes a series of small ones, that enabled the countryside to survive the droughts of 1959–1961. Some examples:

(1) A large commune outside Canton, of 51,000 people, had constructed five reservoirs. The area had a bad history of droughts; there was widespread famine and death from starvation in the early 1900's, in the 1920's, and the 1940's. In 1955 there was a very dry period, with food shortages but with no deaths—because of the rationing system and the fact that supplies of food were sent from other areas. In 1963 there was no rain for seven months, but as the reservoirs which had been built held enough water to last for nine months, there was little diminution in food production.

(2) At the Clay Hill Commune near Peking, water conservation had been carried out under conditions of very poor sandy soil, and the peasants of one brigade dug six wells of 48 cubic meters, which allowed 100 *mou* of land to be irrigated per day, and a waste-land of 504 *mou* to be used to plant 11,000 fruit trees. The Orchard Brigade which accomplished this task insisted that "We destroyed the dogma that you can't dig wells in sandy soil."

(3) At the Yueh Kechuang Commune in the Northeast of Hopei Province, where soil and water are very scarce and rock is the main terrain, the Valley of Stones Brigade had accomplished fantastic feats in the struggle to conserve water. During the Leap Forward some conservation was possible; previously this had not

been true, because ownership of the hills over which water had to be piped to the brigade was dispersed, and not held by the village. A well was dug in 1959 and water was piped into the reservoir from a neighboring commune some three miles away. Nevertheless, the drought of 1960–1962 hit the village hard. In 1965, additional efforts were made to build reservoirs, and, in 1966, to dig further wells in the mountainside in the unpaid labor time of adult male workers, and with the assistance of women and children.

Water conservation remains the foundation of the increase in production and prosperity in agriculture. Larger reservoirs have several functions: they make possible irrigation and flood control, and in many cases they provide fish, fruit, nuts, and timber directly. Many reservoirs are stocked with fish, which are caught with nets at the appropriate season; on one commune near Changsha, which specializes in fish production, research had been done to find out which kind of fish inhabited the upper, middle, and lower levels of the reservoir. It was stocked accordingly, and appropriate methods of catching the various kinds devised. Most of these reservoirs were of the earth-wall variety, and had been built by local labor—often in periods of as short as five or six months, in the off season—but under the direction of engineers sent out to the commune by the State, and with the aid of very little mechanical equipment.

LAND RECLAMATION

In the areas we visited land reclamation consisted of the extensive terracing of hills otherwise unsuitable for cultivation. Some examples:

(1) On a commune near Sian, a very dry and rather poor area, precipitous hillsides were being terraced by teams of workers equipped only with picks and shovels and earth baskets carried on shoulder poles. Laboriously the yellow loess soil was being removed from higher slopes to lower ones, to make the level terraces retained by stone walls that are so characteristic of the landscape of this area. The whole operation had to be carefully engineered for the correct levels and water flows, so that the water pumped up from the irrigation channels would flow correctly from one level

to the next. This commune of 18,000 people had terraced 18,000 *mou* of land since it began.

(2) At Clay Hill Commune near Peking, the soil was so sandy that it would not hold water, while the terrain of part of the commune consisted of a series of clay hills. Brigade labor leveled the sandy-clay hills, and for each piece of soil removed, a new piece was added. After afforestation work it became possible to plant fruit trees in an area which, in feudal times, had been a wall-enclosed hunting ground. Now the wall is a ring of fruit trees.

(3) The Valley of Stones Brigade of Yueh Kechuang Commune gave this account of their struggle for land reclamation:

The "land," if it can be called that, is distributed over nine slopes and eleven small valleys plus one big valley. Most of the valley is rock. At the end of 1957 we launched a collective labor project to cut down the peak of a hill and use the soil to fill in a small valley. This we called "the soil of the youth and the wall of the aged," after those who dug out the hill, and the elderly folk who constructed a rock dam to preserve the new soil. After this we coined the slogan that "Soil is as precious as pearls and water as precious as oil." In 1959 we developed the program of "splitting the mountain, creating the soil so as to alter its face into fertile land." Young people would, in the evening, discuss Chairman Mao's "Foolish Old Man Who Removed the Mountain," and then take up their lanterns, hoes, and picks, and chop off a hill peak to a height of 3½ meters to fill up another small valley with the dirt. In this way, they created land. To fill other valleys we carried soil in iron buckets by donkey from five kilometers away.

We also followed Chairman Mao's advice to "grasp the principal contradiction." We decided that our main one was, on the one hand, we had a shortage of soil and water; on the other hand, when it *did* rain, the water washed away the soil. To solve this we formed shock teams, and in one month created an 80-*mou* area of high quality terrace work. In one area we removed boulders to form 320 *mou* of terracing—this amounted to some 2,000 cubic meters of rock.

After the call to "Learn from Tachai," we scraped more soil from crevices among the rocks. We also strengthened the terraces by removing the very heavy boulders we had left in the soil beds of the terraces, around which weeds were growing. We calculated that one large rock was equivalent to space for ten maize stalks, so we "mopped up" the remaining rocks, except a few which were kept to educate the youngsters. We also widened the edges of the terraces which were not then adequate to protect the soil from heavy watering. Previously we had mistakenly built terrace walls which were too low, due to a short-term emphasis on just expanding extensively and building new terraces as quickly as possible. To correct this, we drew up a program for "a unified plan of mountains, water, forest, terraces, and dams to be transformed in a comprehensive way."

The feats performed here by minute terracing work and care, plus afforestation, paid off in higher yields. In this commune there were only two colors—brown (soil) and white (rock); afforestation added a third—green. It was evident from visits to rural China that this kind of land reclamation by terracing had been going on in most areas, while any plane trip revealed the enormous extent of it.

INCREASES IN PRODUCTION AND YIELDS

Each commune took pride in reciting its increases in production and yields, coupled with its increased use of fertilizer, better seeds, better techniques, and improved organization of collective effort. Some examples:

(1) Commune near Shanghai—yields of rice had doubled since 1957; cotton yield, trebled; pig population, increased sevenfold.

(2) Commune near Hangchow—tea yield had increased by half.

(3) Clay Hill Commune near Peking—yields of vegetables had risen from 80 catties per *mou* in 1958 to 150 in 1966, and 160 in 1967.

(4) Red Star Commune near Peking—yields of rice had risen from 2.5 tons per hectare in 1955 to 5 tons in 1957, and 7 tons in 1967. Wheat yields had risen from 1 ton per hectare in 1958 to 3.1 tons in 1967.

(5) Shashihyi Brigade, Yueh Kechuang County, Hopei Province —grain yield had risen from 80 catties per *mou* in 1947 to 379 catties in 1957, and 500 catties in 1958 and 1968.

These increases had, in most cases, meant that the communes could meet their own food requirements, and also sell food to the "state" purchasing authority, or supply it as payment for the agricultural tax. A number of communes in the poorer areas had previously needed to rely on supplies of food from the "state" to supplement local production, and it was clearly a matter of great pride to be able to announce that those days had passed. No doubt of course there are rural areas still incapable of feeding themselves, but their numbers must be diminishing.

SELF-RELIANCE, LOCAL INITIATIVE, AND INCENTIVES

The matter of local self-sufficiency in food is obviously deliberate policy, and it carries over into other kinds of production as well. It was clear that the utmost local initiative was encouraged, to make the most of local resources. Provided each commune operated within the general framework of the overall plan, and did not require extra resources from outside, it appeared to have a good deal of economic autonomy. Some communes had their own brick and tile factories, using local materials, from which they constructed commune buildings, including houses for the peasants. Others had their own carpentry shops, in which local timbers were used for the construction of small boats, wooden buckets, window and door frames, and similar items. Each had some kind of small tool factory, in which hand tools such as spades and hoes were made and repaired—in some cases from locally smelted iron ore. Although a great deal of local iron produced in "backyard" furnaces during the Great Leap Forward was of poor quality, and has been much ridiculed in the Western press, such production served an educational function. It was no small thing for peasants, with little or no knowledge of iron working, to produce iron and steel and make their own tools; and the experience and knowledge they gained resulted in the local production of good quality tools, and simple food processing equipment, such as rice husking machines.

This knowledge of metal working no doubt helped considerably, too, in the development of the communes' repair and maintenance workshops for the increasing amount of mechanical equipment coming on to the land (although the more complicated units such as tractors and electric pumps require even more specialized knowledge). It is sometimes forgotten in the West that in the early days of farm mechanization, often the only man who was able to service and repair the first simple types of equipment was the village blacksmith.

Most of the small factories or workshops in the communes were catering to the mechanical needs of their own members in the manner just described, but more advanced and larger ones, such as the 55,000-strong Red Star Commune on the outskirts of Peking, had a powdered milk factory, a flour mill, a soybean oil mill, a seed oil mill; all these were for processing the local product for market. In addition, small workshops were producing parts for sewing machines, small cables and wire, and electrical accessories such as light switches and lamp holders. These are highly promising developments, and in them can be seen one aspect of the success of the communes as a form of economic organization: the factories and workshops are all small-scale, and they can utilize the labor which is not required for agriculture in the off-seasons. Thus at busy times, such as spring planting and harvest, most of them can be shut down, and the peasants can work the land; when the pressure is off, they can be reopened, so that no manhours are wasted. No doubt as increasing mechanization on the land releases more labor, more of these commune factories will be developed, bringing a substantial measure of small light industry to the countryside, and rendering unnecessary the large-scale migration to the cities in search of industrial employment that has occurred in other countries.

It would be no exaggeration to say that the desire for self-sufficiency, to be able to "make do" without extensive demands on the "state," is a key element in the motivation of the communes. Its contribution to the stimulus to improve public work projects, and to the communal labor effort to improve facilities and increase yields, can hardly be overestimated. All of the commune leaders were unanimous on this point; perhaps the most graphic account of what is involved comes from the Valley of Stones Brigade:

In 1957 we were trying to raise our efforts by reading Mao's "Foolish Old Man Who Removed the Mountain." We launched a collective labor project to cut down the peak of a hill, and fill in small valleys with the earth. By persevering against Mr. Yen and other doubters, we laid the basis for the commune in 1957.

The three years of drought, 1960–1962, hit us hard, but we based ourselves on self-reliance. In the period of 1961–1964 we operated a work-points system. Today we have individual assessment, followed by mass discussion of the adequacy of the individual's assessment. If someone finishes work early now, he works elsewhere without points and "serves the people."

Political consciousness helped us to master the strong hills and the lack of soil but the key question that has changed the general outlook of the people here is the need to help others. Now people work "for the Revolution" or help those in lands not yet liberated. We consider that one more *mou* ploughed, and one more catty reaped, means another ounce of strength for the Revolution at home and abroad.

We decided to fight the soil shortage under Mao's influence in 1958, and again very enthusiastically after the outbreak of the Cultural Revolution. The Cultural Revolution for us revolves mainly around "fight self" and "serve the people." Two examples will explain this. In 1967 we decided to sell a wild horse to another brigade as we could not spare the time to train it. A brigade of another commune contracted to buy it from us for 1,100 *yuan*. They knew it was wild, but soon had to resell it for a loss of 300 *yuan*. In our brigade we discussed this and three lines emerged: first, that as they knew the risk all along, we do nothing; second, that they should pay us only 800 *yuan* plus 150 to split the burden with them; third, that we should return their 1,100 *yuan*.

We read Chairman Mao's "In Memory of Norman Bethune," and on hearing how Bethune took into account the interests of others, we decided to obtain the horse, and pay them back their 1,100 *yuan*, and we sent them copies of the "three constantly read articles." In this way we both fought self and strengthened friendship.

One household here had grown 3,000 seedlings over some years. Seedlings, generally, were very short; the three children of a medium peasant's family proposed that the seedlings be surrendered to the collectives, but the parents refused. Many study meetings were held until the mother was won over, by the argument that Comrade

Mao's five relatives had all died for the Revolution. After much resistance the father was made to feel ashamed—that he had been using the collective's water and time, yet would not assist the collective in its time of trouble. Finally he agreed.

With this homily, we get an insight into the very simple, if effective, system of moral pressure and persuasion operating within the brigades. In this respect, the main differences between the Cultural Revolution period and the "*san zi yi bao*" period are two. In the earlier period, "state" aid, through machinery, chemical fertilizers, loans, and investments, was stressed to the detriment of the "subjective will of the peasants" and their desire for self-reliance, expressed, in moral incentive terms, as not being "parasitic" on society. Further, in the earlier period private plots provided up to twelve percent of the income of households; now the peasants are being urged to turn their own seedlings, manures, and so forth, over to the collective.

Of course, all of this does not mean that each and every peasant on a commune is inspired to work mainly by reading Mao's thoughts. Such reading, as pointed out earlier, would undoubtedly help to grow better crops, since Mao insists on learning from veteran peasants, applying the more modern seeds and fertilizers, and being persistent in the face of adversity. All that is needed is a core of Maoists, who, by their enthusiasm and example, can influence the remainder of their fellows in the work teams and brigades. That means influencing millions of Chinese peasants and making them feel a part of the Maoist program of agrarian socialism. Village life may be much as it was in previous times, but one sign of change is the sense of a thriving atmosphere —of public works projects completed, of the identification of peasant masses and national goals (rather than their separation by the great gulf caused by lack of education, lack of power to influence events).

The Chinese have formed communes rather than soviets. The communes, in the view of Soviet Communists, are a lower form of political and social organization. But the historical objective of the communes is different from that of the soviets—they are a device to relate town and country, to introduce socialist norms and methods in the country, to sketch an agrarian socialism. The Chinese were able to develop the commune because of the revolutionary traditions and initiative of the masses, and because the leadership did not have any vested interest in preserving the old forms.

Each commune has at least one clinic, reasonably well equipped with simple medical equipment, and capable of performing relatively simple operations such as appendectomies. The largest commune visited, Red Star near Peking, had 9 clinics, with 40 doctors and 60 nurses, to serve a population of 55,000 people.

The educational expansion is detailed with great pride, because in the past rural education was very deficient, and the brightest youngsters had to go elsewhere for education and advancement. This is less true now. Often the growing educational complex in the larger communes includes an agricultural school and an agricultural experimental and research station, for such things as new seeds and better animal husbandry. As such complexes grow, so does employment opportunity for the brighter young people. The developing integration of work and study is exemplified by one class of schoolchildren, who, under the supervision of the teacher, ran a small, high-quality angora rabbit "farm," producing a not inconsiderable income from the output of angora wool. Skilled young people from the cities are encouraged to go to the countryside to teach and work in agricultural research, and to help redress the age-old educational deficiencies of the country areas.

PROBLEMS OF NONHUMAN FACTORS OF PRODUCTION

It is clear that enormous benefits have accrued to the communes from the expenditure of human labor power in cultivation, conservation, and irrigation. Productivity, however, depends also on the supply of fertilizer, seed, and mechanical aids.

There is still a relative shortage of chemical fertilizer. The amount currently applied is two pounds per *mou* or a tenth of the amount used in Japan. This is holding back potential agricultural productivity, and without dramatic improvement it will take at least five to ten years to raise agricultural productivity to a level which can provide China with sufficient capital for a major breakthrough in industrialization. Yet agricultural productivity rose sharply in 1967—by ten percent—and the question of a shortage of chemical fertilizer cannot be judged simply by a comparison with Japan. For "fertilizer" assumes many forms; in most communes, peasants stated that it was necessary to mix chemical fertilizer with organic fertilizer (pig manure especially). There is, of course, a shortage. Production of chemical fertilizer was infinitesimal in 1949, but by 1966 it had risen to 7.5 million tons a year. However, twenty plants under construction have come into operation in the period up to 1970, raising output to 20 million tons as a contribution to the estimated need of 25 million tons. Moreover, in Central and South China, a great deal of attention is being paid to the use of "green" manure, notably to the growing and "ploughing in" of a plant which transforms phosphates naturally into nitrogenous fertilizer, at the rate of 1,010 pounds of plant yielding 22 pounds of fertilizer. This is helping to ease shortages of the output of chemical plants. Moreover, most communes claimed to us that they preferred the use of pig manure, and feared that chemical fertilizer would "burn" the soil. While there are some good reasons for the brigades' opposition to chemical fertilizer and their preference for organic manures, there are also two other reasons—conservatism and making a virtue out of necessity. Many peasants do not want to risk crops by experiments, even though it is recognized increasingly that good results depend on a mixture of organic and chemical fertilizer in the appropriate proportions.

There is a high degree of consciousness in China about the need to apply more fertilizer. Mao's statements that "every pig is a fertilizer factory" and that China's fertilizer needs can be solved by " a pig per person and a pig per *mou*" have been popularized widely. The need for fertilizer varies, of course, according to region. Chemical fertilizer has most potential use in the millet and wheat growing areas of the North. In Southern provinces, like Kiangsi and Kwangtung, on the other hand, the soil is acidic and application of chemical fertilizer only would damage the crop; hence there will be a relatively more intensive use of organic manure.

Mao's program, announced in 1955, called for the mechanization of China's agriculture over twenty-five years. Yet some visiting and local economists have criticized the Chinese concentration on tractor production, on the grounds that labor-saving in agriculture is less urgent than increasing the productivity of the soil. This is true as a generalization, but it is not true of particular locations or particular periods in the rhythm of agriculture. Labor time saved during the transplanting of rice and also during harvests is very valuable in China. For that reason the Chinese are producing mechanical ploughs-cum-hoes, which they are selling for 200 *yuan* to the brigades, and also semimechanized rice-transplanters (selling for 90 *yuan*). The rice-transplanter can do 4 *mou* per day, compared to 1 *mou* done by a small team transplanting by hand, and the results in terms of quality of seedling planting are claimed to be good. Two types available are the Kwangsi 55 Model and the Kwangsi 59 Model. At Leiwang in Hunan Province, since the Cultural Revolution spurred on the project a fully mechanized rice-transplanter is being produced—the Hunan East Wind Model —but it is said to wear out quickly.

In Kwangtung Province in 1967, some 600 rice-transplanters were in use, and 12,000 *mou* were done by this method, by 18 production teams. The advantages claimed for the machine are that it reduces the arduousness of work; that transplanting is done more quickly (by about 30 percent), leaving spare time to finish planting sweet potatoes. In successful experiments, it was also shown that the transplanter machine allows less concentrated planting of roots, which can then spread further, and absorb fertilizer better. On the other hand, planting by this method is not as even as when done manually. Discussions at the Kwangtung Research Institute for Agricultural Machines revealed, however, that no estimates had been kept of social costs and benefits of the rapid development and popularization of the semimechanized rice-transplanter. Yet certainly it would be possible to add up the extra value of output from better planting, plus the extra value of output of other crops produced and harvested, in the labor-days saved by use of mechanized rather than human effort. This would enable economic evaluation of the program.

On the matter of rice strains and other seeds, much scope remains for improvement. Even taking into account the superior quality of Japan's volcanic soil, rice yields in China are well below those in Japan. Probably the future lies in effective mobilization of peasants to use better seeds. A socialist economy, where an attitude of serving the public interest is part of conventional morality, should be able to disseminate effectively new discoveries and new rice seeds; further developments will be needed to raise yields to international levels.

INCOME DISTRIBUTION

In general the production brigade is now the "unit of account," and out of the total product, an effective rate of 5–6 percent is paid as agricultural tax to the "state," although this proportion is reduced if the harvest is poor; 5–6 percent normally is allocated to the public welfare fund of the brigade to provide for the support of the old and the sick who cannot work; another 5–10 percent is allocated to the public accumulation fund of the brigade to purchase tractors, farm machinery, and other equipment. The remainder, 78–85 percent, is distributed among the members of the production brigade. Until 1967 this was done according to the work points, which were assessed by the members themselves. A fully grown man would tally about 10 work points per day, a fourteen-year-old about 5 or 6. At the end of the year all the work points were added up and a final distribution of income was made (preliminary distributions, or advances, being made during the year). Since 1967, however, these distributions have been made by mass decisions, rather than by automatic application of a scale of work points.

The following data was obtained on incomes (the reference is to household or personal incomes, exclusive of food consumption). Red Star Commune near Peking stated that its incomes per head had risen from 180 *yuan* in 1958 to 330 *yuan* in 1967, while 60 percent of its households had radio sets (which cost 100 *yuan*) and 70 percent had bicycles. At the other extreme, the Valley of Stones Brigade in Hopei Province indicated that income per head in 1967 was 120 *yuan*, having risen from 17 *yuan* in 1948, and having reached a peak of 131 *yuan* per head in 1958. Some brigades estimated their incomes per household. At Clay Hill Commune near Peking the per household figure had risen from 400 *yuan* in 1958 to 600 *yuan* in 1967; at Tashih Commune, Kwangtung, a household of five working adults earned more than 2,000 *yuan* per year, and 200 *yuan* from pigs and chickens, while the cost of building its house had been 700 *yuan*.

There are then very big differences in the "share-out" between different brigades; the highest works out at about 1.5 to 1.6 *yuan* per day, the lowest at about one-third of that. Thus the richest brigades might reach the income level of the average worker, after allowing for income in kind, and from the private plot, but there are many more, less fortunate, who would be well below. The reasons for the differences in these rural incomes are many, from location and fertility of soil to variations in the efficiency of organization and in local enthusiasm. So far there is no thought of a differential agricultural tax, that is, a higher tax on the more favorable locations, which would help to even things out; rather, all the emphasis is on improving the efficiency of the less advanced and less fortunate areas, and much use is made of the example of very poor brigades which have "pulled themselves up by their own bootstraps." Such examples, widely publicized by Mao's group, even in 1960–1964, were harbingers of the swing to moral incentives which followed the Cultural Revolution. They also represented, in embryo, Mao's vision of an agrarian socialism which he counterposed to the orthodox path to communist industrialization.

PART III

Chinese Socialism:
Ideology and Politics

Chapter 11

ECONOMIC ASPECTS
OF MAOIST STRATEGY

Western economists encounter great difficulties in interpreting the Chinese system of economic planning. This is because many noneconomic objectives are fed into the Chinese system, and also because of the viewpoint from which Western economists approach economic affairs. Western economists think that society ought to be organized from the point of view of the consumer and that welfare is fully realized when the consumer is satisfied. In the West, the Industrial Revolution exploded in an historical situation in which market institutions, self-interest, and the customs associated with it had already become dominant. This was not true of China. Instead of having a long history of market society behind it (with the exception of the foreign-controlled trading ports), socialist China leaped overnight from essentially feudal or semifeudal relations to commercialized and industrial ones. China as a whole, therefore, lacked the network of economic institutions and relationships on which a market society is built. Lui Shao-chi aimed to inject some of these relationships into an economy in which central planning remained the main guiding force, but this attempt, as we have seen, was short-lived. Maoists, unlike Western economists, hold that society should be organized from the standpoint of the peasants and the working class in the hinterland,[1] so that the general interest is fulfilled only when these groups draw a reasonable share of the social product. To quote Mao on "consumer society": "Only when consumer-cities are transformed into producer-cities can the people's power be consolidated."[2]

Many Western economic models, moreover, conceive of the social structure in terms of a functionally integrated system held in equilibrium by a certain pattern of recurrent processes. But in a society undergoing massive social change, fresh theoretical perspectives are essential. Social movements such as peasant revolution, or the activities of revolutionary cadres, provoke trials of strength between contending forces and ideas, and place enormous strains on the social fabric itself. But through such trials, as tumultuous as the Great Proletarian Cultural Revolution, the list of objectives—economic and noneconomic—is apt to be changed.

For those whose attitudes have been formed in a long established market society, this is very hard to understand and analyze, although even Alfred Marshall—doyen of English economic formalism—warned that economists must concern themselves with "the ultimate aims of man" and not only with production. Only economists such as Weber and Sombart, who were writing in a country (Germany) which remained out of the mainstream of orthodox economic theory and its concomitant assumptions of utilitarian individualism, have made any detailed attempt to integrate the study of economic activities into the broader framework of the social system.[3] Nor have many modern interpreters of communist systems made much of a systematic attempt to integrate economics with other social sciences (such as anthropology), which deal with noneconomic objectives. A favorite way of interpreting China and the Soviet Union has been to set up a "command economy" model, which is then contrasted with the "efficiency" and "rationality" norms of welfare economics. Naturally there are divergences from these norms since price policy, regional autarchy, and technological policy are heavily influenced by noneconomic factors. The "command economy" model, is, in this way, by a sleight of hand, condemned to the "original sin" of irrationality, almost by definition. Yet it should be obvious that neither individual nor social values can be the same in all societies. The notion of "efficiency" or "rationality" therefore has no meaning *until the underlying basis of social values is comprehended.* To postulate a maximum production of goods and services in highly efficient modern factories as a desirable end, for example, reflects an ideological position very different from that of, say, Maoism, for which these same economic activities are subordinated to the aim of securing a political optimum and a certain future shape of society.

These points have to be borne carefully in mind when discussing Chinese policies on regional economic growth, planning, and industrial patterns.

One aspect of economic development that the Maoist strategy seems to have understood well is that one of the foremost tasks of development planning is to bring about a stable pattern of life in the hinterland, outside the main cities, and to ensure that people are not driven to the urban areas by need or frustration. The labor power and productive effort of millions of ordinary people can be successfully mobilized only if new jobs and new work places are created close to where they already live, and not simply in a few big towns. This, naturally, presupposes a decentralized approach supported by a great deal of local initiative, and a feeling of self-reliance inside enterprises and communes.

As we saw in Chapter 9, a striking feature of Chinese technology is the amount of factory self-reliance, and the desire not to be too dependent on the modern machine-tools sector. Reinforced by the military position of encouraging every province to become a self-sufficient "base area," this feature involves a de facto policy of regional autarchy.

The policy of "make your own lathes" is both a cause and an effect of regional autarchy. It is an effect to the extent that in an economy lacking a price mechanism in the factory sector, there is bound to be competition for relatively scarce modern machinery. Rather than let planning be influenced by quarrels over priority allocation or by serious inequalities between regions, it is better, in the Chinese view, to encourage factories within regions to be fairly self-reliant. Even where, as a result of this policy, productivity is lower, by comparison with productivity achieved through specialization and mass production in a modern machine-building sector, there are obvious political and social benefits. Nor is Chinese regional self-sufficiency really so unusual. Even in the West, the whole idea of tariff protection is an interference with the "natural" or "economic" location of industry; indeed Western economies (as shown by the formation of regional trading blocs) do not operate on the model of welfare economics; neither does the Chinese economy.

The decentralization of economic planning to the provincial level proceeded apace in 1960–1965. Provinces obtained the right to make interprovincial deliveries of goods without first going through the center, for approval. Some provinces retained their own foreign exchange holdings. (Tao Chu was criticized for this later—it was alleged that he was obsessed with building up Kwangtung Province's foreign exchange holdings.) Of course, there were a number of centralizing factors at work too, for example, the fact that five out of eleven industrial ministries remained in the State defense sector, and also the supervisory role of the People's Bank. There is, however, some evidence from discussions with Chinese economists that the People's Bank at the provincial level does have a fair amount of de facto authority.[4]

The overwhelming impression is, therefore, of the trend toward regional authority in economic planning. We have mentioned in earlier chapters that the provincial office of the Ministry of Internal Trade operates as a kind of nerve center—as a wholesale agency to place contracts with producers, specifying quality and design in detail and solving the problem of the "assortment-mix" in production. This reinforces regional independence in planning and economic development. The decentralization in the economic sphere, however, built up political autonomy in regions and explains the moves, during the Cultural Revolution, against Party leaders in Kwangtung, Kwangsi, and Szechuan Provinces. Perhaps this could be put in a rather more speculative way: one reason for the strengthening of regional economic self-sufficiency may be that in China, historically, rebellion flared if a certain *sort* of regionalism emerged. The pattern under the Tang and Ching dynasties was that economic development and public administration tended to cluster in the cities where the government was strong. But in the countryside, warlords emerged to replace the weaker regional units of the central government. They, in turn, suppressed the peasantry who were driven to revolt. Mao may have learned from history: certainly, he wants to make sure this pattern is not repeated.

A notable feature of the recent period (1966–1968) is that the formal planning system has not been changed by the Cultural Revolution. What *has* been changed is the motivation.

The major structural lines of the Chinese economic planning system were settled in November 1957, when the State Council issued its decentralization orders. The two main central organs are the State Planning Commission and the State Economic Commission. The former is responsible for the five-year and longer plans, and the latter for the yearly plans. The duties of the Construction Commission, which controlled the investment at the center, were taken over by these two bodies in 1958. In recent times the State Technology Commission has played a larger role in planning.

In 1957, eighty percent of the previously State-controlled enterprises were transferred to provincial authority. This meant in practice that the bulk of medium and small industry was transferred. The center retained control over the major producer goods industries—oil, power, steel, transport, and communications. Generally, consumer rather than producer goods industries were handed over to the provinces. The provinces' powers in planning were augmented. Previously they could not interfere with State-controlled enterprises, and as a result of further moves in 1959, they were able to reallocate resources within the limits of the State plan, even if such resources affected State-controlled enterprises; these had to apply to the provinces for raw materials, and the provinces had considerable power over the selection and promotion of personnel in State-controlled businesses, except for the top people. The provinces could invest beyond the limits of the State plan; they received a share of profits and generally were able to control decision-making at the local level. Mao's thought at the time was "centralized planning, decentralized control."

The reasons for decentralization of planning are important in understanding some of the background to the Cultural Revolution. The decisions were seen to be both necessary and desirable, practically and ideologically. It had become apparent in 1956 that Kao Kang's Soviet-type model of "independent" managers meant too little scope for Party control or for lower level initiative; and the stress on the "mass line" at the Eighth Party Congress served to emphasize Mao's belief that voluntarism and the people's will could overcome objective physical difficulties. Even Li Fu-chun, Kao's successor at the State Planning Commission, said that more participation at the local level was desirable, that progress had been unbalanced, while he also implied that the available statistical sophistication did not match the needs of a country the size of China. So not only was it impracticable to administer China in detail from the center, but it was ideologically sound to trust the people, who would obviously choose the right course in the general interest if they interpreted Marxism-Leninism-Maoism creatively. This decentralization gave greater power to the local Party committees, since planning at the country, district, and provincial levels was naturally subject to the regional Party committee's approval.

Even further, the Party faction in the individual factory, the complex and effective system of dual or triple roles played by Communists in the bureaucracy, in the Party, and in mass organization which influenced all activity, ensured that Party control was not lessened; rather the center of decision-making shifted from the Central Committee to the local Party committee.

These measures were followed by the Great Leap Forward, an example of Maoist voluntarism and faith in the masses, and later by the "three bitter years" (1959–1961) when Mao's political influence in the leadership was temporarily overshadowed by Liu Shao-chi and Teng Hsiao-ping, who led the retreat to a more orderly if less exciting system. In 1958 it was realized that decentralization had produced some unintended and uncontrolled effects. As the power of the State central organs reemerged, the call became: "All the country is a single chessboard." By 1961, there was a definite move to recentralize some of the power. The Rectification Campaign, designed to break some of the hold of the local Party committees on economic affairs, stressed "expertness" rather than "redness," and a manager was tolerated even if he was not a Communist. There was more emphasis on profit as a measure of efficiency, less on quantity and more on quality, and, most important, six regional bureaus of the Party's Central Committee were set up to extend the power of the center. As we saw in Chapter 4, by 1963 things seemed to be returning to some kind of "orderly" pragmatic planning. In 1964 it was announced that the Third Five-Year Plan was being prepared and would start in 1966. But by 1964 the Maoist pendulum had begun to swing back to the Great Leap Forward strategy. The Socialist Education Campaigns, the Learn from the People's Liberation Army Campaign, and the introduction of special political departments into the normal financial, commercial, transport, and communications ministries in 1964, showed that Mao was trying to inculcate the "right" revolutionary spirit, the motivating force of "fight self," and the promotion of the public interest. Afraid of the future generation's becoming soft and "taking the capitalist road," Mao launched the Cultural Revolution in an effort to rid the Party of that section of Party bureaucrats, led by Liu, who seemed to him to be more concerned with maintaining their position, and production, than in making revolution.

During 1966 economic planning was not effected noticeably. Mao urged the Red Guards to "bombard" the Party headquarters but there seemed to be little interference with immediate production. By the end of the year, however, production breaks were getting more serious and Mao was forced to call in the army in 1967 to introduce some order. Although it is difficult to know for certain, it seems that Mao was intent on destroying certain sections of the Party system in an effort to get rid of Liu's bureaucrats, who were, naturally, in positions of considerable power. To this end, he urged the creation of revolutionary committees to take over the jobs of the disgraced Party committees; the PLA, the masses, and the progressive cadres became Mao's allies. During 1967 economic performance was disrupted to a considerable degree. The government was forced to call a halt to the more extreme exchanging of revolutionary experiences, in order to see that the harvest was brought in. The PLA apparently took a more important part in running the economy, but being only three million strong, it could not be expected to replace a Party of twenty million.

Even if the planning system has remained untouched—and there has been little practical interference with the government ministries—the essence of Party control seems to have been gravely disturbed. The Maoist belief that the people can achieve miracles without modern industrialized techniques clearly exercises a powerful motivating force. However, it is fair to add that the motive has not changed as much as it has been reemphasized and brought to the fore, as in 1958–1959. The "mass line," the drive for maximum production, and the ever-present international situation, are some of the dominating forces; Mao has made a virtue of necessity by saying the provinces should become self-sufficient, in part for defense reasons, but the danger is that the thread of central control which has always been the lifeline of the Party, may be broken.

CAPITAL AND LABOR IN PRODUCTIVITY

One explanation sometimes given for the wide proliferation of medium factories and labor-intensive techniques of production in China is that, with only 1.2 million scientists and engineers trained to tertiary level, China cannot absorb a lot of fixed capital in a short time; and hence the absorptive capacity for capital is strictly limited. This is true of particular production functions (combinations of labor and capital) in highly specialized, modern industry. It is not true of China's industry as a whole, for there are millions of technicians trained to secondary level. Rather, the picture is one of a *relative* capital shortage. Naturally, complex capital equipment is put first into defense and heavy industry where highly skilled people work, and there is not enough equipment for the many small and medium factories. That is why those factories make a high proportion of equipment in their own workshops. Such sectors have to wait until sectors with priority, and industries where there are enough partially trained people, have received fixed capital. In agriculture, still the major part of the social product, there is a limit to the amount of fixed capital equipment needed. This is a labor-intensive sector. Mechanization of agriculture demands pumps, irrigation, and small mechanical ploughs—"products" which can be manufactured without a large and highly skilled supply of scientists and technicians.

The major explanation for indigenous small and medium technology is, then, not a shortage of skilled labor alone, but noneconomic factors such as the desirability of self-reliance and mass participation in production. It should be noted that in ten years or so the Chinese will be able to supply much more equipment and much more skill, and thus place China among the industrial powers.

When the Chinese economy eventually produces the same percentage of scientists and technicians as in the Soviet Union and the United States, it will have the biggest absolute concentration of such people anywhere in the world—a fact likely to produce its own dynamic. The kind of scientist will be different too—he will be more practical than his overseas counterparts, more attuned to the specific requirements of his society, and less encumbered by obsolete theoretical baggage. Rote learning of the 1949–1959 period will be gradually abolished. This liberation of the thinking power of the Chinese people will have incalculable effects.

INDUSTRIAL PATTERNS

Chinese manufacturing, as we see it, is featured by the coexistence of enterprises of different technical forms. This reflects the stage of industrialization reached in China, and the fact that, with limited capital resources, the whole structure of industry cannot be changed at one stroke. Further, as already explained, there are social and political reasons for slowing down the rate of change of the industrial structure.

However, the Chinese industrialization program, like all others, is faced with a number of problems—building of infrastructure (railway, ports, marketing systems); the choice of carrying out major extensions to existing factories or constructing modern ones; and the problem of when to wind up the stage of small factories and go over to mass-production-line methods in huge, specialized plants. The main difference between China and other underdeveloped countries is that the reason for increased demand for manufactured goods is not merely the growth of population and higher labor productivity as elemental factors, but the discipline of State plans.

In the field of infrastructure, great achievements have been made in irrigation, power production, and rural electrification works; railways remain the main bottleneck. The organization of marketing is good and plan implementation generally is well organized. Steel, chemicals, and machine building have recorded notable rises. The last fifteen years have also witnessed remarkable improvements in public health and education facilities, without which China's economic growth could not have been as impressive as it is: "China's gains in the medical and public health field are perhaps the most impressive of all." [5]

Basically, the problem of food, shelter, and clothing, at a minimum, but adequate, per capita level has been solved. That in itself is no mean achievement. There has been a very large increase in the per capita availability of mass consumer goods such as bicycles and radios. The improvement in health services and educational facilities has also significantly contributed to the betterment of general living standards.

In the field of investment policy we have already noted, in Chapter 2, that the Chinese method tends to favor quick-yielding projects with high gross output results—for that reason, extension of existing plants and use of existing technology are often preferred to longer-maturing large industrial plants.

However, the question of scale—and of the *definition* of "large" and "small" factories—requires some attention. A plant may be large or small, depending on the criterion used. A Chinese factory, measured in output terms, may be small by Western standards. However, in terms of capital per worker compared to the Chinese average, the same factory may be quite large. Scale is also relevant to the state of technology: a steel mill of 0.25 million tons capacity was once regarded as large by international standards, but now it is thought of as small. In terms of numbers employed (the criterion used in British statistics), most Chinese factories are fairly large. We have already given figures for the factories we saw—any with a staff of around 2,000 are large. It should also be noted that most Chinese plants work three shifts; this is not the case in India or the West. In India small plants coexist with large plants, with restrictions on the output of the latter in order to prevent social dislocation arising from large-scale industry overwhelming the small-scale sector. In China, however, planners can allow both sectors to develop at full potential, since all profits are transferred to the State and investment expansion can be easily controlled.

Chinese industry, then, covers a whole spectrum. Looking at the industry as a whole, the connection between output and scale is not clear. A textile factory with one hundred labor-intensive looms can be large, while a mechanized factory with five hundred looms can be small.

Many Chinese machine tool and truck factories are small in terms of output; a truck factory producing one thousand units per year is common. Naturally its costs are very much higher than those of one with a long through-put. Again, this is not unfamiliar in developing countries. Part of the "infant" industry argument for tariff protection is that where a country does not have enough capital to go in for mass production, a small factory should have the opportunity to develop.

We have noticed, in discussions in many factories, two outstanding features of the Chinese attitude toward rapid industrialization:

(1) Currently there is a drive toward decentralization and ruralization, and some hostility to the "imperatives" of industrialization —notably to the *way of life*, and the need to hand over control to managers and technical experts, which it implies. This also reflects in part Mao's expectation that any war will result in the destruction of China's major industrial sector, so that it is desirable to spread out to the hinterland.

(2) There is some hostility to *crash* industrialization as such: *even the Leap Forward period is not now seen as part of a quicker industrialization program, but really a ruralization program to strengthen local government and collective ways of living in the countryside.*

BALANCE BETWEEN AGRICULTURE AND INDUSTRY

The need to find the correct ratio in the rate of development of agriculture and industry is a familiar one. Taxation of the agricultural surplus, and therefore the size of this surplus, is a crucial underpinning of the financial aspect of industrialization. Agriculture in China contributes two-fifths of total output and half of the State budget. A viable agriculture, by reducing food imports, releases foreign exchange reserves for industrial imports. Agricultural raw materials form the basis of many industries, while rising living standards in agriculture create a market for industrial goods. On the other hand, the transformation of agriculture in a vast and old country is a long-range process requiring development of high-yielding seed strains, machinery, pesticides, and fertilizers. The development of agriculture depends largely on these inputs: agricultural and industrial development have to go side by side. It should be noted that rates of growth of the industrial and agricultural sector, and the basic price ratio between agricultural produce and industrial labor—which affects living standards as well as industrialization—is a political choice according to State plans; it is not subject to the laws of the market.

These facts have been well understood by the Chinese, particularly since the 1960's when the policy of "agriculture as the foundation" began. The events of the Leap Forward showed that the Chinese were not yet ready to push industry far ahead of agriculture. They clearly decided to build up the agricultural base first, and reversed the heavy industry bias of the First Five-Year Plan.

Agricultural output, which reached its lowest point in 1960 at the time of severe drought, is now developing at above the 1953–1957 average levels, due to Herculean efforts in irrigation work. A crucial aspect is Mao's Twenty-five Year Plan for the mechanization of agriculture. The Chinese planners are well aware of how long it would take to supply every brigade with a tractor; that is why a certain inequality between communes is tolerated. Communes decide for themselves what equipment they want, so inequalities have emerged between communes in machinery supplies and in consumption per head. But the alternative would be to pursue a very rapid rate of mechanization, which would only force people to urban areas and produce "mushroom" economic growth. One component of the ideology being promoted in the communes is geared to the reduction of jealousies and rivalries between communes, and the ubiquitous study classes preach not only mechanization, but also the need to identify with the overall goals of Chinese society.

We have already outlined the crucial role played by moral incentives in Chinese economics and noted their ideological basis, but they have also a nonideological basis. In a situation where highly mechanized factories, producing at prices equal to the average cost of small firms, can earn very high profits, there is a need for a check. In the absence of checks or discipline by the price mechanism, there is a need for self-discipline by managers, or for discipline by the mass meeting. Similarly with innovation: where profits are being made in established lines of production, managers will be reluctant to move to new lines or to innovate. Soviet economic practice has faced this problem. In China, moral incentives serve as an automatic check; in any case, China has had fewer problems of corruption in management. Chinese industry, since it is not dominated completely by the large plant, is not so dependent on the managers as is Soviet industry, where often *only* the managers have known what is happening at the enterprise level, and hence cannot be fully accountable to "society."

The use of nonfinancial stimulants in Chinese economic life has been met with a wall of skepticism in the West. We do not share the Chinese view. And critics tend to think only in terms of the societies they know—usually of societies where people have restricted themselves to the inward-looking life of the suburbs, and where the automobile has become a symbol of man's alienation from his neighbor. China, on the other hand, could escape the destiny of becoming such a society. It is a civilization of its own and it is a country little influenced by Western culture. Chinese cadres and politically conscious people do not think of mass consumption in Western terms, and the people in general do not attempt to distinguish themselves from everyone else. So far, they do not clamor for the private automobile or the "washing machine economy."

There are, of course, some who say that at a certain level of economic growth it will be simply impossible for China to resist the "demonstration effect" of living standards and patterns in the West—that when it has ceased making a virtue out of necessity, the government will be unable to resist the drive to mass personal consumption. In that case, it would have to institute a new planning system to cater to increased wants, and the slogan of "fight self," so beloved of Maoists, would be overwhelmed in the drive to satisfy the personal appetites said to lurk just below the consciousness of even the most political man.

Again we do not share this view of Chinese developments. Admittedly no society can run purely on moral or ideological incentives; that, however, is not the issue. The question is—what is the amalgam of material and moral incentives and which way are the proportions moving? On Chinese communes, for example, there is collective free labor time given for the usual reasons, but also there are private household plots. Seedlings are donated to the brigades because households use communal water and other facilities without paying for them. It seems to us unlikely that there will be a dramatic shift to material incentives, or any marked demonstration effect imported from the West—as happened in the Soviet Union. On the contrary, in a world of a changing balance of forces and of ideology, the sheer size and strength of a future Chinese economy may well exert a greater pull on the rest of the world than the rest of the world exerts on it.

Notes

1. "It is the peasants who are the chief concern of China's cultural movement at the present stage. If the 360 million peasants are left out, do not 'the elimination of illiteracy,' 'popularisation of education, literature and art for the masses and public health' become largely empty talk?" Mao Tse-tung, "On Coalition Government," *Selected Works* (Peking: Foreign Languages Press, 1961).

2. Mao made this pungent comment on "consumer" society many years ago in his "Report to the Second Session of the Seventh Central Committee." See *ibid.*, p. 365.
3. The German historical school, however, had a profound effect on the development of the American school of institutional economists, led by Veblen and his followers. This is shown in Joseph Dorfman, *et al.*, *Institutional Economics: Veblen, Commons and Mitchell Reconsidered* (Berkeley: University of California Press, 1963). Also in attempting to integrate the study of economic activities into the broader framework of the social system, the recent works of J. K. Galbraith may be considered to be in this American tradition of institutional economics. And Gunnar Myrdal in his monumental work, *Asian Drama: an Inquiry into the Poverty of Nations* (New York: Twentieth Century Fund, 1968) epitomizes the institutional approach in the field of the economics of development.
4. See also the review by Chao in *Kyklos*, No. 3, 1968, p. 562.
5. John G. Gurley, "The Economic Development of Communist China" (Stanford University, mimeographed), p. 14.

Chapter 12

THE CHINESE "ROAD" TO SOCIALISM

What are the main elements of the Chinese "road" to socialism, and how can we interpret them? These two questions center on the general topic of China's economic and social development.

Some Western commentators[1] like to describe policy differences and ideological clashes as a device by which individual leaders and factions simply legitimize the crudities of the power struggle. This was a typical explanation of the Cultural Revolution—however, only a partial one. Policy disputes spring also from political, economic, and social change, and disagreements about how rapid it should be; leaders are in fact conditioned by ideology. We are still left with the need to understand Chinese socialism (and the Cultural Revolution in particular) as a sociological and ideological phenomenon, and as an aspect of China's path to industrialization.

Another interpretation[2] seeks to downgrade the significance of Marxist-Leninist ideology and socialist aims in China. In this account, the Communist period of power is seen as merely an interlude in the long sweep of the development of a purely Chinese civilization, which is almost untouched by any particular regime. Marxism, in this view, is almost accidental—the way rulers and a section of the people express themselves in a particular period of time is part of a broad historical sweep. Although we have already drawn attention to the "Chineseness" of many of the policies being pursued in contemporary China, and pointed out historical parallels, such an interpretation would be going too far. It underrates the specific power of Marxism to move the masses; in this respect Marxism in China must be likened to a kind of religious revivalist movement, producing cathartic experiences. Seen in this

212

way the present period appears qualitatively different from that of previous Chinese regimes.

A third interpretation, widely distributed over the various Marxist sects in the West, holds that Chinese socialism is simply a political aberration: it cannot be a "socialist" society since, on the criteria of Marxist theory, a certain set of social institutions and a certain level of productivity must be reached before any society can embark upon socialism.[3] Hence China is seen as "Stalinism" rather than as "socialism"—the backwardness of China's economy ensuring a distorted version of traditional Marxism, and depending on a centralized conspiratorial apparatus of control which pursues primarily the development of its own interests as well as national power. Or Maoism is seen as a retreat into a pre-Marxian socialism of the Blanquist*-voluntarist kind,[4] and the Cultural Revolution as an outbreak of revolutionary romanticism.

We shall discuss these views more fully later. Here it will suffice to note that Marx was talking about industrialized societies and wrote very little about peasant societies. In peasant societies, revolution, followed by the construction of socialist values, is at least possible (even if Marx doubted it). This vision is Mao Tse-tung's contribution, and it helps to explain why leadership of the world socialist movement is passing in part from the Soviet Union to China and other peasant countries. To follow the "purist" Marxist line to its logical conclusion it would be necessary to argue that all successful peasant revolutions which establish socialist societies (Cuba, Vietnam, Korea, as well as China) are historical "mistakes." This is a dogmatic approach, which Marx surely would have repudiated.

A common theme pursued by some Marxists and anti-Marxists alike is the "iceberg" theory. According to this, only a vanguard group of three percent of a country's total population is affected by ideology, by moral fervor, and nonfinancial incentives. This "tip of the iceberg" is thought to be unrepresentative, and the

---

* "Blanquist": after French revolutionary Louis Blanqui (1805–1881), who declared the need for permanent revolution as the necessary transit point to the abolition of class distinctions generally, and for conspiratorial activity in the short-term to overthrow the regime.

ninety-seven percent is assumed to want only material goods, and secretly to nurse self-interest. It will be noted that this iceberg theory amounts to saying that human nature does not change. But surely we have learned from a study of history that it does. Moreover this whole theory fails to distinguish between self-interest and selfishness, or to recognize that self-interest, at first harnessed to social ends, can itself be transformed. Stripped right down, the conservative iceberg theory amounts to an assumption that only a capitalist ethos is "natural" and immutable, an assumption on which anthropological and sociological studies have (as we saw in Chapter 8) cast considerable doubt.

We have not said that *everyone* in China is operating on a basis of intense moral fervor. We have said that the vanguard is trying to ensure that Chinese society does operate on this basis, and that in factories and communes the moral fervor does not appear to us to be a mere façade.

We believe that a genuine attempt is being made in China to construct a new morality, a new moral basis for living in socialist society, and on a scale unprecedented in the whole of human history. Can such massive ideological crusades have a deep and lasting effect on people's social values—stir men's souls to their very core—to use favorite Chinese terminology? We do not know. We can only report what we have seen and what we think of it. But one important factor must influence the outcome strongly; we have already noted that Mao, looking for an opportunity to launch reforms and revive revolutionary ideals in 1966, found it in student dissatisfaction. And about forty percent of the population is under the age of eighteen. The older generation may be more cynical and certainly less susceptible to changes in their moral values, but it would be hard for any honest observer of the Chinese scene to deny that the young do feel very strongly the influence of the ideological fervor. An old Chinese proverb says that to teach the old is like writing on water, but to teach the young is like writing on stone.

The attitude toward the Soviet Union which is widely held in China lends indirect support to our view. This is that in the Soviet Union a privileged group now holds power and seeks to perpetuate it by destroying revolutionary spirit, and developing an ethos of self-interest and the consumer society. And it is argued that this would have happened in China if the Chinese had not learned from the Soviet experience.

Finally, there is the interpretation that Maoism (and specifically the Cultural Revolution) is a rejection of Marxism as a Westernizing movement, a reemergence of Chinese peasant anarchism, and of the Luddite Revolt against the machines.[5] This is a challenging, even persuasive view, with much to recommend it. Certainly in our discussions with Chinese academics something similar to it was coming through. We shall analyze this view more fully below. Here let us note that it fails to account for some important aspects of the Cultural Revolution, which started in the cities and in the educational sphere. We have concluded, by contrast, that the Cultural Revolution was not the more narrow revolt of the peasantry against industry, but a broader and more general conflict between revolutionaries and technocrats over the kind of society desirable for China. That is, the Cultural Revolution is not just a crossroad on China's path to industrialization, but a crucial turning point on the Chinese road to socialism.

INDUSTRIALISM AND THE LOCATION OF POWER

Mao believes that a social destiny must be revealed to the Chinese people, and that they must be taught to love and desire that destiny with all the ardor of romantic youth. For the accomplishment of this end, there must exist a unity of action and thought such as common conviction alone cannot confer. Maoism is a sort of religion—a cult with a moral code of its own which holds meetings ("study classes") up and down the country in a genuine burst of religious enthusiasm.

No other meaning can be given to pronouncements such as, in Mao's "Serve the People": "The Chinese people are suffering; it is our duty to save them and we must exert ourselves in struggle. Wherever there is struggle there is sacrifice, and death is a common occurrence, but we have the interests of the people and the sufferings of the great majority at heart and when we die for the people it is a worthy death." Or such as, in his "latest instructions": "The comrades must be helped to remain modest, prudent and free from arrogance and rashness in their style of work. The comrades must be helped to preserve the style of plain living and hard struggle" (1967). Or "We communists seek not official posts, but revolution. Every one of us must be a thoroughgoing revolutionary in spirit and we must never for a moment divorce ourselves from the masses" (April 1968).

Maoists hold that under the previous system (including the years 1952–1957 and 1962–1964), the tendency was to increase the power of the government apparatus and also to establish the ascendancy of the higher classes over the lower. Moreover, they have consistently warned that urban economic life is hierarchically structured. Under the new Maoist system, the aim is to combine the forces of society in such a way as to secure the successful execution of projects which improve the moral and material welfare of the populace; directions from the proletarian headquarters will take the place of commands of the Party, and the character of politics gradually will be transformed by concentrating attention upon matters affecting people's attitudes toward society.

Maoism is not a peasant anarchism, but contains elements of one, in its naive expression of enthusiasm for a new regime, based on a new spirit. There is also something of Babeuf's community of equals about it; it is in the tradition of those elements of Plato, Morley, and Godwin which attack the institution of property and demand social equality. In this, it has to grapple with two "enemies": the imperatives of technology and industrialism, and the concentration of power in the hands of those who promote them.

Maoists recognize that material abundance is made possible by large-scale technology and a sweeping division of labor. But they argue that if industry is allowed to follow its own logic—if technological expansion and economic growth become exclusive objectives to which others are sacrificed, and if politics is kept from interfering with the inner imperatives and "self-evident success" of industrial development, then men will find themselves deprived of effective freedom, even if they reap the indispensable Marxian material conditions of freedom. Men must, therefore, be freed not only from the necessity of eking out a living and finding the means of subsistence, but also from the imperatives of technology. If they are not freed, then they will, as in the Soviet Union, succumb to a new group of governors—technicians who supply material comforts, directors who shape the responses of workers to technological needs. Maoists warn of the centralization of power, entailed by industrial society, and the need to check it by "relying on the masses." Mao said in 1957 that "The organs of state must practice democratic centralism, they must rely on the masses and their personnel must serve the people," [6] and, similarly, that: "The most fundamental principle in the reform of state organs is that they must keep in contact with the masses" (April 1968). He warns that the integrative planning of the manifold activities of an industrial complex requires the centralized governing of men and material; and that *inequality* of responsibility, *inequality* of participation in decisions is a basic condition of societies geared to technological imperatives. Therefore he attempts to suggest a political order which will satisfy the needs in factory and commune, for both material property *and* a meaningful group life, in the face of the necessarily hierarchical organization of industry and government.

To resolve the problem of the concentration of power, dominant political leaders will need to establish new channels of communication and create unique regulatory bodies. Members of a political élite may be challenged by such a process, and they will have to respond. They can resist it, drive it underground, or destroy it. Or, they may try to coopt the movement's leaders by granting them privileges or by accepting parts of its program. The nature of the leadership response is clearly a prime determinant of the tactics and strategies adopted in the economic sphere, of the kind of leadership arising within it, and of the ideological appeals developed by it. In China the established leadership was the Chinese Communist Party. The social movement against it thrown up by the Cultural Revolution was a coalition: youth, underprivileged peasants, those excluded from the education system, those uprooted by industrialism, and a Party minority led by Mao.

In the process, some sections of the Party apparatus were destroyed. In that respect the Communist Party of China (unlike the Communist Party of the Soviet Union) has failed to reestablish a strong central authority in the regions—as many emperors failed earlier. This can be shown by the way in which the Cultural Revolution developed. There was corruption and a partial reversion to "peasant seigneurism" in 1960–1965. A "rational" attack on this problem would have been a reform through the Party organs. When, by contrast, the attack took a populist form, this was an indication, in the clearest possible terms, of a tremendous loss of confidence in the Party structure.

Does the emergence of populism indicate that the Cultural Revolution signified the reemergence of peasant anarchism and the revolt against machinery? Probably this conclusion is too extreme. It is, perhaps, a natural one to draw. The Chinese industrial working class has something to gain from industry; it played a small role in the early stages of the Cultural Revolution. We should remember, however, that while the Chinese working class of the cities was important in the 1920's, it also played a small role in the rise to power of Mao, so that no Party faction could entrench itself with the aim of carrying on the sectional interests of the industrial working class. Moreover, beginning about July 1968, Mao began to involve the industrial working classes more and more in his Cultural Revolution and great strategic plan, with such "instructions" as: "It is essential to bring into full play the leading role of the working class in the great cultural revolution and in all fields of work. On its part, the working class should always raise its political consciousness in the course of struggle" (August 1968). And "In carrying out the proletarian revolution in education, it is essential to have working-class leadership; it is essential for the masses of workers to take part . . ." (September 1968). Besides this, the rural "mob," for the first time in history, have left records of their pamphlets—big character posters and newspapers—which give the outward impression of peasant revolt.

We may conclude, then, that the earlier absence of working-class initiative in the Cultural Revolution does not *necessarily* indicate that the Cultural Revolution is essentially a movement of peasant anarchism. This is not to deny the presence of strong feeling against industrialism as a way of life generally. The harsh realities of industrialization, Mao realizes, demand strong political leadership—not only to initiate and guide the course of economic development, *but to make it last.* As a consequence, many of the policies and programs required for development are likely to be resisted—especially with the ploughing back of surplus into factories, and the growth of conveyer belt production, which means that further improvement in the basic diet, in health, education, and working conditions cannot materialize very quickly.

Mao is certainly in sympathy with resistance to *all-out, or crash, industrialization;* he sees its imperatives as being in conflict with many noneconomic aims he feels China should be pursuing. However this is not the same thing as the Luddite Revolt against technology (especially Western technology) *as such.* Rather, it expresses the desire to keep people in the communes by bringing them carefully rationed samples of the fruits of industrial society.

Such rationings of industrial society into the rural areas have a twofold objective: to bring material benefits to the peasant, and to prevent the dictatorship of the city over the countryside. Mao is saying that the Chinese Revolution was a *peasant* revolution from which the industrial urban workers benefited. Now that the Revolution is in its period of construction, the cities must not rule over the countryside, nor must the education system be dominated by the ethos of cities. Mao's Chinese followers here seem to be getting back to the earlier Marxist notion of breaking down the distinction between town and country life, and between worker and intellectual. According to Marx: "In communist society, where nobody has one exclusive field of activity but each can become accomplished in any branch he wishes, society regulates the general production and thus makes it possible for me to do one thing today and another tomorrow, to hunt in the morning, fish in the afternoon, rear cattle in the evening, criticise after dinner, just as I have a mind, without ever becoming hunter, fisherman, shepherd or critic." [7] Marx also predicted the disappearance of intellectuals as a result of the victory of socialism, saying that philosophy will abolish itself by "realizing" itself.

Marx, then, seemed to hold that the division of labor of industrial society needs to be abolished in communist society. Mao wants to do this *now* by making a peasant also a worker, a soldier, and an intellectual. Most observers cannot understand this, since they view the world through the prism of specialization and maximization of material welfare.

The Chinese, however, have earlier historical lessons before them, from which to learn—and they are good at learning from "negative example." In Britain in the early nineteenth century, there occurred an uprooting of agricultural laborers from the social milieu of the village, a migration of peasants from the village to the town where they found emotional bewilderment and despair. These rapidly growing industrial towns contained large numbers of casually employed laborers, who suffered materially and culturally. This is happening in India today and this the Chinese want to avoid; they are countering this threat by the process of creating a new kind of a peasantry, to be led into political action by a skilled minority vanguard group.

Or, again, take Russian experience in the nineteenth century. Eighty percent of Russian agriculture was owned by peasants but apportioned by a commune authority, partly appointed by the government and partly elected by the peasants. The weakness of this system was that the communes became the object of controversy among the rulers (the paternalists opposing those who wished to unleash capitalist farming), populists, and Marxists. The period before the 1917 Revolution saw rapid social differentiation and unrest and destroyed the possibility (dreamed of by the Narodniks) of skipping the capitalist stage and moving directly from backwardness to agrarian socialism. It seems to us that the Maoists also want to skip the capitalist stage of social differentiation and move directly to agrarian socialism, and that, for members of the Chinese communes, this is the significance of the events of 1958–1959 and 1966–1968.

CHINESE SOCIALISM IN WORLD SOCIALIST THOUGHT

In classical socialist writings four elements have been stressed: (1) public ownership of productive property; (2) an emphasis on equality, fellowship, and brotherhood; (3) maximum opportunity to select and reject people in authority; (4) equality of power over economic and political affairs.

It may fairly be said of the Chinese that whatever is lacking in their practice, their ideology has concentrated on the second, third, and fourth points much more than has the socialist doctrine of

Western political parties or of the Communist Party of the Soviet Union.

A fundamental axiom of Maoist thought is that public ownership is only a technical condition for solving the problems of Chinese society. In a deeper sense, the goal of Chinese socialism involves vast changes in human nature, in the way people relate to each other, to their work, and to society. The struggle to change material conditions, even in the most immediate sense, requires the struggle to change people, just as the struggle to change people depends on the ability to change the conditions under which men live and work. Mao differs from the Russians, and Liu Shao-chi's group, in believing that these changes are simultaneous, not sequential. Concrete goals and human goals are separable only on paper—in practice they are the same. Once the basic essentials of food, clothing, and shelter for all have been achieved, it is not necessary to wait for higher productivity levels to be reached before attempting socialist ways of life.

Revolutionary élan, for Maoists, is the key, and when this flags, it is necessary to seek institutional means of pursuing a permanent revolution, to undertake struggles and reforms which will change people into revolutionaries with a collectivist outlook —for the task of socialism after the revolution is the same as building a socialist movement. As pointed out earlier, this emphasis on moral incentives is very Chinese. The ethical emphasis emerges in every history book. The Chinese traditionally identify politics, government, and morals; a continuing theme has been that the goodness of leaders leads to good government and good morals. Westerners just do not see politics in this way. In China, where ideas of "serve the people" have had a high place among the governing groups, moral incentives are not strange mechanisms for getting things done. Of course Mao is not *only* for moral incentives and Liu *only* for material ones. All societies need *both*. The question is *where does the emphasis lie?* In China between 1961 and 1965 the leaning on material incentives was excessive, and the Maoists felt and argued they couldn't *afford* this policy because of its "demonstration effect." It encourages a high consumption level and puts a strain on the rate of investment that can be carried out. More material incentives imply more inequality and the growth of a new social class. The ideological point is that such a policy works against the construction of socialist society.

Mao argues, then, that in the Chinese "vision," revolution and socialism imply something beyond the physical taking of power: a process of social change involving popular participation in development. He says that "class struggle" refers not merely to an economic condition. It is a struggle to achieve an equality of power within the political framework of the revolution. Therefore it is incorrect to state that the class struggle in China is over, simply because there has been a redistribution of economic wealth —there has not yet been a popular redistribution of political power. The heart and the direction of the Chinese Revolution is popular control over the administration of the State, involving overthrow of the Party and State apparatus, if necessary. And, as already discussed, Maoism is also a revolt against the imperatives of a more technological and industrial way of life. Concretely, this is shown by the process described earlier, by which productivity gains are sacrificed for medium industry, for "make your own lathes" policies. According to the Chinese, the aim of socialism is not the maximizing of economic growth. Once you have reached a level of adequate food, clothing, and shelter, you have a choice: to make socialism a mechanism for forced growth, or to consider socialism as a way of life. Here we are back in the realms of Aristotelian politics, of deciding what is the "good society" and what is the basis of its social organization and needs. The Chinese say, in effect: "We have got 'over the hump' and we can grow without borrowing. Looking at other socialist societies, we see that the Soviet Union is élitist. They have no diffusion of decision-making, and have experienced a loss of revolutionary drive which cuts them off from the rest of the world in the very era of the great world revolution."

The factor of an enormous population is important here. It is not possible centrally to control such a population, as Chinese history demonstrates. There must be a wide diffusion of initiative and considerable local autonomy. The attitudes of large masses of people are crucial, and enforcement is difficult. That is why the issue of motivation is all-pervasive. The government must either bribe people to behave in a certain way through financial incentives, or encourage them to identify their work with the goals of the society.

After all, every society has both moral and material incentives; even in the West, many scientists, engineers, and managers do not operate solely on material incentives; they must cooperate and identify with the goals of the work place and society. In China, the cooperative approach is getting stronger; people are sent from a particular region to learn from other regions; the strong teach the weak and do not try to knock them out. Bourgeois economists, bred on a competitive morality, cannot see that this approach is evangelical and seeks to develop cooperative morality in people. In the West, people brought up to believe in individual, aggressive, competitive values cannot understand it; their social relations have become dominated by the fetishism of commodities and obscured by market relationships.

Western economists who ridicule the ethical aspects of Chinese development fail to look at economic and social development historically. For example, Adam Smith's *Wealth of Nations* preached, for the early stages of British capitalism, a spirit of self-interest, frugality, and parsimony; the Victorian period also emphasized thrift, and the virtues of sturdy independence and self help, as illustrated in the writings of Samuel Smiles. These, along with the values propagated by Methodism, the Salvation Army, and temperance societies were part of the ethical framework of the British capitalist system.

Just as capitalism needed an ideology and an ethical framework suited to its modus operandi, so does socialism. China is trying to substitute, for Adam Smith's principle of private interest guided by the "invisible hand" of competitive market forces as the controlling factor over production, quality, and technology, the visible bond of Mao Tse-tung's policy based on public interest and social cooperation. And this, of course, has to be accomplished within the Chinese context of a traditional identification of politics, law, and morality, within a civilization which invented public administration as we know it—a mandarinate—and which evolved an ideology blending ethics and authoritarianism. Mao's procedure has been to "Sinify" a loose Marxist approach appropriate to a basically peasant society. This has been called a "personality cult." But, as Edgar Snow has remarked:

> The cult was Mao's strongest weapon in his struggle with Shao-ch'i. In one sense, the whole Cultural Revolution, the great purge of the revisionists, was a struggle over whether Mao would command a cult, or whether the Party bureaucracy would utilise the cult, putting Mao on a pedestal where he would have no power . . . Mao is called a visionary, because he adheres to the ideal of the socialist man, selflessly devoted to society and not to the old id or ego. And yet, in China, a leader without principle, and without pretensions to a universal truth or virtue, could not have held the mandate of Heaven—that is, ruled by consensus of the people—during this period. No doubt much of the cult may be retired by Mao's successors. But the China of the visible future will surely emerge as a new society bearing the imprint of Mao's unique personality.[8]

Notes

1. T. Wang, "Power Struggle in Peking: Plot and Counterplots," *Far Eastern Economic Review*, January 25, 1968. This article concludes, after much analysis, but quite incorrectly, that Chiang Ching and Kang Sheng had gone into eclipse and that "with the dawning of 1968 there were signs that power was once again where it had been before the cultural revolution was launched."

2. C. P. Fitzgerald, *The Chinese View of Their Place in the World* (London, New York: Oxford, 1964).

3. A number of Soviet books are shot through with this attitude. See, for example, the argument that "A man's capabilities are in the final analysis determined by . . . the level of development reached by industry, science, technology and culture. History has not given us an example of communal forms of ownership, which are survivals of the clan system, being able to engender a socialist society." V. Afanasyev, *Scientific Communism* (Moscow: 1967).

4. For this interpretation of Maoism see R. Schlesinger, "Socialism Self-Defined," *Monthly Review*, November 1967, p. 90.

5. Alice Teh, "Mystery of Maoland," *The Australian*, November 25, 1967.

6. Mao Tse-tung, *On the Correct Handling of Contradictions Among the People* (Peking: Foreign Languages Press, 1967).
7. Karl Marx and Friedrich Engels, *German Ideology* (New York: International Publishers, 1939), p. 22.
8. Edgar Snow, "Mao's Attributes," *The Listener,* May 29, 1969, p. 757.

THE "LATEST INSTRUCTIONS"
OF MAO TSE-TUNG

This appendix consists of a collection of "instructions" issued by Mao Tse-tung since 1966. Usually they appeared as explicit instructions; at other times, they were issued after first having run as anonymous editorials in *People's Daily* or *Red Flag*. Those that have been collected here do not appear either in *Quotations from Chairman Mao* or in any consolidated form as a booklet issued by the Chinese authorities. It has not been possible to give precise dates for every "instruction." Mao's messages to heads of State, or to fraternal movements abroad, dealing with international problems, have not been included, for the collection aims to show Mao's influence on internal developments.

The collection does not include the programmatic documents issued by the Central Committee in August 1966 and November 1968 (said to have been drafted by Mao), nor his critique of the "Group of Five Report" (May 1966); these are readily available as booklets.

(1) Bombard the Headquarters! In the last fifty days or so some leading comrades from the center down to the local levels have acted in a diametrically opposite way. Adopting the reactionary stand of the bourgeoisie, they have enforced a bourgeois dictatorship and struck down the surging movement of the great cultural revolution of the proletariat. They have stood facts on their heads and juggled black and white, encircled and suppressed revolutionaries, stifled opinions differing from their own, imposed a White terror and felt very pleased with themselves. They have puffed up the arrogance of the bourgeoisie and deflated the morale of the proletariat. How poisonous! Viewed in connection with the

Right deviation in 1962 and the wrong tendency of 1964 which was "Left" in form but Right in essence, shouldn't this prompt one to deep thought? (August 5, 1966)

(2) The period of schooling should be shortened, education should be revolutionized, and the domination of our schools by bourgeois intellectuals should by no means be allowed to continue. (1966)

(3) The Party organization should be composed of the advanced elements of the proletariat; it should be a vigorous vanguard organization capable of leading the proletariat and the revolutionary masses in the fight against the class enemy.

(4) The correct handling of cadres is the key question in forming the revolutionary "three-in-one" combination, consolidating the revolutionary great alliance and making a success of struggle-criticism-transformation in each unit, and it must be solved properly. Through the rectification in Yenan, our Party educated the masses of cadres and united the whole Party, thus ensuring the victory of the War of Resistance Against Japan and the War of Liberation. We must carry forward this tradition.

(5) The "four firsts" is good; it is an invention. Since Comrade Lin Piao put forward the "four firsts" and the "three-eight" working style, the ideological-political work of the People's Liberation Army, as well as its military work, has developed remarkably, has become more concrete and at the same time has been raised to a higher theoretical plane than in the past.

(6) One must not always think himself in the right, as if he had all the truth on his side. One should not always think that only he is capable and everybody else is capable of nothing, *as if the earth could not turn if he were not there.* (1967)

(7) The two groupings should talk less about others' shortcomings and faults, and let each talk about its own. They should make more self-criticism and seek common ground on major questions while reserving differences on minor ones.

(8) Fighters should be included in the study classes sponsored by the army.

(9) People do different types of work at various posts, but no matter how high-ranking an official anyone is, he should be like an ordinary worker among the people. It is absolutely impermissible for him to put on airs.

(10) Solve the problem of relations between the higher and lower levels effectively and harmonize relations between cadres and the masses. From now on, cadres should go in turn to the lower levels and see what's happening; they should persist in the mass line, always consult the masses and be their pupils. In a sense, the fighters with the most practical experience are the wisest and the most capable.

(11) Support the army and cherish the people, grasp revolution and promote production and other work, promote preparations against war and achieve still better results in all fields.

(12) The proletarian revolution in education should be carried out by relying on the mass of revolutionary students, teachers and workers in the schools, by relying on the activists among them, namely, those proletarian revolutionaries who are determined to carry the great proletarian cultural revolution through to the end.

(13) Resume classes in all colleges, middle schools and primary schools while carrying on the revolution.

(14) The situation of the great proletarian cultural revolution throughout the country is not just good, it is excellent. The whole situation is better than ever before. The key indication of this excellent situation is that the masses have been fully aroused. Never before in any mass movement have the masses been aroused so thoroughly and on so broad a scale.

Given a few more months, the whole situation will be still better.

(15) 1. It is imperative to combat selfishness and criticize and repudiate revisionism.

2. Fight self, repudiate revisionism.

3. Fight self-interest, repudiate revisionism.

(16) The revolutionary Red Guards and revolutionary student

organizations should realize the revolutionary great alliance. So long as both sides are revolutionary mass organizations, they should realize the revolutionary great alliance in accordance with revolutionary principle.

(17) Taking a firm hold of grain, cotton and cotton cloth production, practice economy in carrying out revolution.

(18) There is no fundamental clash of interest within the working class. Under the dictatorship of the proletariat, there is no reason whatsoever for the working class to split into two big irreconcilable organizations.

(19) We must have faith in and rely on the masses, have faith in and rely on the People's Liberation Army and have faith in and rely on the great majority of the cadres.

(20) Remain one of the common people while serving as an official.

(21) We must be good at guiding people with petty-bourgeois thinking in our ranks on to the path of the proletarian revolution. This is a key to the success of the great proletarian cultural revolution.

(22) The veteran cadres made contributions in the past but they must not rest on their laurels. They should strive to temper themselves in the great proletarian cultural revolution and make new contributions. (March 1967)

(23) We communists seek not official posts, but revolution. Every one of us must be a thoroughgoing revolutionary in spirit and we must never for a moment divorce ourselves from the masses. So long as we do not divorce ourselves from the masses, we are certain to be victorious.

(24) Unity—criticism and self-criticism—unity.

(25) Don't rest on your laurels, make new contributions.

(26) Never forget class struggle.

(27) Preparedness against war, preparedness against natural calamities, and everything for the people.

(28) There is no construction without destruction. Destruction means criticism and repudiation; it means revolution. It involves reasoning things out, which is construction. Put destruction first, and in the process you have construction.

(29) The present great cultural revolution is only the first; there will inevitably be many more in the future. In the last few years Comrade Mao Tse-tung has said repeatedly that the issue of who will win in the revolution can only be settled over a long historical period. If things are not properly handled, it is possible for a capitalist restoration to take place at any time. It should not be thought by any Party member or any one of the people in our country that everything will be all right after one or two great cultural revolutions, or even three or four. We must be very much on the alert and never lose vigilance.

(30) It is an excellent idea to send army cadres to train revolutionary teachers and students. There is a tremendous difference between those who have had such training and those who have not. For through this training, they learn about political and military affairs from the liberation army, they learn its "four firsts," its "three-eight" working style and the three main rules of discipline and the eight points for attention and they thereby strengthen their sense of organization and discipline.

(31) In every place or unit where power must be seized, it is necessary to carry out the policy of the revolutionary "three-in-one" combination in establishing a provisional organ of power which is revolutionary and representative and enjoys proletarian authority. This organ of power should preferably be called the Revolutionary Committee.

(32) We must work conscientiously to unite all those who can be united. The proletariat must emancipate not only itself but also mankind as a whole. Without emancipating the whole of mankind the proletariat cannot finally emancipate itself.

(33) They [the cadres] should be allowed to correct their errors and be encouraged to make amends for their crimes by good deeds, unless they are anti-Party, anti-socialist elements who persist in their errors and refuse to correct them after repeated education.

(34) Having committed errors, one should make a self-criticism.

(35) The army should give military and political training in the universities, middle schools and the higher classes of primary schools, stage by stage and group by group. It should help in re-opening school classes, strengthening organization, setting up the leading bodies on the principle of the "three-in-one" combination and carrying out the task of "struggle-criticism-transformation." It should first make experiments at selected points and acquire experience and then popularize it step by step. And the students should be persuaded to implement the teaching of Marx that only by emancipating all mankind can the proletariat achieve its own final emancipation, and in military and political training, they should not exclude those teachers and cadres who have made mistakes. Apart from the aged and the sick, these people should be allowed to take part so as to facilitate their remolding. (March 7, 1967)

(36) As far as the great proletarian cultural revolution is concerned, the situation throughout the country is not just good, it is excellent. The whole situation is better than ever before.

In a few more months, the whole situation will become better still. (December 1967)

(37) The People's Liberation Army should help the broad masses of the Left. (January 1968)

(38) Grasp class struggle and all problems can be solved.

(39) The struggle has to be conducted by reasoning and not by coercion or force.

(40) You must concern yourselves with state affairs and carry the great proletarian cultural revolution through to the end!

(41) We must know how to judge cadres. We must not confine our judgment to a short period or a single incident in a cadre's life, but should consider his life and work as a whole. This is the principal method of judging cadres.

(42) On the problem of cadres, make education the starting point and help more cadres through education.

(43) Concerning cadres who have committed serious mistakes, provided they do not persist in their mistakes but make earnest efforts to correct them and have received the forgiveness of the broad revolutionary masses, they can still stand up and join the revolutionary ranks.

(44) Learn from past mistakes to avoid future ones.

(45) Cure the sickness to save the patient.

(46) Observe and help.

(47) Political work is the life-blood of all economic work.

(48) The aim of every revolutionary struggle in the world is the seizure and consolidation of political power.

(49) Either the East wind prevails over the West wind, or the West wind prevails over the East wind; there is no room for compromise on the question of the two lines.

(50) This change in world outlook is something fundamental.

(51) Listen patiently to all dissenting views raised by people at lower levels and give them due consideration. Don't fly into a temper or consider it a sign of disrespect when you hear views different from yours.

(52) The proletariat seeks to transform the world according to its own world outlook, and so does the bourgeoisie. In this respect, the question of which will win out, socialism or capitalism, is still not really settled.

(53) If the army and the people are united as one, who in the world can match them?

(54) Serve the people whole-heartedly and never for a moment divorce ourselves from the masses.

(55) Politics is the commander, the soul in everything, and political work is the life-blood of all work.

(56) We must firmly believe that the great majority of the masses are good and that bad elements only make up a very small fraction.

(57) Our point of departure is to serve the people whole-heartedly and never for a moment divorce ourselves from the masses, to proceed in all cases from the interests of the people and not from one's self-interest or from the interests of a small group, and to identify our responsibility to the people with our responsibility to the leading organs of the Party.

(58) All our cadres, whatever their rank, are servants of the people, and whatever we do is to serve the people. How then can we be reluctant to discard any of our bad traits?

(59) Wherever our comrades go, they must build good relations with the masses, be concerned for them and help them overcome their difficulties. We must unite with the masses; the more of the masses we unite with, the better.

(60) The cadres of our Party and state are ordinary workers and not overlords sitting on the backs of the people. By taking part in collective productive labor, the cadres maintain extensive, constant and close ties with the working people. This is a major measure of fundamental importance for a socialist system; it helps to overcome bureaucracy and to prevent revisionism and dogmatism.

(61) Apply the working method of "from the masses, to the masses."

(62) The comrades must be helped to remain modest, prudent and free from arrogance and rashness in their style of work. The comrades must be helped to preserve the style of plain living and hard struggle.

(63) Blame not the speaker but be warned by his words.

(64) Not to have a correct political point of view is like having no soul.

(65) Successors to the revolutionary cause of the proletariat come forward in mass struggles and are tempered in the great storms of revolution.

(66) Marxism consists of thousands of truths, but they all boil

down to one sentence, "It is right to rebel." . . . And from this truth there follows resistance, struggle, the fight for socialism.

(67) Veteran cadres and young new cadres work together in the revolutionary committees, learn from each other and help each other so that, as Chairman Mao teaches, *the veterans are not divorced from the masses and the young people are tempered.*

(68) The basic experience of revolutionary committees is this— they are threefold: they have representatives of revolutionary cadres, representatives of the armed forces and representatives of the revolutionary masses. This forms a revolutionary "three-in-one" combination. The revolutionary committee should exercise unified leadership, do away with redundant or overlapping administrative structures, have "better troops and simpler administration" and organize a revolutionized leading group which is linked with the masses. (January 1968)

(69) Running study classes is a good method; you can arrive at a solution of many problems in these classes. (February 1968)

(70) The great proletarian cultural revolution is a great revolution that touches people to their very souls and aims at solving the problem of their world outlook. (March 1967)

(71) The great proletarian cultural revolution is in essence a great political revolution under the conditions of socialism made by the proletariat against the bourgeoisie and all other exploiting classes; it is a continuation of the prolonged struggle between the Chinese Communist Party and the masses of revolutionary people under its leadership on the one hand and the Kuomintang reactionaries on the other, a continuation of the class struggle between the proletariat and the bourgeoisie. (April 1968)

(72) The "three-in-one" revolutionary committee is a creation of the working class and the masses in the current great cultural revolution.

The most fundamental principle in the reform of State organs is that they must keep in contact with the masses. (April 1968)

(73) To protect or to suppress the broad masses of the people—

this is a fundamental distinction between the Communist Party and the Kuomintang, between the proletariat and the bourgeoisie, and between the dictatorship of the proletariat and the dictatorship of the bourgeoisie. (June 1968)

(74) It is still necessary to have universities; here I refer mainly to colleges of science and engineering. However, it is essential to shorten the length of schooling, revolutionize education, put proletarian politics in command and take the road of the Shanghai Machine Tools Plant in training technicians from among the workers. Students should be selected from among peasants and workers with practical experience, and they should return to production after a few years' study. (July 1968)

(75) All people who have had some education ought to be very happy to work in the countryside if they get the chance. In our vast rural areas there is plenty of room for them to develop their talents to the full. (July 1968)

(76) Our country has 700 million people, and the working class is the leading class. It is essential to bring into full play the leading role of the working class in the great cultural revolution and in all fields of work. On its part, the working class should always raise its political consciousness in the course of struggle. (August 1968)

(77) The struggle-criticism-transformation in a factory, on the whole, goes through the following stages: establishing a revolutionary committee based on the "three-in-one" combination, mass criticism and repudiation, purifying the class ranks, rectifying the Party organization, simplifying organizational structure, changing irrational rules and regulations and sending people who work in offices to grass-roots levels. (August 1968)

(78) In carrying out the proletarian revolution in education, it is essential to have working-class leadership; it is essential for the masses of workers to take part and, in cooperation with Liberation Army fighters, bring about a revolutionary "three-in-one" combination, together with the activists among the students, teachers and workers in the schools who are determined to carry the pro-

letarian revolution in education through to the end. The workers' propaganda teams should stay permanently in the schools and take part in fulfilling all the tasks of struggle-criticism-transformation in the schools, and they will always lead the schools. In the countryside, the schools should be managed by the poor and lower-middle peasants—the most ' reliable ally of the working class. (September 1968)

(79) What is the situation as regards the engineering and technical personnel in factories in our big, medium-sized and small industrial cities throughout the country? How is the revolution in education going in the colleges and secondary schools of science and engineering? We hope that the revolutionary committees in all parts of the country will send out people to make some typical investigations and report the results to the Party Central Committee. Here we wish to raise the question of giving attention to reeducating the large numbers of college and secondary school graduates who started work quite some time ago as well as those who have just begun to work, so that they will integrate with the workers and peasants. Some of them are sure to make a success of this integration and achieve something in regard to inventions and innovations. Mention should be made of these people as encouragement. Those who are really impossible, that is, the diehard capitalist roaders and bourgeois technical authorities who have incurred the extreme wrath of the masses and therefore must be overthrown, are very few in number. Even they should be given a way out. To do otherwise is not the policy of the proletariat. The above-mentioned policies should be applied to both new and old intellectuals, whether working in the arts or sciences. (September 1968)

(80) The majority or the vast majority of the students trained in the old schools and colleges can integrate themselves with the workers, peasants and soldiers, and some have made inventions or innovations; they must, however, be reeducated by the workers, peasants and soldiers under the guidance of the correct line, and thoroughly change their old ideology. Such intellectuals will be welcomed by the working peasants, and soldiers. (September 1968)

(81) The current great proletarian cultural revolution is absolutely necessary and most timely for consolidating the dictatorship of the proletariat, preventing capitalist restoration and building socialism. (October 1968)

(82) Sending the masses of cadres to do manual work gives them an excellent opportunity to study once again; this should be done by all cadres except those who are too old, weak, ill or disabled. Functioning cadres should also go by group to do manual work. (October 1968)

(83) A human being has arteries and veins and his heart makes the blood circulate; one breathes through the lungs, exhaling carbon dioxide and inhaling oxygen afresh, that is, getting rid of the waste and letting in the fresh. A proletarian party must also get rid of the waste and let in the fresh for only in this way can it be full of vigor. Without eliminating waste and getting fresh blood the party has no vigor. (October 1968)

(84) Our power, who gives it to us? The working class gives it, the poor and lower-middle peasants give it, and the masses of laboring people who comprise over 90 percent of the population give it. We represent the proletariat and the masses, and have overthrown the enemies of the people; the people therefore support us. One of the basic principles of the Communist Party is to rely directly on the revolutionary masses. (October 1968)

(85) It is necessary to maintain the system of cadre participation in collective productive labor. The cadres of our Party and State are ordinary workers and not overlords sitting on the backs of the people. By taking part in collective productive labor, the cadres maintain extensive, constant and close ties with the working people. This is a major measure of fundamental importance for a socialist system; it helps to overcome bureaucracy and to prevent revisionism and dogmatism. (Restated November 1968—originally published anonymously in *On Khrushchev's Phoney Communism and Its Historical Lessons for the World*, July 14, 1964.)

(86) The fighters with the most practical experience are the wisest and most capable. The lowly are most intelligent; the élite are most ignorant. (November 1968)

(87) Historical experience merits attention. Line and viewpoint must be talked over constantly and repeatedly. It won't do to talk them over with only a few people; they must be known to all the revolutionary masses. (November 1968)

(88) It is very necessary for educated young people to go to the countryside to be reeducated by the poor and lower-middle peasants. Cadres and other people in the cities should be persuaded to send their sons and daughters who have finished junior or senior middle school, college or university to the countryside. It is necessary for educated young people to be reeducated by the poor and lower-middle peasants. Let us mobilize. Comrades throughout the countryside should welcome them. (December 1968)

(89) As for purifying the class ranks, first we must grasp this work firmly; second we must pay attention to policy. (December 1968)

(90) We must pay attention to policy in dealing with counter-revolutionaries and those who have made mistakes. The scope of attack must be narrow and more people must be helped through education. The stress must be on the weight of evidence and on investigation and study. It is strictly forbidden to extort confessions and accept such confessions. As for good people who have made mistakes, we must give them more help through education. When they are awakened, we must liberate them without delay. (December 1968)

(91) In medical and health work, put the stress on the rural areas. (January 1969)

(92) Serious attention must be paid to policy in the stage of struggle-criticism-transformation in the great proletarian cultural revolution. (February 1969)

(93) In making plans, it is essential to mobilize the masses and see to it that there is enough leeway. (February 1969)

(94) It is necessary to sum up experience conscientiously.
    When one goes to a unit to get to know the situation there, one must become acquainted with the whole process of the movement —its inception, its development and its present state, how the

masses have acted and how the leadership has acted, what contradictions and struggles have emerged and what changes have occurred in these contradictions, and what progress people have made in their knowledge—so as to find out its laws. (March 1969)

(95) The proletariat is the greatest class in the history of mankind. It is the most powerful revolutionary class ideologically, politically and in strength. It can and must unite the overwhelming majority of people around itself so as to isolate the handful of enemies to the maximum and attack them. (May 1969)

(96) Unite to win still greater victories.

In speaking of victory we mean to ensure that the masses of the people throughout the country are united under the leadership of the proletariat to win victory. (June 1969)

(97) Unite for the purpose of consolidating the dictatorship of the proletariat. This must be realized in every factory, village, office and school. (June 1969)

(98) Every Party branch must reconsolidate itself in the midst of the masses. This must be done with the participation of the masses and not merely a few Party members; it is necessary to have the masses outside the Party attend the meetings and give comments. (July 1969)

(99) In the great proletarian cultural revolution, some tasks have not yet been fulfilled and they should now be carried on, for instance, the tasks of struggle-criticism-transformation. (July 1969)

INDEX

Academy of Science: 173
Adler, S.: 45
Advanced School for Party Cadres: 88
Agrarian communism *see* Agrarian socialism
Agrarian socialism (*see also* Cooperatives *and* Communes): 43, 88, 220
  development of, 26–27
  communes as, 49, 189–90, 194
  NEP as threat to, 88
Agricultural Equipment Ministry: 167
Agriculture (*see also* Agrarian socialism *and* Communes *and* Cooperatives *and* Land reform): 52, 140, 182–88
  balance between industry and, 209–10
  before land reforms, 32
  capitalism in, 37, 67–68, 145, 155
  crisis years (1959–61), 54, 58–60
  Cultural Revolution's effects *see* Communes
  First Five-Year Plan, 35, 36–41
  as the foundation of the economy, 54, 58–59, 66, 86, 140, 208
  incentives, 38–39, 40, 78, 187–90
  san zi yi bao policy, 67–68, 73
  Bukharinism, 86
  and industrialization, 37, 191, 219–20
  land reclamation, 37, 183–85
  Mao's policies, 37, 189, 191, 192, 194
  market forces in, 67–68, 78, 145
  mechanization, 192, 204–05, 208–09
  New Economic Policy, 66, 67–68, 73–74
  productivity and output
    before land reform, 32
    First Five Year Plan, 39–40
    under Cultural Revolution, 185–86, 190–93
  regionalism, 61–62
  san zi yi bao policy, 67–68, 73–74, 155
    compared to Cultural Revolution, 189
    Mao's criticism of, 91, 92, 93
  socialist transformation of, 33–34, 36–41
    Cultural Revolution, 182–93
    First Five Year Plan, 36–41
  surplus, 40, 54, 62
  taxation, 40, 194, 208, 210
  water conservation, 182–83, 208
All Men Are Brothers: 21, 22
Anshan Iron and Steel Mill: 132
Anthropology: 150, 198, 214
Army *see* People's Liberation Army (PLA)
Arts *see* Cultural affairs
Ashbrook, Arthur G., Jr.: 34, 39–40
August 1958 Resolution: 145
Automation: 148
Automobile industry: 171

Babeuf, François Emile: 216
Backyard iron and steel campaign: 43, 48–49, 186
Banking (*see also* People's Bank): 33
Blanquism: 213
Bonuses *see* Material incentives
Bourgeois economics: 79, 87, 223
Bourgeois ideology: 71, 101, 108, 110
Bourgeoisie (*see also* Bourgeois ideology *and* Capitalism *and* Class and class struggle): 89
  and Cultural Revolution, 117, 125, 126

241

dictatorship of, 125, 126
leaders, 102
Mao on, 110, 124, 125, 218
in Paris Commune, 117
Propaganda Department of the Party
Central Committee: 90, 115
Provinces and provincial government
(*see also* Regionalism): 116,
123
as base areas, 199
planning role, 129–30, 133, 134–
35, 137, 140, 141, 200, 201
technological policy, 163, 167, 168
Public health services: 36, 75, 104,
206
Public housing: 13
Public ownership: 106, 107, 220
law of value and, 83
Maoist view, 221
Purges: 102, 122

Railways (*see also* Transport system):
33, 60
Rectification Campaign: 99, 202–03
Red Guards: 19, 101, 110–14, 135,
176, 177, 203
ideology, 110–12
membership conditions, 111
origins, 105, 110–11
violence, 111, 112
in Western press, 112, 113
"Redness" vs. "expertness" controversy: 68–73, 115, 132, 163,
168–69, 202–03
Red Star Commune: 130–31, 185,
187, 190, 193–94
Regionalism (*see also* Decentralization *and* Provinces): 15, 23–
26, 41, 45, 222–23
Maoist policy, 24–25, 198, 199–201
peasant revolt and, 24, 200–01,
217–18
physical basis for, 60–62
planning and, 129–30, 133, 134–
35, 137, 140, 141, 200, 201
pricing and, 137–38
Rehabilitation of 1949–52: 32–34
Research: 173
Resource allocation *see* Priorities
Retail trade: 134, 137

Revisionism (*see also* Capitalism,
reversion to): 93, 101–03,
107–08, 121
Soviet, 101–03
Revolution (*see also* Chinese Revolution *and* Great Proletarian
Cultural Revolution *and* Peasant revolution):
human values and, 99–100
Maoist strategy, 21, 26, 99–100,
115–16, 146–47, 221, 222
in peasant societies, 213
Revolutionary committees: 154, 174,
181, 203
factory, 118–20, 121, 126, 165
Provincial, 62, 126, 129–30
three-in-one, 27, 123, 124
authority, 132–33
planning role, 129, 132, 141
Revolutionary socialism: 101, 103
Rightists: 91, 92, 93, 113, 114, 116,
122, 125, 126, 163
Right to rebel: 125, 144, 151–52
Robinson, Joan: 20
Russia *see* Union of Soviet Socialist
Republics (U.S.S.R.)

San zi yi bao policy: 67–68, 73–74,
155, 189
compared to Cultural Revolution
policy, 189
Mao's criticism of, 91, 92, 93
Scale standards: 206–07
Scholars, The: 19
Schools (*see also* Education):
Academy of Science, 173
Advanced School for Party Cadres,
88
Central China Engineering Uni-
versity, 174–75
May 7 School, 177
Peking University, 108–11
Shanghai, 174, 177
Tsinghua University, 111
Tungchia Architectural University,
174
Wukeu Part-Time Tea Growing
and Part-Time Study Middle
School, 177
Schurmann, Franz: 69